WASHBACK IN LANGUAGE TESTING

Research Contexts and Methods

WASHBACK IN LANGUAGE TESTING

Research Contexts and Methods

Edited by

Liying Cheng
Queen's University

Yoshinori Watanabe
Akita National University

With

Andy Curtis
Queen's University

LAWRENCE ERLBAUM ASSOCIATES, PUBLISHERS
2004 Mahwah, New Jersey London

Lawrence Erlbaum Associates, Inc., Publishers
10 Industrial Avenue
Mahwah, New Jersey 07430

Cover design by Kathryn Houghtaling Lacey

Library of Congress Cataloging-in-Publication Data

Washback in language testing : research contents and methods / edited by Liying Cheng, Yoshinori J. Watanabe, with Andy Curtis.
p. cm.
Includes bibliographical references and indexes.
ISBN 0-8058-3986-0 (cloth : alk. paper) – ISBN 0-8058-3987-9 (pbk. : alk. paper)
1. English language–Study and teaching–Foreign speakers. 2. Language and languages–Ability testing. 3. English language–Ability testing. 4. Test-taking skills. I. Cheng, Liying, 1959– II. Watanabe, Yoshinori J., 1956– III. Curits, Andy.

PE1128.A2W264 2003
428'.0076–dc22

2003061785
CIP

Books published by Lawrence Erlbaum Associates are printed on acid-free paper, and their bindings are chosen for strength and durability.

Printed in the United States of America
10 9 8 7 6 5 4 3 2

To Jack and Andy for their love, support, and understanding with this washback book, and to those who have conducted and will conduct washback research
—Liying

To my parents, Akiko, and all the friends and teachers who made this project possible
—Yoshinori (Josh)

To Manboadh Sookdeo and his family, for the tragic and testing times of 2002
—Andy

Contents

Foreword

J. Charles Alderson
Lancaster University

Washback and the impact of tests more generally has become a major area of study within educational research, and language testing in particular, as this volume testifies, and so I am particularly pleased to welcome this book, and to see the range of educational settings represented in it. Exactly ten years ago, Dianne Wall and I published an article in the journal *Applied Linguistics* which asked the admittedly somewhat rhetorical question: "Does Washback Exist?" In that article, we noted the widespread belief that tests have impact on teachers, classrooms, and students, we commented that such impact is usually perceived to be negative, and we lamented the absence of serious empirical research into a phenomenon that was so widely believed to exist. Hence, in part, our title: How do we know it exists if there is no research into washback? Ten years on, and a slow accumulation of empirical research later, I believe there is no longer any doubt that washback does indeed exist. But we now know that the phenomenon is a hugely complex matter, and very far from being a simple case of tests having negative impact on teaching. The question today is not "does washback exist?" but much rather what does washback look like? What brings washback about? Why does washback exist?

We now know, for instance, that tests will have more impact on the content of teaching and the materials that are used than they will on the teacher's methodology. We know that different teachers will teach to a particular test in very different ways. We know that some teachers will teach to very different tests in very similar ways. We know that high-stakes tests—

tests that have important consequences for individuals and institutions—will have more impact than low-stakes tests, although it is not always clear how to identify and define the nature of those stakes, since what is a trivial consequence for one person may be an important matter for another.

Although the possibility of positive washback has also often been mooted, there are, interestingly, few examples of this having been demonstrated by careful research. Indeed, the study that Dianne Wall and I conducted in Sri Lanka (Wall & Alderson, 1993; Wall, 1996, 1999) was initially expected to show that introducing new tests into the curriculum would reinforce innovations in teaching materials and curricula and produce positive washback. We were therefore surprised to discover that the impact of the introduction of new tests was much more limited than expected, and we were forced to re-examine our beliefs about washback. I cite this as an example of how important it is to research one's beliefs, rather than simply to accept what appear to be truisms. But I also cite it because it was during this research that we came to realize more deeply the complexity of the matter, and the importance of understanding the nature of washback effects. It was in that research, for example, that we first became aware of the importance of distinguishing between impact on teaching content and impact of teaching methodology.

In subsequent research (Alderson & Hamp-Lyons, 1996) into the impact of the TOEFL test on teaching (and incidentally and curiously, this is the only published research to date into the washback of a test that is very widespread and almost unanimously believed to have negative impact on teachers and learner as well as materials) I became aware of the teacher factor in washback, when I discovered how differently two teachers taught toward the same test. And it was during that same research that I began to realize that the crucial issue is not to ask whether washback exists, but to understand why it has what effects it does have. I will never forget one of the teachers I observed replying to the question: "Is it possible to teach TOEFL communicatively?" by saying: "I never thought of that." Which I interpreted as meaning that he had not given much thought as to what might be the most appropriate way to teach toward such an important test. And when I interviewed a group of teachers about what they thought about teaching toward TOEFL, I was surprised to learn that two things they liked most about teaching TOEFL (there were, of course, many things they did not like) was that they did not have to plan lessons, and they did not have to mark homework. Two of the most important things teachers do is prepare their lessons and give students feedback, and yet when teaching toward TOEFL some teachers at least do not feel that this is necessary. In short, it is at least as much the teacher who brings about washback, be it positive or negative, as it is the test.

In current views of the nature of test validity, the "Messickian view" of construct validity, it is commonplace to assert the need for test validation to include a consideration of the consequences of test use. Morrow goes so far as to call this "washback validity." I have serious problems with this view of a test's influence, not only because it is now clear that washback is brought about by people in classrooms, not by test developers, but also because it is clearly the case that there is only so much that test developers can do to influence how people might prepare students for their test. I accept that it is highly desirable for test developers to consider the likely impact—negative as well as positive—of the test they are designing on teaching and learning, and seeking to engineer positive washback by test design (as Messick, 1996, put it) is certainly a sensible thing to do. But there are limits to what a test developer can achieve, and much more attention needs to be paid to the reasons why teachers teach the way they do. We need to understand their beliefs about teaching and learning, the degree of their professionalism, the adequacy of their training and of their understanding of the nature of and rationale for the test.

Equally, as is attested by several authors in this book, educational authorities and politicians can be seen as responsible for the nature of washback, because tests are frequently used to engineer innovation, to steer and guide the curriculum. Tests are often intended as "levers for change" (Pearson, 1988), in a very naïve fashion. Curricular innovation is, in fact, a very complex matter, as Fullan (1991) has clearly shown, and washback studies need to take careful account, not only of the context into which the innovation is being introduced, but of all the myriad forces that can both enhance and hinder the implementation of the intended change. Wall (1996, 1999) shows clearly how innovation theory, and a study of innovation practice, can increase our understanding of how and why washback comes about.

If I may permit myself the luxury of a footnote, in reference to the use of two terms to refer to the same phenomenon, namely *backwash* and *washback*, I should explain that one of the reasons why the Alderson and Wall article was entitled "Does Washback Exist?" was because it seemed to us that the word *washback* was commonly used in discussions, in presentations at conferences and in teacher training. When I was studying at the University of Edinburgh, Scotland, for example, Alan Davies, the doyen of British language testing, frequently used the term *washback* and I do not recall him ever using *backwash*. Whereas in what literature there was at the time, the word "backwash" seemed much more prevalent. Hence another reason for our question: "Does Washback Exist?" But to clarify the distinction between the terms *backwash* and *washback*: there is none. The only difference is that if somebody has studied at the University of Reading, UK, where Arthur Hughes used to teach, they are likely to use the term *backwash*. If they have studied language testing anywhere else, but especially in Edinburgh or Lancaster in the UK, they will almost certainly use the term *washback*.

I would like to congratulate the editors on their achievement in commissioning and bringing together such a significant collection of chapters on washback. I am confident that this volume will not only serve to further our understanding of the phenomenon, but I also hope it will settle once and for all that washback, not backwash, does indeed exist, but that its existence raises more questions than it answers, and that therefore we need to study the phenomenon closely, carefully, systematically, and critically in order better to understand it. For that reason, I am very pleased to welcome this publication and I am honored to have been invited to write this Foreword.

REFERENCES

Alderson, J. C., & Hamp-Lyons, L. (1996). TOEFL preparation courses: A study of washback. *Language Testing, 13*, 280–297.

Fullan, M. G., with Stiegelbauer, S. (1991). *The new meaning of educational change* (2nd ed.). London: Cassell.

Messick, S. (1996). Validity and washback in language testing. *Language Testing, 13*, 241–256.

Pearson, I. (1988). Tests as levers for change. In D. Chamberlain & R. J. Baumgardner (Eds.), *ESP in the classroom: Practice and evaluation* (pp. 98–107). London: Modern English.

Wall, D. (1996). Introducing new tests into traditional systems: Insights from general education and from innovation theory. *Language Testing, 13*, 334–354.

Wall, D. (1997). Impact and washback in language testing. In C. Clapham & D. Corson (Eds.), *Encyclopedia of language and education: Vol. 7. Language testing and assessment* (pp. 291–302). Dordrecht: Kluwer Academic.

Wall, D. (1999). *The impact of high-stakes examinations on classroom teaching: A case study using insights from testing and innovation theory.* Unpublished doctoral dissertation, Lancaster University, UK.

Wall, D., & Alderson, J. C. (1993). Examining washback: The Sri Lankan impact study. *Language Testing, 10*, 41–69.

Preface

We live in a testing world. Our education system is awash with various high-stakes testing, be it standardized, multiple-choice testing or portfolio assessment. *Washback*, a term commonly used in applied linguistics, refers to the influence of language testing on teaching and learning. The extensive use of examination scores for various educational and social purposes in society nowadays has made the washback effect a distinct educational phenomenon. This is true both in general education and in teaching English as a second/foreign language (ESL/EFL), from Kindergarten to Grade 12 classrooms to the tertiary level. Washback is a phenomenon that is of inherent interest to teachers, researchers, program coordinators/directors, policymakers, and others in their day-to-day educational activities.

Despite the importance of this issue, however, it is only recently that researchers have become aware of the importance of investigating this phenomenon empirically. There are only a limited number of chapters in books and papers in journals, except for the notable exception of a special issue on washback in the journal *Language Testing* (edited by J. C. Alderson and D. Wall, 1996). Once the washback effect has been examined in the light of empirical studies, it can no longer be taken for granted that where there is a test, there is a direct effect. The small body of research to date suggests that washback is a highly complex phenomenon, and it has already been established that simply changing test contents or methods will not necessarily bring about direct and desirable changes in education as intended through a testing change. Rather, various factors within a particular educational context seem to be involved in engineering desirable washback. The question then is what factors are involved and under which conditions beneficial washback is most likely to be generated. Thus, researchers have started to pay attention to the specific educational contexts and testing cultures within which different types of tests are being used for different purposes, so that implications and recommendations can be made available to education and testing organizations in many parts of the world.

In the field of language testing, researchers' major interest has been to address issues and problems inherent in a test in order to increase its reliability and validity. However, washback goes well beyond the test itself. Researchers now need to take account of a plethora of variables, including school curriculum, behaviors of teachers and learners inside and outside the classroom, their perceptions of the test, how test scores are used, and so forth. This volume is at the intersection of language testing and teaching practices and aims to provide theoretical, methodological, and practical guidance for current and future washback studies.

STRUCTURE OF THE BOOK

The purpose of the present volume, then, is twofold; first to update teachers, researchers, policymakers/administrators, and others on what is involved in this complex issue of testing and its effects, and how such a phenomenon benefits teaching and learning, and second, to provide researchers with models of research studies on which future studies can be based. In order to address these two main purposes, the volume consists of two parts. Part I provides readers with an overall view of the complexity of washback, and the various contextual factors entangled within testing, teaching, and learning. Part II provides a collection of empirical washback studies carried out in many different parts of the world, which lead the readers further into the heart of the issue within each educational context.

Chapter 1 discusses washback research conducted in general education, and in language education in particular. The first part of the chapter reviews the origin and the definition of this phenomenon. The second examines the complexity of the positive and negative influence of washback, and the third explores its functions and mechanisms. The last part of the chapter looks at the concept of bringing about changes in teaching and learning through changes in testing.

Chapter 2 provides guidance to researchers by illustrating the process that the author followed to investigate the effects of the Japanese university entrance examinations. Readers are also introduced to the methodological aspects of the second part of this volume.

Chapter 3 examines the relationship between washback and curricular innovation. It discusses theories of research on washback from both general education and language education, and relates that discussion to what we now know about innovation, especially educational innovation.

Chapter 4 reports on a survey research study conducted in Washington State to examine the effects of the state's standards-based reform on school and classroom practices. The chapter reports on a variety of changes in classroom practices that occurred following the reform, including changes in curriculum and in instructional strategies. However, the core of writing instruction continued to be writing conventions and the writing process, as it had been before the new tests were introduced. This study concludes that both the standards and the tests appeared to influence practice, but it is difficult to determine their relative impact.

Chapter 5 describes the development of data collection instruments for an impact study of the International English Language Testing System (IELTS). Among a broad range of test impact areas the study covers, this chapter concentrates on the impact study instrument for the evaluation of textbooks and other materials, tracing its design, development, and validation through iterative processes of trailing and focus group analyses. Key issues of data collection instrumentation classifications, format, and scale are exemplified and discussed, and the finalized instrument for the analysis of textbook materials is presented.

Chapter 6 reports on research in New Zealand on the washback effects of preparation courses for the IELTS. The study involves intensive classroom observation of two IELTS courses over a 4-week period. The results show clear differences between the two courses. One was strongly focused on familiarizing students with the test and practicing test tasks, while the other covered a wider range of academic study tasks. The research highlights both the potential and the limitations of this kind of study in the investigation of washback.

Chapter 7 is a report of the study that provides an examination of the washback effect in the context of classroom-based, achievement assessment in Australia. Using conceptualization derived from a survey, interviews, and classroom observations based on structured observation instruments, the author proposes a new model for washback, which places the teacher, and the teacher's beliefs, assumptions, and knowledge (Woods, 1996), at the center of the washback effect.

Chapter 8 reports on part of a large project investigating the effect of the Japanese university entrance examinations on secondary level classroom instructions. The results of observation studies accompanied with teacher interviews indicate that teacher factors, such as personal beliefs and educational background, are important in the process of producing examination effects. To induce beneficial washback in light of the results, an argument is made for the importance of incorporating a type of re-attribution training in teacher development courses, and of taking account of a type of face validity during the test development process.

Chapter 9 investigates washback by identifying the ways in which an examination reform influenced teachers and their classroom teaching within the context of teaching English as a second language (ESL) in Hong Kong secondary schools. It reports comparative survey findings from teachers' perspectives in relation to their reactions and attitudes, and day-to-day classroom teaching activities, toward an examination change. The findings illustrate certain washback effects on teachers' perceptions toward the new examination, although teachers' daily teaching did not seem to be much influenced by the examination at the time of the research.

Chapter 10 investigates the intended washback of the National Matriculation English Test in China (NMET) with a view to deepening our understanding of the washback phenomenon through new empirical evidence. Analyses of interview data reveal that there is considerable discrepancy between the test constructors' intentions and school practice. The study concludes that the NMET has achieved very limited intended washback and is an inefficient tool for bringing about pedagogical changes in schools in China.

Chapter 11 examines the washback effects of the Israeli national EFL oral matriculation test immediately following its administration. The study attempts to find whether this high-stake test affects the educational processes, the participants and the products of teaching and learning in Israeli high schools, and if so, how. The study examines various factors that have been found to be involved in the process of generating washback.

This volume is intended for a wide variety of audiences, in particular, language teachers and testing researchers who are interested in the application of findings to actual teaching and learning situations, researchers who wish to keep abreast of new issues in this area, researchers and graduate students in broader language education and educational measurement and evaluation areas who wish to conduct washback research in their own contexts, policy and decision makers in educational and testing organizations, comparative education audiences, and language teachers, who would like to know what washback looks like and who would like to carry out washback research in their own context.

ACKNOWLEDGMENTS

The volume could not have been completed without the contributions of a group of dedicated researchers who are passionate about washback research. We thank you all for going through the whole process with us in bringing this book to the language testing and assessment community. We are grateful to so many individuals including:

- Professor J. C. Alderson for his Foreword to this book, and as a pioneer in the field of washback research
- Hong Wang at Queen's University, Rie Koizumi and Yo In'nami at University of Tsukuba for proofing and printing the drafts
- Naomi Silverman, Senior Editor, and Lori Hawver, Assistant Editor, at Lawrence Erlbaum Associates for supporting us in completing this book project
- Antony Kunnan, California State University, Los Angeles; James D. Brown, University of Hawai'i, and one anonymous reviewer for detailed and constructive feedback

Finally, our greatest thanks go to our families, for their patience, encouragement, and support while we were working on this book.

—Liying Cheng
—Yoshinori Watanabe
—Andy Curtis

About the Authors

THE EDITORS

Liying Cheng is an assistant professor and a member of the Assessment and Evaluation Group (AEG) at the Faculty of Education, Queen's University in Canada. Before she joined Queen's University, she was a Killam postdoctoral fellow in the Center for Research in Applied Measurement and Evaluation, University of Alberta. Her doctoral dissertation—*The Washback Effect of Public Examination Change on Classroom Teaching*—from the University of Hong Kong won the seventh TOEFL Award for Outstanding Doctoral Dissertation Research on Second/Foreign Language Testing.

Yoshinori Watanabe is an associate professor of the Faculty of Education and Human Studies at Akita University, Japan. He is also a research fellow of the Japanese Ministry of Education, Science and Culture, investigating the issue of new curricular innovation implemented in 2002. His long-standing research interest lies in language learning strategies, classroom observation, examination washback, and research methodology of ESL.

Andy Curtis is the Director of the School of English at Queen's University in Canada, where international students from around the world are tested, taught, and assessed. Before he joined Queen's University, he was an associate professor in the Department of Language Teacher Education at the School for International Training in Vermont. He has published research on change and innovation in language education, and he has worked with language teachers and learners in Europe, Asia, North, South, and Central America.

THE CONTRIBUTORS

Stephen Andrews heads the language and literature division in Hong Kong University's Faculty of Education. He has extensive involvement in assessment as was previously Head of the TEFL Unit at the University of Cambridge Local Examinations Syndicate. He has been involved in washback research for more than 10 years.

Sheila Barron is an assistant professor of educational measurement and statistics at the University of Iowa. While doing a postdoctoral fellowship at RAND, she began a series of research studies with Dan Koretz and Brian Stecher investigating the consequences of high stakes testing on school and classroom practices.

Catherine Burrows is the Manager of the TAFE Strategic Services Unit in the New SouthWales Department of Education and Training. Her doctoral research, which forms the basis of her chapter in this book, was undertaken when she was the Coordinator of Staff and Curriculum Development in NSW Adult Migrant English Service.

Tammi Chun is the Director of Project Evaluation for Gaining Early Awareness and Readiness for Undergraduate Programs (GEAR UP) at the University of Hawai'i at Manoa. Chun's research includes study of the implementation of standards-based reform, including assessment, accountability, and instructional guidance policies, in America.

Irit Ferman is an instructor and English Center Director, at the English Department, Levinsky College of Education, Tel-Aviv, Israel. She graduated the Language Education Program, School of Education, Tel-Aviv University, 1998, with distinction. Her washback-related research has focused on the impact of tests on EFL teaching–learning–assessment practices and the perceptions of those involved.

Roger Hawkey is a consultant on testing and evaluation, currently working on several test validation research projects for the University of Cambridge ESOL Examinations. These include the IELTS impact study described in this volume, and a study of the impact of the *Progetto Lingue 2000* language teaching reform program in Italy.

Belinda Hayes is a senior lecturer at the Auckland University of Technology, New Zealand, where she teaches international students, creates courses, and trains teachers.

John Read teaches courses in applied linguistics, TESOL, and academic writing at Victoria University of Wellington, New Zealand. His research interests are in testing English for academic purposes and second language vocabulary assessment. He is the author of *Assessing Vocabulary* (Cambridge University Press, 2000) and coeditor of the journal *Language Testing*.

Nick Saville is Director of Research and Validation for Cambridge ESOL Examination where he coordinates the research and validation program. He has worked on several impact studies, including the IELTS impact project reported in this volume, and a study of the impact of the *Progetto Lingue 2000* in Italy.

Brian Stecher is a senior social scientist in the education program at RAND. His research emphasis is applied educational measurement, including the implementation, quality, and impact of state assessment and accountability systems; and the cost, quality, and feasibility of performance-based assessments.

Luxia Qi is an associate professor of English at the Guangdong University of Foreign Studies in China. Her teaching and research areas include language testing, reading in a foreign language, and second language acquisition. Her doctoral studies at City University of Hong Kong focused on the issue of washback in language testing.

PART

I

CONCEPTS AND METHODOLOGY OF WASHBACK

CHAPTER

1

Washback or Backwash: A Review of the Impact of Testing on Teaching and Learning

Liying Cheng
Andy Curtis
Queen's University

Washback or backwash, a term now commonly used in applied linguistics, refers to the influence of testing on teaching and learning (Alderson & Wall, 1993), and has become an increasingly prevalent and prominent phenomenon in education–"what is assessed becomes what is valued, which becomes what is taught" (McEwen, 1995a, p. 42). There seems to be at least two major types or areas of washback or backwash studies–those relating to traditional, multiple-choice, large-scale tests, which are perceived to have had mainly negative influences on the quality of teaching and learning (Madaus & Kellaghan, 1992; Nolan, Haladyna, & Haas, 1992; Shepard, 1990), and those studies where a specific test or examination[1] has been modified and improved upon (e.g., performance-based assessment), in order to exert a positive influence on teaching and learning (Linn & Herman, 1997; Sanders & Horn, 1995). The second type of studies has shown, however, positive, negative, or no influence on teaching and learning. Furthermore, many of those studies have turned to focus on understanding the mechanism of how washback or backwash is used to change teaching and learning (Cheng, 1998a; Wall, 1999).

[1]In this chapter, the terms "test" and "examination" are used interchangeably to refer to the use of assessment by means of a test or an examination.

WASHBACK: THE DEFINITION AND ORIGIN

Although washback is a term commonly used in applied linguistics today, it is rarely found in dictionaries. However, the word *backwash* can be found in certain dictionaries and is defined as "the unwelcome repercussions of some social action" by the *New Webster's Comprehensive Dictionary*, and "unpleasant after-effects of an event or situation" by the *Collins Cobuild Dictionary*. The negative connotations of these two definitions are interesting, as they inadvertently touch on some of the negative responses and reactions to the relationships between teaching and testing, which we explore in more detail shortly.

Washback (Alderson & Wall, 1993) or *backwash* (Biggs, 1995, 1996) here refers to the influence of testing on teaching and learning. The concept is rooted in the notion that tests or examinations can and should drive teaching, and hence learning, and is also referred to as *measurement-driven instruction* (Popham, 1987). In order to achieve this goal, a "match" or an overlap between the content and format of the test or the examination and the content and format of the curriculum (or "curriculum surrogate" such as the textbook) is encouraged. This is referred to as *curriculum alignment* by Shepard (1990, 1991b, 1992, 1993). Although the idea of alignment–matching the test and the curriculum–has been descried by some as "unethical," and threatening the validity of the test (Haladyna, Nolen, & Haas, 1991, p. 4; Widen, O'Shea, & Pye, 1997), such alignment is evident in a number of countries, for example, Hong Kong (see Cheng, 1998a; Stecher, Barron, Chun, Krop, & Ross, 2000). This alignment, in which a new or revised examination is introduced into the education system with the aim of improving teaching and learning, is referred to as *systemic validity* by Frederiksen and Collins (1989), *consequential validity* by Messick (1989, 1992, 1994, 1996), and *test impact* by Bachman and Palmer (1996) and Baker (1991).

Wall (1997) distinguished between test impact and test washback in terms of the scope of the effects. According to Wall, *impact* refers to ". . . any of the effects that a test may have on individuals, policies or practices, within the classroom, the school, the educational system or society as a whole" (see Stecher, Chun, & Barron, chap. 4, this volume), whereas *washback* (or *backwash*) is defined as "the effects of tests on teaching and learning" (Wall, 1997, p. 291).

Although different terms are preferred by different researchers, they all refer to different facets of the same phenomenon–the influence of testing on teaching and learning. The authors of this chapter have chosen to use the term *washback*, as it is the mostly commonly used in the field of applied linguistics.

The study of washback has resulted in recent developments in language testing, and measurement-driven reform of instruction in general education. Research in language testing has centered on whether and how we assess the specific characteristics of a given group of test takers and whether and how we can incorporate such information into the ways in which we design language tests. One of the most important theoretical developments in language testing in the past 30 years has been the realization that a language test score represents a complex of multiple influences. Language test scores cannot be interpreted simplistically as an indicator of the particular language ability we think we are measuring. The scores are also affected by the characteristics and contents of the test tasks, the characteristics of the test takers, the strategies test takers employ in attempting to complete the test tasks, as well as the inferences we draw from the test results. These factors undoubtedly interact with each other.

Nearly 20 years ago, Alderson (1986) identified *washback* as a distinct—and at that time emerging—area within language testing, to which we needed to turn our attention. Alderson (1986) discussed the "potentially powerful influence offsets" (p. 104) and argued for innovations in the language curriculum through innovations in language testing (also see Wall, 1996, 1997, 2000). At around the same time, Davies (1985) was asking whether tests should necessarily follow the curriculum, and suggested that perhaps tests ought to lead and influence the curriculum. Morrow (1986) extended the use of washback to include the notion of *washback validity*, which describes the relationship between testing, and teaching and learning (p. 6). Morrow also claimed that "... in essence, an examination of washback validity would take testing researchers into the classroom in order to observe the effects of their tests in action" (p. 6). This has important implications for test validity.

Looking back, we can see that examinations have often been used as a means of control, and have been with us for a long time: a thousand years or more, if we include their use in Imperial China to select the highest officials of the land (Arnove, Altback, & Kelly, 1992; Hu, 1984; Lai, 1970). Those examinations were probably the first civil service examinations ever developed. To avoid corruption, all essays in the Imperial Examination were marked anonymously, and the Emperor personally supervised the final stage of the examination. Although the goal of the examination was to select civil servants, its washback effect was to establish and control an educational program, as prospective mandarins set out to prepare themselves for the examination that would decide not only their personal fate but also influence the future of the Empire (Spolsky, 1995a, 1995b).

The use of examinations to select for education and employment has also existed for a long time. Examinations were seen by some societies as ways to encourage the development of talent, to upgrade the performance of schools and colleges, and to counter to some degree, nepotism, favoritism, and even outright corruption in the allocation of scarce opportunities

(Bray & Steward, 1998; Eckstein & Noah, 1992). If the initial spread of examinations can be traced back to such motives, the very same reasons appear to be as powerful today as ever they were. Linn (2000) classified the use of tests and assessments as key elements in relation to five waves of educational reform over the past 50 years: their tracking and selecting role in the 1950s; their program accountability role in the 1960s; minimum competency testing in the 1970s; school and district accountability in the 1980s; and the standards-based accountability systems in the 1990s (p. 4). Furthermore, it is clear that tests and assessments are continuing to play a crucial and critical role in education into the new millennium.

In spite of this long and well-established place in educational history, the use of tests has, constantly, been subject to criticism. Nevertheless, tests continue to occupy a leading place in the educational policies and practices of a great many countries (see Baker, 1991; Calder, 1997; Cannell, 1987; Cheng, 1997, 1998a; Heyneman, 1987; Heyneman & Ransom, 1990; James, 2000; Kellaghan & Greaney, 1992; Li, 1990; Macintosh, 1986; Runte, 1998; Shohamy, 1993a; Shohamy, Donitsa-Schmidt, & Ferman, 1996; Widen et al., 1997; Yang, 1999; and chapters in Part II of this volume). These researchers, and others, have, over many years, documented the impact of testing on school and classroom practices, and on the personal and professional lives and experiences of principals, teachers, students, and other educational stakeholders.

Aware of the power of tests, policymakers in many parts of the world continue to use them to manipulate their local educational systems, to control curricula and to impose (or promote) new textbooks and new teaching methods. Testing and assessment is "the darling of the policy-makers" (Madaus, 1985a, 1985b) despite the fact that they have been the focus of controversy for as long as they have existed. One reason for their longevity in the face of such criticism is that tests are viewed as the primary tools through which changes in the educational system can be introduced *without having to change other educational components* such as teacher training or curricula. Shohamy (1992) originally noted that "this phenomenon [washback] is the result of the strong authority of external testing and the major impact it has on the lives of test takers" (p. 513). Later Shohamy et al. (1996; see also Stiggins & Faires-Conklin, 1992) expanded on this position thus:

> the power and authority of tests enable policy-makers to use them as effective tools for controlling educational systems and prescribing the behavior of those who are affected by their results—administrators, teachers and students. School-wide exams are used by principals and administrators to enforce learning, while in classrooms, tests and quizzes are used by teachers to impose discipline and to motivate learning. (p. 299)

One example of these beliefs about the legislative power and authority of tests was seen in 1994 in Canada, where a consortium of provincial ministers of education instituted a system of national achievement testing in the areas of reading, language arts, and science (Council of Ministers of Education, Canada, 1994). Most of the provinces now require students to pass centrally set school-leaving examinations as a condition of school graduation (Anderson, Muir, Bateson, Blackmore, & Rogers, 1990; Lock, 2001; Runte, 1998; Widen, O'Shea, & Pye, 1997).

Petrie (1987) concluded that "it would not be too much of an exaggeration to say that evaluation and testing have become the engine for implementing educational policy" (p. 175). The extent to which this is true depends on the different contexts, as shown by those explored in this volume, but a number of recurring themes do emerge. Examinations of various kinds have been used for a very long time for many different purposes in many different places. There is a set of relationships, planned and unplanned, positive and negative, between teaching and testing. These two facts mean that, although washback has only been identified relatively recently, it is likely that washback effects have been occurring for an equally long time. It is also likely that these teaching–testing relationships are likely to become closer and more complex in the future. It is therefore essential that the education community work together to understand and evaluate the effects of the use of testing on all of the interconnected aspects of teaching and learning within different education systems.

WASHBACK: POSITIVE, NEGATIVE, NEITHER OR BOTH?

Movement in a particular direction is an inherent part of the use of the washback metaphor to describe teaching–testing relationships. For example, Pearson (1988) stated that "public examinations influence the attitudes, behaviors, and motivation of teachers, learners and parents, and, because examinations often come at the end of a course, this influence is seen working in a backward direction—hence the term 'washback' " (p. 98). However, like Davies (1985), Pearson believed that the direction in which washback actually works must be forward (i.e., testing leading teaching and learning).

The potentially bidirectional nature of washback has been recognized by, for example, Messick (1996), who defined washback as the "extent to which a test influences language teachers and learners to do things they would not necessarily otherwise do that *promote or inhibit* [emphasis added] language learning" (p. 241, as cited in Alderson & Wall, 1993, p. 117). Wall and Alderson also noted that "tests can be powerful determiners, *both positively and negatively,* [emphasis added] of what happens in classrooms" (Alderson & Wall, 1993, p. 117; Wall & Alderson, 1993, p. 41).

Messick (1996) went on to comment that some proponents have even maintained that a test's validity should be appraised by the degree to which it manifests positive or negative washback, which is similar to Frederiksen and Collins' (1989) notion of *systemic validity*.

Underpinning the notion of direction is the issue of what it is that is being directed. Biggs (1995) used the term *backwash* (p. 12) to refer to the fact that testing drives not only the curriculum, but also the teaching methods and students' approaches to learning (Crooks, 1988; Frederiksen, 1984; Frederiksen & Collins, 1989). However, Spolsky (1994) believed that "backwash is better applied only to accidental side-effects of examinations, and not to those effects intended when the first purpose of the examination is control of the curriculum" (p. 55). In an empirical study of an intended public examination change on classroom teaching in Hong Kong, Cheng (1997, 1998a) combined movement and motive, defining washback as "an intended direction and function of curriculum change, by means of a change of public examinations, on aspects of teaching and learning" (Cheng, 1997, p. 36). As Cheng's study showed, when a public examination is used as a vehicle for an intended curriculum change, unintended and accidental side effects can also occur, that is, both negative and positive influence, as such change involves elaborate and extensive webs of interwoven causes and effects.

Whether the effect of testing is deemed to be positive or negative should also depend on *who* it is that actually conducts the investigation within a particular education context, as well as *where*, the school or university contexts, *when*, the time and duration of using such assessment practices, *why*, the rationale, and *how*, the different approaches used by different participants within the context.

If the potentially bidirectional nature of washback is accepted, and movement in a positive direction is accepted as the aim, the question then becomes methodological, that is, how to bring about this positive movement. After considering several definitions of washback, Bailey (1996) concluded that more empirical research needed to be carried out in order to document its exact nature and mechanisms, while also identifying "concerns about what constitutes both positive and negative washback, as well as about how to promote the former and inhibit the latter" (p. 259).

According to Messick (1996), "for optimal positive washback there should be little, if any, difference between activities involved in learning the language and activities involved in preparing for the test" (pp. 241–242). However, the lack of simple, one-to-one relationships in such complex systems was highlighted by Messick (1996): "A poor test may be associated with positive effects and a good test with negative effects because of other things that are done or not done in the education system" (p. 242). In terms of complexity and validity, Alderson and Wall (1993) argued that washback is "likely to be a complex phenomenon which cannot be related directly to a test's validity" (p. 116). The washback effect should, therefore, refer to the effects of the test itself on aspects of teaching and learning.

The fact that there are so many other forces operating within any education context, which also contribute to or ensure the washback effect on teaching and learning, has been demonstrated in several washback studies (e.g., Anderson et al., 1990; Cheng, 1998b, 1999; Herman, 1992; Madaus, 1988; Smith, 1991a, 1991b; Wall, 2000; Watanabe, 1996a; Widen et al., 1997). The key issue here is how those forces within a particular educational context can be teased out to understand the effects of testing in that environment, and how confident we can be in formulating hypotheses and drawing conclusions about the nature and the scope of the effects within broader educational contexts.

Negative Washback

Tests in general, and perhaps language tests in particular, are often criticized for their negative influence on teaching—so-called "negative washback"—which has long been identified as a potential problem. For example, nearly 50 years ago, Vernon (1956) claimed that teachers tended to ignore subjects and activities that did not contribute directly to passing the exam, and that examinations "distort the curriculum" (p. 166). Wiseman (1961) believed that paid coaching classes, which were intended for preparing students for exams, were not a good use of the time, because students were practicing exam techniques rather than language learning activities (p. 159), and Davies (1968) believed that testing devices had become teaching devices; that teaching and learning was effectively being directed to past examination papers, making the educational experience narrow and uninteresting (p. 125).

More recently, Alderson and Wall (1993) referred to negative washback as the undesirable effect on teaching and learning of a particular test deemed to be "poor" (p. 5). Alderson and Wall's *poor* here means "something that the teacher or learner does not wish to teach or learn." The tests may well fail to reflect the learning principles or the course objectives to which they are supposedly related. In reality, teachers and learners may end up teaching and learning toward the test, regardless of whether or not they support the test or fully understand its rationale or aims.

In general education, Fish (1988) found that teachers reacted negatively to pressure created by public displays of classroom scores, and also found that relatively inexperienced teachers felt greater anxiety and accountability pressure than experienced teachers, showing the influence of factors such as age and experience. Noble and Smith (1994a) also found that high-stakes testing could affect teachers directly and negatively (p. 3), and that "teaching test-taking skills and drilling on multiple-choice worksheets is likely to boost the scores but unlikely to promote general understanding" (1994b, p. 6). From an extensive qualitative study of the role of external testing in elementary schools in the United States, Smith (1991b) listed a number of damaging effects, as the "testing programs substantially reduce the time available for instruction, narrow curricular offerings and modes of instruction, and potentially reduce the capacities of teachers to teach content and to use methods and materials that are incompatible with standardized testing formats" (p. 8).

This narrowing was not the only detrimental effect found in a Canadian study, in which Anderson et al. (1990) carried out a survey study investigating the impact of re-introducing final examinations at Grade 12 in British Columbia. The teachers in the study reported a narrowing to the topics the examination was most likely to include, and that students adopted more of a memorization approach, with reduced emphasis on critical thinking. In a more recent Canadian study (Widen et al., 1997), Grade 12 science teachers reported their belief that they had lost much of their discretion in curriculum decision making, and, therefore, much of their autonomy. When teachers believe they are being circumscribed and controlled by the examinations, and students' focus is on what will be tested, teaching and learning are in danger of becoming limited and confined to those aspects of the subject and field of study that are testable (see also Calder, 1990, 1997).

Positive Washback

Like most areas of language testing, for each argument in favor or opposed to a particular position, there is a counterargument. There are, then, researchers who strongly believe that it is feasible and desirable to bring about beneficial changes in teaching by changing examinations, representing the "positive washback" scenario, which is closely related to "measurement-driven instruction" in general education. In this case, teachers and learners have a positive attitude toward the examination or test, and work willingly and collaboratively toward its objectives.

For example, Heyneman (1987) claimed that many proponents of academic achievement testing view "coachability" not as a drawback, but rather as a virtue (p. 262), and Pearson (1988) argued for a mutually beneficial arrangement, in which "good tests will be more or less directly usable as teaching-learning activities. Similarly, good teaching-learning tasks will be more or less directly usable for testing purposes, even though practical or financial constraints limit the possibilities" (p. 107). Considering the complexity of teaching and learning and the many constraints other than those financial, such claims may sound somewhat idealistic, and even open to accusations of being rather simplistic. However, Davies (1985) maintained that "creative and innovative testing . . . can, quite successfully, attract to itself a syllabus change or a new syllabus which effectively makes it into an achievement test" (p. 8). In this case, the test no longer needs to be just an obedient servant. It can also be a leader.

As the foregoing studies show, there are conflicting reactions toward positive and negative washback on teaching and learning, and no obvious consensus in the research community as to whether certain washback effects are positive or negative. As was discussed earlier, one reason for this is the potentially bidirectional nature of an exam or test, the positive or negative nature of which can be influenced by many contextual factors.

According to Pearson (1988), a test's washback effect will be negative if it fails to reflect the learning principles and course objectives to which the test supposedly relates, and it will be positive if the effects are beneficial and "encourage the whole range of desired changes" (p. 101). Alderson and Wall (1993), on the other hand, stressed that the quality of the washback effect might be independent of the quality of a test (pp. 117–118). Any test, good or bad, may result in beneficial or detrimental washback effects.

It is possible that research into washback may benefit from turning its attention toward looking at the complex causes of such a phenomenon in teaching and learning, rather than focusing on deciding whether or not the effects can be classified as positive or negative. According to Alderson and Wall (1993), one way of doing this is to first investigate as thoroughly as possible the broad educational context in which an assessment is introduced, since other forces exist within the society and the education system that might prevent washback from appearing (p. 116). A potentially key societal factor is the political forces at work. As Heyneman (1987) put it: "Testing is a profession, but it is highly susceptible to political interference. To a large extent, the quality of tests relies on the ability of a test agency to pursue professional ends autonomous" (p. 262). If the consequences of a particular test for teaching and learning are to be evaluated, the educational context in which the test takes place needs to be fully understood. Whether the washback effect is positive or negative will largely depend on where and how it exists and manifests itself within a particular educational context, such as those studies explored in this volume.

WASHBACK: FUNCTIONS AND MECHANISMS

Traditionally, tests have come at the end of the teaching and learning process for evaluative purposes. However, with the widespread expansion and proliferation of high-stakes public examination systems, the direction seems to have been largely reversed. Testing can come first in the teaching and learning process. Particularly when tests are used as levers for change, new materials need to be designed to match the purposes of a new test, and school administrative and management staff, teachers, and students are generally required to learn to work in alternative ways, and often work harder, to achieve high scores on the test. In addition to these changes, many more changes in the teaching and learning context can occur as the result of a new test, although the consequences and effects may be independent of the original intentions of the test designers, due to the complex interplay of forces and factors both within and beyond the school.

Such influences were linked to test validity by Shohamy (1993a), who pointed out that "the need to include aspects of test use in construct validation originates in the fact that testing is not an isolated event; rather, it is connected to a whole set of variables that interact in the educational process" (p. 2). Similarly, Linn (1992) encouraged the measurement research community "to make the case that the introduction of any new high-stakes examination system should pay greater attention to investigations of both the intended and unintended consequences of the system than was typical of previous test-based reform efforts" (p. 29).

As a result of this complexity, Messick (1989) recommended a unified validity concept, which requires that when an assessment model is designed to make inferences about a certain construct, the inferences drawn from that model should not only derive from test score interpretation, but also from other variables operating within the social context (Bracey, 1989; Cooley, 1991; Cronbach, 1988; Gardner, 1992; Gifford & O'Connor, 1992; Linn, Baker, & Dunbar, 1991; Messick, 1992). The importance of collaboration was also highlighted by Messick (1975): "Researchers, other educators, and policy makers must work together to develop means of evaluating educational effectiveness that accurately represent a school or district's progress toward a broad range of important educational goals" (p. 956).

In exploring the mechanism of such an assessment function, Bailey (1996, pp. 262–264) cited Hughes' trichotomy (1993) to illustrate the complex mechanisms through which washback occurs in actual teaching and learning environments (see Table 1.1). Hughes (1993) explained his model as follows:

> The trichotomy . . . allows us to construct a basic model of backwash. The nature of a test may first affect the perceptions and attitudes of the participants towards their teaching and learning tasks. These perceptions and attitudes in

TABLE 1.1
The Trichotomy Backwash Model

(a) Participants—students, classroom teachers, administrators, materials developers and publishers, whose perceptions and attitudes toward their work may be affected by a test
(b) Processes—any actions taken by the participants which may contribute to the process of learning
(c) Products—what is learned (facts, skills, etc.) and the quality of the learning

Note. Adapted from Hughes, 1993, p. 2. Cited in Bailey (1996).

> turn may affect what the participants do in carrying out their work (process), including practicing the kind of items that are to be found in the test, which will affect the learning outcomes, the product of the work. (p. 2)

Whereas Hughes focused on participants, processes, and products in his model to illustrate the washback mechanism, Alderson and Wall (1993), in their Sri Lankan study, focused on micro aspects of teaching and learning that might be influenced by examinations. Based on that study, they drew up 15 hypotheses regarding washback (pp. 120–121), which referred to areas of teaching and learning that are generally affected by washback. Alderson and Wall concluded that further research on washback is needed, and that such research must entail "increasing specification of the Washback Hypothesis" (p. 127). They called on researchers to take account of findings in the research literature in at least two areas: (a) motivation and performance, and (b) innovation and change in the educational settings.

One response to Alderson and Wall's (1993) recommendation was a large-scale quantitative and qualitative empirical study, in which Cheng (1997, 1998a) developed the notion of "washback intensity" to refer to the degree of the washback effect in an area or a number of areas of teaching and learning affected by an examination. Each of the areas was studied in order to chart and understand the function and mechanism of washback—the participants, the processes, and the products—that might have been brought about by the change of a major public examination within a specific educational context (Hong Kong).

Wall (1996) stressed the difficulties in finding explanations of how tests exert influence on teaching (p. 334). Wall (1999, 2000) used the innovation literature and incorporated findings from this literature into her research areas to propose ways of exploring the complex aspect of washback:

- The writing of detailed baseline studies to identify important characteristics in the target system and the environment, including an analysis of current testing practices (Shohamy et al., 1996), current teaching practices, resources (Bailey, 1996; Stevenson & Riewe, 1981), and attitudes of key stakeholders (Bailey, 1996; Hughes, 1993).
- The formation of management teams representing all the important interest groups, for example, teachers, teacher trainers, university specialists, ministry officials, parents and learners, etc. (Cheng, 1998a).

Fullan with Stiegelbauer (1991) and Fullan (1993), also in the context of innovation and change, discussed changes in schools, and identified two main recurring themes:

- Innovation should be seen as a process rather than as an event.

- All the participants who are affected by an innovation have to find their own "meaning" for the change.

Fullan explained that the "subjective reality" which teachers' experience would always contrast with the "objective reality" that the proponents of change had originally imagined. According to Fullan, teachers work on their own, with little reference to experts or consultation with colleagues. They are forced to make on-the-spot decisions, with little time to reflect on better solutions. They are pressured to accomplish a great deal, but are given far too little time to achieve their goals. When, on top of this, they are expected to carry forward an innovation that is generally not of their own making, their lives can become very difficult indeed. This may help to explain why intended washback does or does not occur in teaching and learning. If educational change is imposed upon those parties most directly affected by the change, that is, learners and teachers, without consultation of those parties, resistance is likely to be the natural response (Curtis, 2000). In addition, it has also been found that there tend to be discrepancies between the intention of any innovation or curriculum change and the understanding of teachers who are tasked with the job of implementing that change (Andrews, 1994, 1995; Markee, 1997).

Andrews (1994, 1995) highlighted the complexity of the relationship between washback and curriculum innovation, and summarized three possible responses of educators in response to washback: fight it, ignore it, or use it (see also Andrew's chap. 3 in this volume; Heyneman, 1987, p. 260). By "fight it," Heyneman referred to the effort to replace examinations with other sorts of selection processes and criteria, on the grounds that examinations have encouraged rote memorization at the expense of more desirable educational practices. In terms of "ignoring it," Andrews (1994) used the metaphor of the ostrich pretending that on-coming danger does not really exist by hiding its head in the sand (pp. 51–52). According to Andrews, those who are involved with mainstream activities, such as syllabus design, material writing, and teacher training, view testers as a "special breed" using an obscure and arcane terminology. Tests and exams have been seen as an occasional necessary evil, a dose of unpleasant medicine, the taste of which should be washed away as quickly as possible.

The third response, "use it," is now perhaps the most common of the three, and using washback to promote particular pedagogical goals is now a well-established approach in education (see also Andrews & Fullilove, 1993, 1994; Blenkin, Edwards, & Kelly, 1992; Brooke & Oxenham, 1984; Pearson, 1988; Somerset, 1983; Swain, 1984). The question of who it is that uses it relates, at least in part, to the earlier discussion of the legislative power of tests as perceived by governments and policymakers in many parts of the world (see also Stecher, Chun, & Barron, chap. 4, this volume).

WASHBACK: THE CURRENT TRENDS IN ASSESSMENT

One of the main functions of assessment is generally believed to be as one form of leverage for educational change, which has often led to top-down educational reform strategies by employing "better" kinds of assessment practices (James, 2000; Linn, 2000; Noble & Smith, 1994a). Assessment practices are currently undergoing a major paradigm shift in many parts of the world, which can be described as a reaction to the perceived shortcomings of the prevailing paradigm, with its emphasis on standardized testing (Biggs, 1992, 1996; Genesee, 1994). Alternative or authentic assessment methods have thus emerged as systematic attempts to measure learners' abilities to use previously acquired knowledge in solving novel problems or completing specific tasks, as part of this use of assessment to reform curriculum and improve instruction at the school and classroom level (Linn, 1983, 1992; Lock, 2001; Noble & Smith, 1994a, 1994b; Popham, 1983).

According to Noble and Smith (1994b), "the most pervasive tool of top-down policy reform is to mandate assessment that can serve as both guideposts and accountability" (p. 1; see also Baker, 1989; Herman, 1989, 1992; McEwen, 1995a, 1995b; Resnick, 1989; Resnick & Resnick, 1992). Noble and Smith (1994a) also pointed out that the goal of current measurement-driven reforms in assessment is to build better tests that will drive schools toward more ambitious goals and reform them toward a curriculum and pedagogy geared more toward thinking and away from rote memory and isolated skills.

Beliefs about testing tend to follow beliefs about teaching and learning (Glaser & Bassok, 1989; Glaser & Silver, 1994), as seen, for example, in the shift from behaviorism to cognitive–constructivism in teaching and learning beliefs. According to the more recent psychological and pedagogical cognitive–constructivist views of learning, effective instruction must mesh with how students think. The direct instruction model under the influence of behaviorism—tell-show-do approach—does not match how students learn, nor does it take into account students' intentions, interests, and choices. Teaching that fits the cognitive–constructivist view of learning is likely to be holistic, integrated, project-oriented, long-term, discovery-based, and social. Likewise, testing should aim to be all of these things too. Thus cognitive–constructivists see performance assessment[2] as par-

[2]Performance assessment based on the constructivist model of learning is defined by Gipps (1994) as "a systematic attempt to measure a learner's ability to use previously acquired knowledge in solving novel problems or completing specific tasks. In performance assessment, real life or simulated assessment exercises are used to elicit original responses, which are directly observed and rated by a qualified judge" (p. 99).

allel in terms of beliefs about how students learn and how their learning can be best supported.

It is possible that performance-based assessment can be designed to be so closely linked to the goals of instruction as to be almost indistinguishable from them. If this were achieved, then rather than being a negative consequence, as is the case now with many existing high-stakes standardized tests, "teaching to these proposed performance assessments, accepted by scholars as inevitable and by teachers as necessary, becomes a virtue, according to this line of thinking" (Noble & Smith, 1994b, p. 7; see also Aschbacher, 1990; Aschbacher, Baker, & Herman, 1988; Baker, Aschbacher, Niemi, & Sato, 1992; Wiggins, 1989a, 1989b, 1993). This rationale relates to the debates about negative versus positive washback, discussed earlier, and may have been one of the results of public discontent with the quality of schooling leading to the development of measurement-driven instruction (Popham, Cruse, Rankin, Standifer, & Williams, 1985, p. 629). However, such a reform strategy has been challenged, for example, described by Andrews (1994, 1995) as a "blunt instrument" for bringing about changes in teaching and learning, since the actual teaching and learning situation is far more complex, as discussed earlier, than proponents of alternative assessment appear to suggest (see also Alderson & Wall, 1993; Cheng, 1998a, 1999; Wall, 1996, 1999).

Each different educational context (including school environment, messages from administration, expectations of other teachers, students, etc.) plays a key role in facilitating or detracting from the possibility of change, which support Andrews' (1994, 1995) beliefs that such reform strategies may be simplistic. More support for this position comes from Noble and Smith (1994a), whose study of the impact of the Arizona Student Assessment Program revealed "both the ambiguities of the policy-making process and the dysfunctional side effects that evolved from the policy's disparities, though the legislative passage of the testing mandate obviously demonstrated Arizona's commitment to top-down reform and its belief that assessment can leverage educational change" (pp. 1–2). The chapters in Part II of this volume describe and explore what impact testing has had in and on those educational contexts, what factors facilitate or detract from the possibility of change derived from assessment, and the lessons we can learn from these studies.

The relationship between testing and teaching and learning does appear to be far more complicated and to involve much more than just the design of a "good" assessment. There is more underlying interplay and intertwining of influences within each specific educational context where the assessment takes place. However, as Madaus (1988) has shown, a high-stakes test can lever the development of new curricular materials, which can be a positive aspect. An important point, though, is that even if new materials are produced as a result of a new examination, they might not be molded according to the innovators' view of what is desirable in terms of teaching, and might instead conform to publishers' views of what will sell, which was shown to be the case within the Hong Kong education context (see Andrews, 1995; Cheng, 1998a).

In spite of the reservations about examination-driven educational reform, measurement-driven instruction will occur when a high-stakes testing of educational achievement influences the instructional program that prepares students for the test, since important contingencies are associated with the students' performance in such a situation, as Popham (1987) has pointed out:

> Few educators would dispute the claim that these sorts of high-stakes tests markedly influence the nature of instructional programs. Whether they are concerned about their own self-esteem or their students' well being, teachers clearly want students to perform well on such tests. Accordingly, teachers tend to focus a significant portion of their instructional activities on the knowledge and skills assessed by such tests. (p. 680)

It is worthwhile pointing out here that performing well on a test does not necessarily indicate good learning or high standards, and it only tells part of the story about the actual teaching and learning. When a new test emerging—a traditional type or an alternative type of assessment emerging—is introduced into an educational context as a mandate and as an accountability measure, it is likely to produce unintended consequences (Cheng & Couture, 2000), which goes back to Messick's (1994) consequential validity. Teachers do not resist changes. They resist being changed (A. Kohn, personal communication, April 17, 2002). As English (1992) stated well, the end point of educational change—classroom change—is in the teachers' hands. When the classroom door is closed and nobody else is around, the classroom teacher can then select and teach almost any curriculum he or she decides is appropriate, irrespective of reforms, innovations, and public examinations.

The studies discussed in this chapter highlight the importance of the educational community understanding the function of testing in relation to the many facets and scopes of teaching and learning as mentioned before, and the importance of evaluating the impact of assessment-driven reform on our teachers, students, and other participants within the educational context. This chapter serves as the starting point, and the linking point to other chapters in this volume, so we can examine the nature of this washback phenomenon from many different perspectives (see chaps. 2 and 3) and within many different educational contexts around the world (chaps. in Part II).

CHAPTER

2

Methodology in Washback Studies

Yoshinori Watanabe
Akita National University

The writing of research methodology puts researchers in a dilemma. A description that is too specific to one context makes it hard to generalize to other contexts, whereas too generalized a description makes it difficult to apply to any particular research context. In the paper entitled "Investigating washback in Japanese EFL classrooms: Problems of methodology" (Watanabe, 1996a), I argued for the importance of incorporating an ethnographic or qualitative approach to the research into washback, and described the process that I followed to investigate the washback effect in the context of the Japanese university entrance examination system (Watanabe, 1997b). Whereas the description of my 1996a paper was highly contextualized, the present chapter attempts to render the description usable in other contexts. In so doing, reference is made to the other chapters of this book where appropriate.

COMPLEXITY OF WASHBACK AS A PHENOMENON

One of the key findings of the research in the field to date is that washback is a highly complex rather than a monolithic phenomenon. The influence has been observed on various aspects of learning and teaching (Bailey, 1996; Cheng, 1997; Watanabe, 1996b), and the process of washback being generated is mediated by numerous factors (Brown, 1997; Shohamy, Donitsa-Schmidt, & Ferman, 1996; Wall, 1996; Wall & Alderson, 1993). Washback is also conceptualized on several dimensions (Watanabe, 2000). Accordingly, the methodology that attempts to disentangle the complexity has inevitably to be multifarious. There is no one single correct methodology, which automatically leads everyone to a solution. Hayek (1952) once stated that the "*scientistic* [italics added] as distinguished from the *scientific* [italics added] view is not an unprejudiced but a very prejudiced approach which, before it has considered its subject, claims to know what is the most appropriate way of investigating it" (p. 24). The approach taken to investigate washback ought to be scientific rather than scientistic. Therefore, I begin with an outline of the complexity of the phenomenon called washback.

(a) Dimensions

Watanabe (1997b) conceptualized washback on the following dimensions, each of which represents one of the various aspects of its nature.

Specificity. Washback may be *general* or *specific*. General washback means a type of effect that may be produced by any test. For example, if there is a hypothesis that a test motivates students to study harder than they would otherwise, washback here relates to any type of exam, hence, general washback. Specific washback, on the other hand, refers to a type of washback that relates to only one specific aspect of a test or one specific test type. For example, a belief that if a listening component is included in the test, the students and teachers will emphasize this aspect in their learning or teaching.

Intensity. Washback may be *strong* or *weak*. If the test has a strong effect, then it will determine everything that happens in the classroom, and lead all teachers to teach in the same way toward the exams. On the other hand, if a test has a weak effect, then it will affect only a part of the classroom events, or only some teachers and students, but not others. If the examination produces an effect only on some teachers, it is likely that the effect is mediated by certain teacher factors. The research to date indicates the presence of washback toward the weak end of the continuum. It has also been suggested that the intensity of washback may be a function of how high or low are the stakes (Cheng, 1998a).

Length. The influence of exams, if it is found to exist, may last for a *short* period of time, or for a *long* time. For instance, if the influence of an entrance examination is present only while the test takers are preparing for the test, and the influence disappears after entering the institution, this is short-term washback. However, if the influence of entrance exams on students continues after they enter the institution, this is long-term washback.

Intentionality. Messick (1989) implied that there is *unintended* as well as *intended* washback when he wrote, "Judging validity in terms of whether a test does the job it is employed to do ... requires evaluation of the intended or unintended social consequences of test interpretation and use. The appropriateness of the intended testing purpose and the possible occurrence of unintended outcomes and side effects are the major issues" (p. 84). McNamara (1996) also holds a similar view, stating that "High priority needs to be given to the collection of evidence about the intended and unintended effects of assessments on the ways teachers and students spend their time and think about the goals of education" (p. 22). The researcher has to investigate not only intended washback but also unintended washback.

Value. Examination washback may be *positive* or *negative*. Because it is not conceivable that the test writers intend to cause negative washback, intended washback may normally be associated with positive washback, while unintended washback is related to both negative and positive washback. When it comes to the issue of value judgment, the washback research may be regarded as being a part of evaluation studies. The distinction between positive and negative could usefully be made only by referring to the audience. In other words, researchers need to be ready to answer the question, "who the evaluation is for" (Alderson, 1992). For example, one type of outcome may be evaluated as being positive by teachers, whereas the same outcome may be judged to be negative by school principals. Thus, it is important to identify the evaluator when it comes to passing value judgment (see also chap. 1, this volume).

(b) Aspects of Learning and Teaching That May Be Influenced by the Examination

A test can influence various aspects of learning and teaching. Bailey (1996), referring to Hughes' (1993) trichotomy (i.e., participants, process, and product) and Alderson and Wall's (1993) 15 Washback Hypotheses, proposes that these variables be divided into "washback to the learner" and "washback to the programme." The former involves what learners learn, how learners learn, the rate and sequence of learning, and the degree and depth of learning, while the latter is concerned with what teachers teach, how teachers teach, the rate and sequence of teaching, and the degree and depth of teaching. Relatively well explored is the area of washback to the program, while less emphasis has been given to learners, perhaps because of the difficulty of getting access to the participants.

(c) Factors Mediating the Process of Washback Being Generated

The research to date suggests that various factors seem to be mediating the process of washback. The factors may include the following (Alderson & Hamp-Lyons, 1996; Brown, 1997; Cheng, chap. 9, this volume; Shohamy et al., 1996; Wall, 1997): *test factors* (e.g., test methods, test contents, skills tested, purpose of the test, decisions that will be made on the basis of test results, etc.); *prestige factors* (e.g., stakes of the test, status of the test within the entire educational system, etc.); *personal factors* (e.g., teachers' educational backgrounds, their beliefs about the best methods of teaching/learning, etc.); *micro-context factors* (e.g., the school setting in which the test preparation is being carried out); and *macro-context factors*, that is, the society where the test is used.

Given these complexities of this phenomenon called washback, it becomes important that the researcher should take account of the whole context wherein the test is used. As Alderson and Wall (1993) pointed out, research into washback needs to examine the tests that "are used regularly within the curriculum and which are perceived to have educational consequences" (p. 122). Under artificial conditions, the test is likely to be perceived by the participants as having little educational consequence, which is unlikely in actual situations. These requirements necessitate using qualitative research methodology, rather than a traditional experimental approach, although this does not preclude the use of quantitative data.

QUALITATIVE RESEARCH METHODOLOGY

The qualitative or ethnographic research has been increasingly widely used among researchers in the field of language teaching and learning (Watson-Gegeo, 1988). According to LeCompte and Preissle (1993), qualitative or ethnographic research[1] is characterized by the following strategies, which are relevant to the research into washback.

1. Ethnography (or qualitative research) elicits phenomenological data that represent the worldview of the participants being investigated and participants' constructs are used to structure the research. Because tests are used in a particular context for a specific purpose, it is important to identify

[1]LeCompte and Preissle (1993) use these two terms interchangeably.

problems that are recognized by test users in the context. Otherwise, the research could not help to solve the problem test users are acutely aware of, and the research results are likely to be sterile, having little implication for the context.

2. The researcher employs participant and nonparticipant observation to acquire firsthand, sensory accounts of phenomena as they occur in real-world settings. If the washback research were not to gather firsthand data, it would be necessary to take at face value what teachers and students say about how they feel about the effects of examinations. However, such perceptions may not reflect what they are actually doing (Hopkins, 1985, p. 48). Qualitative research also stresses gathering data in "real," that is, nonexperimental, settings. The test always plays a certain role in a specific context, so even if it were found that a test has some impact on teaching and learning under controlled settings, it is likely that the result would not apply to situations where the teaching is actually being done for test preparation.

3. The researcher seeks to construct descriptions of total phenomena within their various contexts and to generate from these descriptions the complex interrelationship of causes and consequences that affect human behavior toward and beliefs about particular phenomena. As Wall and Alderson (1993) pointed out, the exam may be only one of the factors that affect how innovations succeed or fail. In other words, numerous factors other than the exam are involved in determining what happens in the classroom. This type of insight could not be gained without an attempt to describe the total phenomena of the classroom, including a teacher's perceptions about his or her teaching.

4. The researcher uses a variety of research techniques to amass their data. Despite the importance of direct observations of the situation where a test is used, this does not mean that observation is the single method to be employed in washback research. Rather, various research methods, including interviews and questionnaires in particular, should be considered to complement each other. If it were not for interviews or questionnaires, for example, it would not be possible to gather public opinions, nor would it be possible to find out about reasons (or intentions) behind behaviors of teachers in the classroom. The question is which method should be employed.

Identifying Researcher Bias

Virtually all the researchers must have taken a test, and thus, it is very likely they are biased by their own experience when they embark on the research. To increase the degree of reliability or "trustworthiness" (Eisenhart & Howe, 1992) of the research, it is important to make one's "base line" explicit. Allwright and Bailey's (1991) comments are worth quoting:

> Anthropologists sometimes use . . . the "base line", to refer to the pre-existing framework researchers bring with them to an observational setting . . . As researchers, we need to be aware that our previous training, experiences, and attitudes all contribute to the way we view the events we observe. This awareness is especially important to keep in mind in doing classroom research, because virtually all researchers have themselves been learners, and most have also been teachers. And when we, as teachers, get involved in doing classroom research, of course we cannot divest ourselves completely of our attitudes as teachers. Thus, it is important for all classroom researchers, especially those who are also teachers, to be aware of their own predispositions, their "base line", before they begin to collect and analyze classroom data. (pp. 74–75)

The foregoing advice is intended for observation studies in general, but it also applies to any type of research that is conducted by a human being. A base line may be raised to awareness through a casual talk with a colleague, students, test writers, administrators, and so forth. In one such example, I gained insight for my research. One of my students said he had not studied for the listening section of the entrance examination of a university, half of which was devoted to testing listening, because he deemed it to be too difficult for him. This type of information, though anecdotal, highlights the influence and the importance of washback. In this regard, the distinction between the two types of questions identified by LeCompte and Preissle (1993) is crucial: ". . . the first question with which ethnographers begin their work is, '*Is* there anything going on out there?' The second question, then, is '*What* is going on out there?' " In this way, "one avoids the danger of assuming the presence of a phenomenon which may not, in fact, exist in the given setting" (p. 120). In this respect, the question that Alderson and Wall (1993) posed in the title of their article—Does washback exist?—becomes relevant.

Identify the Problem in the Society and the Research Circle

However interesting it might be, the research remains valueless until its significance in the society and in the academic circle is proven. The questions that ought to be asked to render the research meaningful are:

- What research would be useful and meaningful to the society?
- How would the research most usefully be conducted in the society?
- What would be useful to the research community?

The specific tasks that ought to be done to answer these questions involve identifying the areas in which the empirical research is required. When addressing the first two questions regarding the society, useful information may be gathered by seeking public opinions as reflected in various media, such as newspapers, magazines, TV programs, etc. Besides these, it is important to confirm the claims and assertions made by listening to the teachers and students who are or have been actually involved in test preparation. These data sets are subsequently to be combined with the information gathered from the mass media and the description of the target exams, to derive a set of predictions for the research (see the following).

When seeking the information as to what has been done in the field to date, there are two things the researcher should note. First, he or she needs to seek the information not only in the ESL/EFL literature, but also in other fields related to educational studies. Such an important source of information as Smith (1991b) could not be found otherwise. Second, it is imperative to differentiate between claims or assertions on the one hand, and empirically grounded research results on the other. Whatever authority one might hold and however convincing his or her opinion might sound, the claim remains a surmise until empirical evidence is provided.

Describing the Context

In parallel with identifying the problems in the society, the context where the test is used must also be described in detail. Thus, the questions that should be asked are:

- What does the educational system look like?
- What role does the test play in the system?

It is crucial to describe the context as explicitly as possible (i.e., *thick description*, Geertz, 1973), not only to help readers understand the role of the test in that context, but also to establish *transferability* or "the demonstration of the generalizability, or applicability of the results of a study in one setting to another context, or other contexts" (Brown, 2001, p. 226). This task is not as easy as one might imagine, however. Paradoxically, it becomes particularly difficult when the researcher is an insider within the context, since the insider is likely to take many things for granted.

The context can be divided into *micro* and *macro* levels (Cheng, chap. 9, this volume). Micro context is the immediate environment where the test is put to use, such as a school system or a classroom setting. Macro context refers to a larger environment that surrounds the research site. To undertake a research study on low-stakes tests, such as in-class tests, a description of the micro-context only would be sufficient, whereas research on high-stakes tests, that involve a large number of people and which are used for making major decisions, requires that the macro-context as well as the micro-context be taken into account. It may even be necessary to consider a history of an educational context where the test is employed, one of the components of what Henrichsen (1989) referred to as "antecedents" in her hybrid model of educational innovation.

Identifying and Analyzing the Potentially Influential Test(s)

There are cases where the test, the effects of which are to be investigated, is very clear in the researcher's mind at the time when embarking on the research. However, there may also be cases where the researcher has to seek to examine the effect of various types of examinations at a time. For example, in the context where the present author conducted his research, it was difficult to identify a single influential exam, since there are more than 1,000 universities and junior colleges in Japan, and each of these produces its own examinations. In order to identify the target examination of the research in such a situation, the researcher has to start by asking test users about what exams they consider to be influential. In either case, it is important to ask at least two questions:

- What content does the test have?
- For what purpose is the test used?

The first of these questions is important particularly in a situation where the structure of a new test is substantially different from the previous test and the washback of the new test need to be established. Unless the differences in the content of the examination have been specified prior to the research, it is not possible to establish washback. The second question should be asked, since the nature of washback may vary according to the purpose of the test. If a test is used to make an important or high-stakes decision, the test is expected to have a greater effect than the one that is used to make a less important or low-stakes decision. The task at this stage involves then describing "the nature of the decisions that are taken on the basis of the test results" (Alderson & Wall, 1993, p. 127).

Producing Predictions

The question to be asked at this stage is:

- What would washback look like?

Where there are specific intentions on the part of test constructors and where they are made public (i.e., intended washback as defined earlier), to produce predictions is a relatively straightforward task. However, where such intentions are absent, not clearly defined or not clearly articulated, useful sources may involve general public opinions about the influence of the test, a theory of washback, and a description of the test content. When producing predictions, an attempt needs to be made to specify which aspects of learning and teaching will be influenced (e.g., use of language, classroom organization, etc.) and how they will be influenced. Here, it would be useful to ask the following set of questions (Alderson & Wall, 1993, p. 127).

- What scope should the notion of washback have?
- Where should its limits lie?
- What aspect of impact might we not wish to include in the concept of washback?

In order to answer these questions, it would be helpful to refer to the dimensional analysis of the notion of washback and a description of various factors involved in the process of washback being generated, which were presented at the beginning of this chapter. Note that the research is recursive, and the formulation of predictions is not a one-time or one-off event. As the research progresses, new predictions are formulated, subsequently tested, and the results are used to inform subsequent stages of the research.

Designing Research

Once predictions have been formulated, the next thing to do is to design the research. The aim of the research may be to investigate how tests influence, for instance, teachers' internal factors, such as personal beliefs about teaching, motivation, and so forth. For such a purpose, it may be possible to explore teachers' internal factors by administering interviews or questionnaires. Nevertheless, the present chapter argues that eventually it becomes crucial to examine how these internal factors are revealed in the form of actual teaching and learning behaviors, as argued by Alderson and Wall (1993). In other words, an attempt should be made to establish *credibility* or to demonstrate "that the research was conducted in a way that maximizes the accuracy of identifying and describing the object(s) of study" (Brown, 2001, p. 225). Thus, the questions that need to be asked for designing observation research include:

- What would be necessary to establish washback?
- What evidence would enable us to say whether washback exists or not?

In order to prove that washback exists, it is necessary to exclude all the possibilities other than exams that may potentially influence the teaching and learning, and it is important to "weigh the potential social consequences of *not* testing at all" (Ebel, 1966, as cited in Messick, 1989, p. 86). The research design based on this assumption could usefully be constructed by taking account of the dimension of specificity as defined earlier, which is depicted in Figs. 2.1 and 2.2.

Washback on a *general* dimension (Fig. 2.1) addresses the question, "would teaching/learning become different if there were no exams?" Washback is considered to exist on this dimension if at least the following conditions are met:

(A) Teaching, learning, and/or textbooks are different in exam-preparation and in non-exam preparation classes, both of which are taught by the same teacher.

(B) Teaching, learning, and/or textbooks are similar in exam-preparation classes, which are taught by two different teachers, and teaching,

	Teacher A		Teacher B
Exam prep. lessons	↑	←(2) [Same]→	↑
	(1) [Different]		(1) [Different]
Non-exam lessons	↓		↓

FIG. 2.1. Diagrammatic representation of washback on general dimension. Note: In exam preparation lessons, teachers aim at a variety of target exams. Teacher A is different from Teacher B. Each shaded cell represents classroom events and materials being used.

	Teacher A		Teacher B
Exam C	↑	←(2) [Same]→	↑
	(1) [Different]		(1) [Different]
Exam D	↓	←(2) [Same]→	↓

FIG. 2.2. Diagrammatic representation of washback on specific dimension. Note: Exam C is different from Exam D in their contents and methods. Exam C may be being used at the same time when Exam D is being used (Cross-sectional study). Exam D may be a revised version of Exam C (Longitudinal study). Teacher A is different from Teacher B. Each shaded cell represents classroom events and materials being used.

learning and/or textbooks are those which can be predicted from the target exams.

On the other hand, washback on a *specific* dimension addresses the question, "would teaching/learning become different if the exams were to change?" Here, washback is considered to exist on this dimension if at least the following conditions are met:

(A) Teaching, learning, and/or textbooks are different in the courses which are taught by the same teacher.
(B) Teaching, learning, and/or textbooks are similar in the courses which are taught by two different teachers.

This is, of course, an apparently idealistic research assumption. However, the reality is far more complex. The ideal cases that fall into one of the cells of the earlier diagram rarely occur, and the researcher is required to interpret the data he or she collects by considering various factors (as defined earlier) within the context where the test is used.

Selecting Participants

Next, participants are selected in order to examine the validity of predictions. The questions that may be asked at this stage and could include the following:

- What would be necessary to establish access to participating schools?
- What ethical concerns would need to be taken into account?

Note that "selection" rather than "sampling" is being used here, the difference being explained by LeCompte and Preissle (1993) as: "Selection refers to a more general process of focusing and choosing what to study; sampling is a more specialized and restricted form" (p. 57). In other words, as the research progresses and the focus is shifted or expands, an appropriate population may need to be re-selected. Thus, the selection is not to be made at random, but purposefully, "selecting *information-rich cases* for study in depth" (Patton, 1987, p. 52). As is illustrated in each chapter in Part II of this book, in the research into washback, it is normal to select various groups of participants rather than one single population. In this way, an attempt is made to examine washback from different perspectives (i.e., data triangulation), as it may be the case that some aspects of washback exist for learners but not for teachers, whereas other aspects exist for teachers but not for learners.

Meanwhile, the researcher has to decide whether or not he or she should reveal the purpose of the research to the participants. There is no reason why the purpose of the research should be kept confidential. Nor is it ethical to deceive the participants. The question is how much the researcher should and can let them know. However, revealing too much about the exam should be avoided, since this may excessively raise participants' awareness, which in turn may contaminate the data. In many cases, a very broad description of the purpose would suffice (e.g., the study is intended to gather information about the use of tests in the classroom). But it is far more important to emphasize the value of the research, and to promise the confidentiality of all the data to be gathered.

Observations

The observation task is divided into several subtasks, typically involving construction of observation instruments, preobservation interviews, recording classroom events, and postobservation interviews.

To carry out an observation study, a set of data-gathering instruments needs to be constructed. The type of instrument varies according to the context, the purpose of the research, and the examination being investigated. An ideal instrument may be available for some research contexts, but in many cases researchers have to develop their own tools (see chapters in this volume by Stecher, Chun, & Barron, chap. 4; Saville & Hawkey, chap. 5; Cheng, chap. 9; Qi, chap. 10; Ferman, chap. 12), or others may have to modify an instrument that is available (see Hayes & Read, chap. 7; Burrows, chap. 8).

Before entering the classroom, a variety of information needs to be gathered about the school (e.g., educational policy, academic level, etc.) and the teacher whose lesson is to be observed (e.g., education, age/experience, major field of study, etc.). The researcher has to prepare specific sets of questions in advance, as the teachers are likely to be busy, so it is important that they feel their time spent helping the researcher is time well spent. A valuable piece of information, such as teachers' personal beliefs about education, may also be obtained through casual conversations with teachers. All these pieces of information will become an important source for interpreting the observation data.

What the researcher is trying to do in the observation is to find answers to the question:

- What is happening in the classroom under the influence of the examination as it is predicted?

At the same time, the observer should not neglect those aspects of teaching/learning, which are *not* observed, though they are predicted to be observed. Thus, it is important to ask a corollary of the earlier question:

- What is not happening, though it is predicted to be happening?

The observer's task is not only to establish the presence of washback, but also the absence of predicted types of test effects.

The observer should also take account of *unintended* as well as *intended* washback in the sense defined earlier. In order to identify unintended washback, it may be useful to consider the following logical possibilities, as suggested by D. Allwright (personal communication, October 24, 1994). First, learners may be "angling their learning in terms of the exam, even if the teacher [is] not apparently intending to help them." Second, a teacher may be "using exam-related task types but will simply wish to deny any suggestion that he or she is exam-influenced." Third, there may be a teacher "who proclaims he or she is exam-influenced, but whose teaching exhibits nothing that can be related by observation to exam content." Thus, it is important for the observer to explore, during postobservation interviews, unintended washback by identifying the intention of the teachers and/or learners underlying their behaviors in the classrooms.

Upon completion of the observation, interviews are held with the teacher for his or her reaction to the teaching that was observed. The purpose is to gather information that will be used to interpret the observation data. The types and contents of questions to be asked will vary greatly depending upon what has been observed. Postobservation interviews are becoming increasingly important, as a number of research results indicate that the teachers are prominent factors mediating the process of washback being produced (e.g., Burrows, chap. 6; Cheng, 1999; Qi, chap. 11; Wall, 1999; Wall & Alderson, 1993; Watanabe, 1996a). (See Briggs, 1986; Oppenheim, 1992; and Cohen, Manion, & Morrison, 2000, for details of how to conduct interviews.)

This chapter emphasizes the importance of observation in the research exploring washback, but it does not intend to serve as a research manual for observations studies in general. For more detailed explanations about a variety of observation techniques, instruments, and useful advice, readers are referred to standard textbooks on observation studies, such as Allwright and Bailey (1991), Chaudron (1988), Nunan (1989), and van Lier (1988).

Analyzing the Data

What the researcher has at hand now is a bulky set of information, consisting of classroom materials, audio- and/or video-recordings, field notes, interview data, various memos, e-mails, and computer files. In principle, however, the data analysis has already begun when recording classroom events during observations. The observer has looked at the lesson, decided which event is more important than others, and selected the events to record. It would be advisable that the data set that has been collected at each observation session be analyzed without waiting until all data sets are in. An observation of one single lesson may provide an enormous amount of information, which may appear overwhelming to the researcher.

While engaging in the data analysis, it may be worthwhile to keep asking the following question:

- How could the collected data be analyzed most usefully to test predictions?

The initial data analysis at this stage may not necessarily have to be in-depth. It may involve reviewing the field notes, and filling in the information that has not been recorded by listening to the audiotape or watching the video. In the research conducted by the present author, the analysis of the classroom events was conducted twice for two different purposes; first, to identify relevant categories to examine the presence or absence of washback (e.g., interaction done in English, group work, etc.), and second, to count the frequency of incidents which belong to each of the derived categories. The first-stage analysis was carried out immediately after the lesson, whereas the second analysis was carried out after all the observations were finished. In other words, what I did was "qualitative refinement of the relevant categories" at the first stage, and "quantitative analysis of the *extent* of relevance" at the second stage (Chaudron, 1986, p. 714).

One practical problem for the researcher to solve regarding data analyses is that it usually takes a long time to generate results in the case of qualitative or ethnographic research, whereas the most useful interviews are carried out only *after* the results of the data analyses have been studied. To address this type of problem, the researcher may want to employ computer software, such as NUD*IST (Wall, 1999), WinMax (Qi, chap. 10, this volume), The Ethnograph, which will greatly facilitate the data processing (see Miles & Huberman, 1994). Note that the use of qualitative research does not necessarily mean that the researcher should not deal with numerical data. Watson-Gegeo (1997) stated: "Four current trends in classroom ethnography can be expected to intensify over the next few years. ... First, classroom ethnographers can be expected to incorporate quantitative techniques in their analyses more than they have in the past ... classroom ethnography will need to become more quantitative if it is to produce theory" (p. 141). Nevertheless, it should be emphasized that computing frequency data and qualitative data should also be examined in parallel. While analyzing the qualitative data, it may be useful to note: "... human endeavors such as classroom language learning cannot simply be reduced to a set of incontrovertible facts without missing out on a great deal of what is humanly interesting and probably pedagogically important" (Allwright & Bailey, 1991, p. 64). Thus, the researcher needs to keep an eye on the whole range of data sets he or she has gathered while looking into the details. Analyses may involve examining whether there is any innovative use of tests for teaching, describing and analyzing the materials used, etc.

Interpreting Results and Drawing Implications

Interpretation is not an independent activity. Rather, it runs through all of the research activities, particularly in the process of collecting and analyzing the data. When interpreting the results of the data analysis, the following questions should be considered:

- What implications can be drawn for teachers, students, test developers, administrators, and future researchers?
- Which action plan can be proposed?
- What would be the best way to report the results to the audience?

Interpretation is made through interplay of data and theory, whereby the researcher "look[s] for patterns in the data, validate[s] initial conclusions by returning to the data or collecting more data, recycle[s] through the process or the data" (Seliger & Shohamy, 1989, pp. 121–124). By the time the researcher has gathered data, he or she is very likely to have formulated a certain notion that might be slanted in favor of his or her own interpretation of the data. In order to minimize such a bias, it would be helpful to go back to the teacher for his or her reaction immediately after analyzing the data, that is, *member check*. If the classroom events have been video-recorded, it would be useful to watch it together with the teacher whose lessons were recorded, that is, *investigator triangulation*. The researcher should always be ready to accept and change his or her interpretation when "rival explanations" (Miles & Huberman, 1994, pp. 274–275) are suggested.

This type of research is usually addressed to a wide variety of audiences, and thus the researcher needs to be ready to provide different sets of information for different audiences. This means that various implications need to be drawn from the results for teachers, researchers, test constructors, and material developers. When preparing reports for a group of teachers, for example, technical terms may be better avoided, but suggestions for teaching may need to be specified, whereas for policymakers, action plans may need to be included. For the researchers in the field, details of the reliability and validity of instruments employed need to be provided in greater detail.

Verification of the Research

In the foregoing discussion, the issue of verification has been dealt with, but in a somewhat unsystematic manner. The researcher's experience needs to be examined in order to minimize his or her bias; the reliability of a coding scheme needs to be confirmed by multiple coders; interviews should follow specific guidelines; findings need to be sent to the participants for their reactions and responses, etc. All these are attempts to establish reliability (or the consistency of data analysis) and validity (the relevance of the data) in the quantitative research tradition, and credibility, transferability, dependability, and confirmability in the qualitative research tradition. In this regard, the second part of this book contains much useful information.

One strength running through all the chapters of Part II of this book is their attempt to establish credibility and dependability by employing various types of triangulation. Stecher, Chun, and Barron (chap. 4) examine the effect of the Washington Assessment of Student Learning by administering surveys to school principals as well as teachers based on a stratified random sample (data triangulation). Saville and Hawkey (chap. 5) describe the process of developing an instrument to examine the impact of IELTS. During the process, the authors incorporated multiple views of experts (investigator triangulation) as well as a large number of test users. Their description of the process itself serves as an effective illustration of establishing the dependability of the research. Burrows (chap. 6) demonstrates the importance of complementary quantitative and qualitative data collection by means of interviews, questionnaires, and observations (methodological triangulation). In her research, feedback from each stage was carefully examined, the results of which were used to inform subsequent stages, enabling the author to formulate a new conceptualization of washback by drawing on Woods' (1996) theory (theory triangulation). Hayes and Read (chap. 7) not only used two observation instruments to confirm their results (methodological triangulation), but referred to test scores (data triangulation), which enabled them to shed light on one of the most important aspects of washback, that is, the effectiveness of the exam class. Watanabe (chap. 8) incorporated interview data gathered from teachers whose lessons were observed (data triangulation), and used the information to understand each teacher's intentions behind his/her teaching behaviors in light of attribution theories of motivation (theory triangulation). Cheng (chap. 9) administered a set of questionnaires to teachers twice, before and after the implementation of the Hong Kong Certificate Examinations in English, to investigate changes in the teachers' perceptions of this particular examination (time triangulation). Qi (chap. 10) interviewed test constructors to reveal what type of washback they intended to produce (i.e., intended washback), incorporating teachers' and inspectors' perceptions of the effects of the target examination (data triangulation) by carrying out open-ended and semi-open ended interviews with them. These data were further confirmed by classroom observations (methodological triangulation). Ferman (chap. 12) administered structured questionnaires, structured interviews, and open interviews (methodological triangulation) to various types of participants, including students as well as teachers and inspectors (data triangulation), collecting data from a group of students of various ability levels, making her research unique.

In addition to a variety of triangulation types, each chapter provides a detailed description of the context where the target examination was used. This type of "thick description" helps assess the potential transferability of the results to other contexts.

Finally, one of the most important requirements of the qualitative research process that could not be fully presented in this book is *confirmability*, which "involves full revelation or at least the availability of the data upon which all interpretations are based" (Brown, 2001, p. 227). Due to space limitation, it is not usually possible to provide readers with the full data sources. However, it is important to store the data sources until the researcher makes sure that it is no longer needed. This is important not only for establishing confirmability, but also for an occasion where the researcher is going to publish the report, when he or she may need to examine the relevance of the data by returning to the source, or he or she may have to analyze the data from a new angle.

Readers are referred to standard textbooks, such as LeCompte, Millroy, and Preissle (1992), Miles and Huberman (1994), Cohen, Manion, and Morrison (2000) for a further discussion of the issue of verification in the area of qualitative research in social sciences. Miles and Huberman (1994) listed useful sets of checklists for establishing verifiability in qualitative research, and for the use of qualitative research in ESL/EFL, Davis (1995), Lazaraton (1995), and Brown (2001) are strongly recommended.

FINAL REMARKS

Maeher and Fyans (1989) once stated that "many educational doctrines have become axiomatic not by being correct but by being repeated so often that it seems they *must* be correct" (p. 203). The claims held by the public to be true are likely to be the educational doctrine, and become *ipse dixit*. The role of washback research is to set us free from these types of axioms and provide a specific set of guidelines for the future. It is perhaps worth remembering the distinction Hayek made between *scientific* and *scientistic* research methodology, referred to at the beginning of this chapter: It is impossible to know the most appropriate method of investigating the subject before considering this distinction. The process that has been described in this chapter is one that was employed to investigate the washback effect of the examination being employed to select candidates for Japanese universities. Obviously, methodologies need to vary according to a given situation, where different uses of the methodologies are put to the test. Nevertheless, it is hoped that this chapter may be useful for future researchers to find the most appropriate method for their own unique context. It is left to them to examine how the research results actually apply to their own context. The various instruments that were used in each research project are given in the Appendices of each chapter, which will help the reader to experiment, contextualize, and adapt the research designs.

CHAPTER

3

Washback and Curriculum Innovation

Stephen Andrews
The University of Hong Kong

The present chapter explores the relationship between washback and curricular innovation. The chapter begins by examining the assertions that have been made about the nature of that relationship. It then goes on to consider the related research evidence. In the following discussion, the term *washback* is interpreted broadly. Instead of adopting Wall's (1997, p. 291) distinction between test impact and test washback, the present chapter uses *washback* to refer to the effects of tests on teaching and learning, the educational system, and the various stakeholders in the education process. Where the word "impact" occurs in the chapter, it is used in a non-technical sense, as a synonym for "effect."

The discussion focuses specifically on the washback associated with "high-stakes tests." High-stakes tests are so labeled because their results "are seen—rightly or wrongly—by students, teachers, administrators, parents, or the general public, as being used to make important decisions that immediately and directly affect them" (Madaus, 1988, p. 87). The primary use of such tests is "to ration future opportunity as the basis for determining admission to the next layer of education or to employment opportunities" (Chapman & Snyder, 2000, p. 458).

It is precisely the power of high-stakes tests (or the strength of the perceptions which are held about them) that makes them potentially so influential upon the curriculum and curricular innovation. It is recognition of this power that has led educators to use such tests as a force for promoting curricular innovation. The present chapter examines the influence of high-stakes tests upon curricular innovation: both how it is alleged to work, and how research suggests it works in practice. The definition of curricular innovation adopted in this chapter is that of Markee (1997), who describes it as "a managed process of development whose principal products are teaching (and/or testing) materials, methodological skills, and pedagogical values that are perceived as new by potential adopters" (p. 46).

The discussion begins by reviewing the claims (within both the general education and the language education literature) concerning the relationship between washback and curricular innovation. Those claims are then related to the research evidence from studies of the effects of high-stakes tests, first in language education and then in general education. Finally, the results of those studies are considered in the light of ideas from the emerging literature on innovation in language education.

WASHBACK AND CURRICULUM INNOVATION: WHAT HAS BEEN CLAIMED?

Over the years there has been extensive discussion, in both the general education and language education literature, of the influence of examinations on teaching and learning (see, e.g., Alderson & Wall, 1996; Chapman & Snyder, 2000; Davies, 1968; Dore, 1976, 1997; Frederiksen & Collins, 1989; Heyneman, 1987; Kellaghan, Madaus, & Airasian, 1982; Madaus, 1988; Morris, 1985; Oxenham, 1984; Swain, 1985; Wall, 1997, 2000; Wall & Alderson, 1993; Wiseman, 1961). Madaus (1988) expressed the assumption underlying much of the washback debate: "It is testing, not the 'official' stated curriculum, that is increasingly determining what is taught, how it is taught, what is learned, and how it is learned" (p. 83).

The Negative Impact of Tests

In the past, most discussion of the influence of examinations emphasized their supposed harmful effects. Oxenham (1984) described these as follows: "The harm of centralized examinations is said to spring from the restrictions they will impose upon curricula, teachers and students. . . . Their almost inescapable bias is to encourage the most mechanical, boring and debilitating forms of teaching and learning" (p. 113). Such concerns are far from new: For example, Wall (1997) quoted reported comments from 1802 about an examination that had been newly introduced at Oxford University, which was claimed to have the effect that "the student's education became more narrow than before, since he was likely to concentrate only on examined subjects" (Simon, 1974, p. 86, as cited in Wall, 1997, p. 291). At the same time, these negative perceptions about the influence of examinations appear to be no less prevalent today, as illustrated by Chapman and Snyder's (2000) observation that: "teachers' tendencies to teach to the test are often cited as an impediment to introducing new instructional practices" (p. 460).

Tests as a Strategy to Promote Curricular Innovation

In recent years, however, alongside continuing recognition of the potential for tests to have a negative influence on the curriculum, attention has increasingly been paid to the possibility of turning the apparently powerful effect of tests to advantage, and using it to exert a positive influence in support of curriculum innovation. Elton and Laurillard (1979) summarized the strategy very succinctly: "The quickest way to change student learning is to change the assessment system" (p. 100, as cited in Tang & Biggs, 1996, p. 159). Such thinking lies behind what is sometimes referred to as measurement-directed instruction (MDI), which "occurs when a high-stakes test of educational achievement . . . influences the instructional program that prepares students for the test" (Popham, 1993, as cited in Chapman & Snyder, 2000, p. 460).

Using tests as a mechanism to drive instruction is a strategy that has aroused strong emotions. Popham's (1987) argument in support of MDI (as summarized in Wall, 2000) was that if tests were properly conceived (i.e., criterion-referenced and focusing on appropriately selected content and skills) and sensibly implemented (with, for example, sufficient support for teachers), then aligning teaching with what such tests assessed was likely to have positive educational outcomes. However, while MDI has its advocates, it has also attracted fierce opposition. Madaus (1988), for instance, decried it as "psychometric imperialism," by which tests become "the ferocious master of the educational process" (pp. 84–85). Shepard (1991a, p. 27) claimed that such an approach disempowers the great majority of teachers, while Shohamy (2000) suggested it may even be seen as an "unethical and undemocratic way of making policy" (p. 11).

In spite of such opposition, the use of assessment as a strategy for promoting change across education systems has become increasingly widespread. James (2000), for example, charted its adoption as a change strategy by successive governments in England since the late 1980s, in an article entitled "Measured Lives: The Rise of Assessment as the Engine of Change in English Schools." Meanwhile, Chapman and Snyder (2000) reported the experiences (discussed later in the chapter) from a number of countries where tests and the data from tests have been used as levers of instructional reform.

In language education, too, several testing developments have been based on the belief that examination reform can act as a "lever for change"

(Pearson, 1988, p. 101). For example, Pearson (1988) and Wall and Alderson (1993) both discussed modifications to Sri Lankan public examinations of English intended to reinforce textbook innovations and teacher-training innovations. Swain (1985) talked about "working for washback" in the development of a test of French in Canada (pp. 43–44), while Andrews and Fullilove (1994) described the development of an oral English test in Hong Kong specifically intended to influence teaching and learning.

Washback: From "Assumed Truth" to Research Area

Until very recently, the influence of tests on the curriculum (whether positive or negative) has been treated as an "assumed truth" rather than the subject of empirical investigation, both in language education and in general education. Thus we find, from the general education literature, Elton and Laurillard's claim (cited earlier), while Swain (1985), in the field of language education, reminds us that "It has frequently been noted that teachers teach to a test" (p. 43). Assertions have also been made about the pervasiveness of washback, that it affects not just teachers and students, but also every other stakeholder in the education process. In the context of second language education, for example, Johnson (1989) suggested that: "In many education systems the key question for students, teachers, parents, school administrators, and even inspectors is not, 'Are students gaining in communicative competence?' but, 'Are they on course for the examination?' " (p. 6).

In the past 10 years, the washback effect of tests on teaching and learning has begun to be examined much more seriously, both theoretically and empirically, becoming a major issue in the assessment literature (Berry, Falvey, Nunan, Burnett, & Hunt, 1995, p. 31). Important theoretical contributions have been made in the field of language education by, for instance, Alderson and Wall (1993), who first unpacked the number of different hypotheses associated with the concept of washback, by Bailey (1996), who distinguished between "washback to the learners" and "washback to the program," and by Messick (1996), who situated discussion of washback within the broader context of construct validity.

This burgeoning interest in washback has given rise to a number of research studies (in language education, see, e.g., Alderson & Hamp-Lyons, 1996; Andrews, 1995; Andrews & Fullilove, 1997; Cheng, 1997, 1998a; Hughes, 1988; Wall 1999; Wall & Alderson, 1993; Watanabe, 1997b). It is therefore timely to consider what the reports of these and other studies (in both language education and general education) tell us about the relationship between washback and curricular innovation. This is discussed in the next two sections of the chapter.

WASHBACK AND CURRICULAR INNOVATION: RESEARCH IN LANGUAGE EDUCATION

As Alderson and Wall (1993) pointed out, there were very few empirical studies of the impact of assessment on the curriculum before the 1990s. In their review of research into washback, they note that one of the first systematic attempts in language education to engineer curriculum change via an innovation in test design was that reported by Hughes (1988) at an English-medium university in Turkey. In order to raise the lamentably low standard of English of students emerging from their preparatory year at the Foreign Language School, a high-stakes test was introduced, the results of which would determine whether students could begin undergraduate studies. The test was designed to reflect the language needs of students studying at an English-medium university, the intention being that the high stakes associated with the test would have a powerful washback effect on teachers (as well as students), and push them to teach toward "the proper objectives of the course" (p. 145). The test impacted upon the curriculum in a number of ways, directly causing changes to the teaching syllabus and the textbooks. It also appeared to bring about substantial improvements in students' English proficiency.

Alderson and Wall (1993) noted that Hughes' study (in common with other early washback studies in the field of language education, such as Khaniyah [1990]) did not incorporate classroom data, an omission they sought to rectify in their own Sri Lanka study. This research, described in detail in Wall and Alderson (1993), investigated the washback from the revised Sri Lankan "O" level English exam, which focused on reading and writing for a purpose. In contrast with previous washback studies in language education, classroom observation was a major component of the methodology employed, with over 300 observations being conducted. Wall (1996) summarized the results of the study as follows: "The main findings . . . were that the examination had had considerable impact on the content of English lessons and on the way teachers designed their classroom tests (some of this was positive and some negative), but it had had little to no impact on the methodology they used in the classroom or on the way they marked their pupils' test performance" (p. 348).

Cheng's study of the washback associated with changes to the Hong Kong Certificate of Education Examination (HKCEE) English Language (see, e.g., Cheng, 1997, 1998a, 1998b, 1999) made use of a number of research techniques, including questionnaire, interview, and classroom observation. As with the changes to the Sri Lankan "O" level exam, there was a deliberate attempt in Hong Kong to engineer "a top-down intended washback on English language teaching and learning . . . in accord with a target-oriented curriculum development . . ." (Cheng, 1997, p. 38). Changes to English examinations in Hong Kong have typically been motivated by the desire to exert positive washback: "throughout the 18-year history of the HKEA [Hong Kong Examinations Authority], all development work on English Language syllabuses has been aimed at improving the washback effect of the exam on classroom teaching" (King, 1997, p. 34). Cheng's findings revealed that changes to the "what" of teaching and learning (i.e., the content of teaching, the materials used) occurred quickly. However, the intended changes to the "how" of teaching and learning appeared in the main to have been only at a superficial level (additional classroom activities reflecting the content of the revised examination). There was little evidence of fundamental changes in either teacher behavior (e.g., lessons continued to be dominated by teacher talk) or in student learning. Cheng (1998b) concluded that "A change in the examination syllabus itself will *not* alone fulfill the intended goal. Washback effect as a curriculum change process works slowly" (p. 297). As Cheng (personal communication) noted, in order for the longer term effects of washback to be properly evaluated, investigations of the curriculum changes associated with test innovations need to be afforded a relatively long time span.

Andrews (1995) conducted a small-scale study comparing the perceptions of examination designers (i.e., those aiming to use exam washback as a catalyst for curriculum innovation), with the perceptions and experiences of teachers (i.e., the receivers/implementers of that innovation). In this case, the critical examination change involved the addition of an oral component to the Hong Kong Use of English (UE) examination, taken by approximately 20,000 students a year at the end of Secondary 7 (year 13). Andrews (1995) found similar patterns to those noted by Cheng (1998b), and concluded that "As a tool to engineer curriculum innovation, ... washback seems to be a very blunt instrument, one which may have relatively predictable quantitative effects on, for example, the time allocated to different aspects of teaching and on the content of that teaching, but rather less predictable qualitative effects upon the teaching-learning process and what actually takes place in classrooms" (p. 79).

Other recent studies of washback in language education have confirmed that while tests may indeed affect teaching and learning, those effects are unpredictable. Watanabe (1996b), for example, found that the form of university entrance examinations in Japan exerted a washback effect on some teachers, but not on others (p. 330). Watanabe (1996b) commented that "teacher factors may outweigh the influence of an examination ..." suggesting that teacher education should play a vital role in relation to any assessment innovation (p. 331; see also Andrews, 1994, pp. 54–55). Alderson and Hamp-Lyons' (1996) study of the washback from the TOEFL test came to similar conclusions about the unpredictability of washback, and the variability of its effects from teacher to teacher: "Our study shows clearly that the TOEFL affects both *what* and *how* teachers teach, but the effect is not the same in degree or in kind from teacher to teacher, and the simple difference of TOEFL versus non-TOEFL teaching does not explain *why* they teach the way they do" (p. 295).

Wall (2000) commented that little research attention has been paid to the impact of tests on the "products of learning" (although see Hughes, 1988): "What is missing . . . are analyses of test results which indicate whether students have learned more or learned better because they have studied for a particular test" (p. 502). Andrews and Fullilove (1997) reported one such study, in which an attempt was made to measure empirically the effect of the introduction of a new test (the Hong Kong UE Oral exam, referred to earlier) on student learning. A specially designed oral test, reflecting the aims of the curriculum and (like the UE Oral) involving both monologue and group discussion, was administered over a 3-year period to batches of students from three Secondary 7 cohorts. The 1993 cohort was the last not specifically prepared for an oral examination (the first administration of the UE Oral was in 1994). The 1994 and 1995 cohorts were the first two to take the UE oral. The performance on the specially designed test of the students from all three cohorts was videotaped. Three matched groups of 31 students were selected from the three cohorts. The videotaped oral performances of these 93 students were jumbled and then rated by eight experienced and trained UE Oral assessors. The mean ratings of the three cohorts were then compared. Comparison revealed what appeared to be a substantively significant difference in mean performance between the 1993 and 1995 cohorts, suggesting that the introduction of the test might have had a positive influence on students' oral proficiency. The differences were not, however, statistically significant, possibly due to the relatively small size of the sample.

Follow-up analysis (Andrews, Fullilove, & Wong, 2002) of the language used by the subjects in both parts of the test revealed clear evidence of washback upon some students, though not necessarily of a positive kind. Within the two cohorts who had prepared for the UE Oral, for example, there were a number of uses of formulaic phrases, which, while appropriate for the format of the UE Oral, were quite inappropriate for the oral tasks performed as part of the study. However, the analysis so far suggests that washback on student learning is just as unpredictable and variable as the washback on teacher behavior noted in other studies.

WASHBACK AND CURRICULAR INNOVATION: RESEARCH IN GENERAL EDUCATION

A number of recent studies in general education have also shed light on the relationship between assessment and the curriculum. In this section, discussion centers first on the situation in England, which, according to Whetton (1999), currently subjects its school population to more external tests than any other country in the world (as cited in James, 2000). The focus then switches to recent experience in a number of countries around the world where attempts have been made to use high-stakes national assessment to improve classroom practices and thereby student learning.

According to Broadfoot (1999), "assessment procedures in England have always played a key role in controlling an otherwise almost anarchic system" (as cited in James, 2000, p. 351). James describes how both teachers and students have been affected by the amount of statutory assessment that now forms part of education in England. The cohort of 16-year-olds who took General Certificate of Secondary Education (GCSE) examinations in 2000, for example, had already taken three mandatory sets of tests (beginning at the age of 7) to measure their attainment against specified targets. In a climate of external accountability, such assessments have been used to monitor and evaluate the performance of teachers, schools, and local education authorities.

James cites evidence from the Primary Assessment, Curriculum and Experience (PACE) research project, which monitored the impact of policy changes on the experience of English primary headteachers, teachers, and students from 1989 to 1997. The longitudinal study of students, for example, revealed a number of negative effects on attitude and behavior attributable to external and overt assessment, such as becoming "performance orientated" rather than "learning orientated," and avoiding challenge (Broadfoot, 1998, as cited in James, 2000). The findings from the PACE project showed external accountability (via, for example, League Tables comparing primary schools' published results on Standard Assessment Tests) to be having an equally negative impact upon a number of teachers, especially older ones: "Some teachers expressed fragmented identities, torn between a discourse which emphasized technical and managerial skills and values which continued to emphasize the importance of an emotional and affective dimension to teaching" (Broadfoot, 1998, p. 12, as cited in James, 2000, p. 350).

In the same paper, however, James (2000) reported the findings of Black and Wiliam's (1998) review of research evidence on the impact of formative assessment on children's learning across subject areas, which concluded that "The research reported here shows conclusively that formative assessment does improve learning. The gains in achievement appear to be quite considerable, and ... among the largest ever reported for educational interventions" (p. 61, as cited in James, 2000, p. 359).

Given the evidence about the negative impact of summative assessment, and the positive impact which certain other forms of assessment appear to have on learning, James and Gipps (1998) proposed that, in the English context at least, there is a powerful argument to justify a reduction in the amount of summative assessment (thereby reducing the pressures on both students and teachers), and a broadening of the forms of assessment employed, in order to encourage and support "strategic learning," the "judicious mix of surface and deep learning" (p. 288) described in Marton, Hounsell, and Entwistle (1984).

The assessment experiences in a number of other countries are described in the recent paper by Chapman and Snyder (2000), referred to earlier. Chapman and Snyder (2000) reported on the mixed outcomes of attempts in various parts of the world to use high-stakes tests to improve instruction. They evaluated the success of five propositions emerging from the international educational development literature concerning the contribution of assessment to improvements in student performance:

(a) Education officials can use test scores to target educational resources to low achieving schools or geographic areas;
(b) Testing can be used to shape and "pull" teachers' pedagogical practices in desirable ways;
(c) Testing can be used to motivate teachers to improve their teaching;
(d) Testing gives teachers information with which they can target remediation; and
(e) National assessments can support cross-national comparisons which can lead governments to commit a larger share of the national budget to education. (pp. 458–466)

The following discussion focuses on Propositions (b) and (c), since they are the most directly linked to teaching and learning.

In relation to Proposition (b), which encapsulates the principles of MDI, as mentioned earlier, Chapman and Snyder (2000) noted that the changes to the tests are generally intended "to raise the cognitive complexity of students' thinking and problem-solving processes by concentrating the questions on the application of knowledge rather than information recall" (p. 460). Their descriptions of the consequences of employing this change strategy in Trinidad and Tobago (London, 1997) and in Uganda (Snyder et al., 1997) reveal mixed success. In the former case, the Government changed its Eleven-Plus examination in response to criticism from education professionals, only to encounter a number of unexpected difficulties, including accusations that the new examination (with the inclusion of essay writing) discriminated against the poor. As Chapman and Snyder (2000) reported (p. 461), changes in instructional practices occurred over time, but at a cost. In the case of Uganda, changes to the national examination did not lead to the intended adjustments in teachers' instructional practices, either because teachers could not understand the requirements of the new exam, or because they were unwilling to risk taking chances with new classroom techniques.

Chapman and Snyder (2000) concluded that changing national exams *can* shape teachers' instructional practices, but that success is by no means assured: "It depends on the government's political will in the face of potentially stiff opposition and the strategies used to help teachers make the transition to meet the new demands" (p. 462). They put forward three other important propositions:

(a) The connection between changing tests and teachers' changing instructional practices is not a technical relationship, where a change of test format automatically leads to changes in the dynamic patterns of classroom behavior.
(b) Changing the behavior of individual teachers does not automatically lead to changes in student learning.
(c) Well-intentioned changes to tests may generate considerable opposition, often among those with seemingly most to gain from improving educational quality (i.e., teachers, parents, and students). (pp. 462–463)

Proposition (c) explored by Chapman and Snyder (2000) is premised on one of the central assumptions of external accountability: Disseminating test scores will generate competition between schools and thus motivate teachers in low achieving schools to improve their instructional practices. In other words, the washback on teaching and learning is planned to operate less directly than in Proposition (b). Again, the findings reported show mixed results. In Kenya (Bude, 1989; Somerset, 1983), the experience was generally successful, illustrating "the positive impact of feedback coupled with specific information to teachers on how to change their instruction in order to raise test scores" (Chapman & Snyder, p. 463). In Chile, on the other hand, the widespread dissemination of test scores was an unsuccessful strategy (Schiefelbein, 1993), partly because teachers tended to blame poor results on factors beyond their control, rather than consider possible inadequacies in their instructional practices.

WASHBACK AND CURRICULAR INNOVATION: LESSONS FROM INNOVATION STUDIES

Wall (1996), referring back to Alderson and Wall (1993), suggested that in order to understand how washback works (or fails to work), it is important to take account of what we know about innovation, particularly innovation in educational settings (p. 338). The work of Fullan (e.g., Fullan with Stiegelbauer, 1991) in general education, and of White (1988, 1991), Kennedy (1988), Cooper (1989), Stoller (1994), and Markee (1993, 1997) in language education have all helped to clarify the complexity of the innovation process, and the various factors which inhibit or facilitate successful implementation. Among the points emerging from that literature are the importance of understanding both the sociocultural context and the concerns of the stakeholders in the innovation process, the length of time that is often required for successful innovation, and the odds against actually achieving success. The latter point is noted by a number of writers, among them Markee (1997), who cited Adams and Chen's (1981) estimate that roughly 75% of all innovations fail to survive in the long term (as cited in Markee, 1997, p. 6).

Wall (2000) developed these arguments, describing the use of a "diffusion-of-innovations" model (Henrichsen, 1989) to analyze attempts to employ washback as a strategy to influence teaching in Sri Lanka (via the testing innovation discussed earlier). The analysis underlines the need to introduce innovations in assessment with just as much care as innovations in any other field, by taking full account of "Antecedent" conditions (such as the characteristics of the context, and of the participants within the innovation process) as well as of "Process" factors likely to facilitate or inhibit the implementation of the intended changes (see, e.g., Rogers, 1983 for a discussion of "Process" factors such as relative advantage, compatibility, complexity, trialability, and observability) (Wall, 2000, p. 506).

Chapman and Snyder's (2000) review of international educational development research (pp. 470–471) resonates with much that is discussed in the educational innovation literature in general, and in Wall (2000) in particular. This can be seen both in their conclusion that "changing tests to change instructional practices can work in some settings, that its impact on instructional practices is more indirect than is widely understood, and that its success is not necessarily assured," and also in the five emerging issues which, they suggest, must be borne in mind when any attempt is made to use high-stakes tests as a lever for educational improvement:

(a) Teachers do not necessarily understand which of their instructional practices, if changed, might lead to improvements in student test scores.
(b) Teachers may not have the necessary content knowledge or pedagogical skills to meet new demands.
(c) Changing the test in order to change instruction, if not done with care, may cause students, teachers, and parents to consider the system as unfair.
(d) "The logical path by which information on test results is expected to impact teacher behavior is often indirect; much of the voltage is lost during the transmission." (Chapman & Snyder, p. 471)
(e) Enlisting teacher and parental support for the changes may not succeed as a strategy, if the changes are too complex, or are perceived as

adversely affecting the balance of advantage across test takers. (Chapman & Snyder, p. 471)

Based on the innovation literature and her own research (e.g., Wall, 1999), Wall (2000) also made a number of observations about the impact of test reform. She expressed them as recommendations addressed to researchers investigating washback. They seem, however, to be equally valuable as guidelines for anyone contemplating the introduction of an assessment innovation as a strategy to promote changes in instructional practices:

(a) Analyze the "Antecedent" situation to ensure that the change is desirable, and the education system is ready and able to take on the burden of implementation.
(b) Involve teachers (and other stakeholders, including students) in all stages of planning.
(c) Incorporate stakeholder representatives in the design team to ensure that the test is both comprehensible to teachers, and acceptable to other stakeholders.
(d) Provide draft test specifications for all key stakeholders, and carefully pilot the new test before its introduction.
(e) Build on-going evaluation into the implementation process.
(f) Do not expect either an instant impact on instructional practices, or the precise impact anticipated. (pp. 506–507)

CONCLUSION

The aim in this chapter has been to consider the relationship between washback and curricular innovation. To that end, theory and research on washback from both general education and language education have been examined, and related to what is now understood about innovation, with particular reference to educational innovation.

It is clear from the preceding discussion that the relationship between assessment and the curriculum arouses great passion, not least because high-stakes tests are potentially a very powerful tool. The use (or abuse) of tests by governments and/or examination agencies has been noted, and the conflicting results of attempts to use tests as a strategy for promoting curricular innovation have only served to underline both the complexity of washback, and the dangers of an oversimplistic, naive reliance on high-stakes tests as a primary change strategy.

In the light of the available evidence, what lessons can be learned by testers, examination agencies, educators, and governments? Perhaps the first and most important lesson is that governments need to learn from the less than successful attempts to use assessment (via MDI) as a power-coercive strategy for change (Chin & Benne, 1976). As Markee (1997) reported, research in North America, Britain, and Australia suggests that the power-coercive approach "does not promote long-lasting, self-sustaining innovation effectively" (p. 64). The findings from the studies reported earlier serve to confirm this. James (2000) raised pertinent questions in this regard: "If assessment is a lever for change in schools, should more attention be paid to the models of change that underpin this assumption? In particular, should the limits of coercive strategies be recognized and should attention turn to developing powerful approaches to formative assessment as a central dimension of effective pedagogy?" (p. 361).

The second lesson to be learned, as Andrews (1994) and Wall (1996, 2000) made clear, is that those responsible for assessment innovations, and all other forms of curricular innovation, need to take full and careful account of the context within which the innovation is to be introduced. They also need to acknowledge and to work within the constraints imposed by the complexity of the innovation process: the time that it takes, the depths of the changes that successful implementation might entail, and the concerns of the various stakeholders. The experiences of assessment reform described by Chapman and Snyder (2000) confirmed the importance of such considerations, while at the same time reinforcing Wall's (1996, 2000) suggestions that, even with the most careful and sensitive planning and implementation, the effects of a new test may not be as intended or anticipated.

The third lesson, which is especially important for testers and examination agencies, is that whatever the objections to measurement-driven instruction as a change strategy, the strength of the potential influence of assessment on the curriculum is something that cannot be ignored. It therefore behooves testers to try to ensure, at the very least, that every effort is made to minimize the unintended negative effects of any assessment innovation upon teaching and learning. The desirable objective would seem to be an alignment of curriculum and assessment—not with the essentially negative connotations of "curricular alignment" noted by Hamp-Lyons (1997, p. 295), which associate it with a narrowing of the curriculum in response to a test, but rather in the sense with which Biggs (1999) talks of "constructive alignment," where the various elements of the curriculum (including assessment) work in harmony to promote deep learning (pp. 11–32). This reflects the view of Glaser (1990), that: "Testing and learning should be integral events, guiding the growth of competence" (p. 480, as cited in Biggs, 1998, p. 358). However, it is clear from the various studies described earlier that such an ideal may be very hard to attain in practice.

The fourth lesson—one that has clearly been borne in mind by the editors of this volume—is that there is still a great need for further research into the complex and varied ways in which tests affect the curriculum and curricular innovation. It is to be hoped that the range of studies reported in this volume will both raise awareness of the issues associated with washback and inspire more research activity in this area. There is in particular a continuing need for studies incorporating first-hand evidence of classroom events, as Alderson and Wall (1993) noted in their seminal paper. Our understanding of washback and its relationship with curricular innovation has advanced considerably in the past 10 years, but there are still many aspects of this elusive phenomenon that remain to be investigated.

PART

II

WASHBACK STUDIES FROM DIFFERENT PARTS OF THE WORLD

CHAPTER

4

The Effects of Assessment-Driven Reform on the Teaching of Writing in Washington State

Brian Stecher
The RAND Corporation

Tammi Chun
University of Hawaii

Sheila Barron
University of Iowa

Although the term *washback* is not widely used in the United States, the concept is clearly understood. As far back as the 1980s, researchers identified many undesirable consequences of testing on curriculum and instruction. These effects included "narrowing" of the curriculum, changes in course objectives, and revisions in the sequence of the curriculum (Corbett & Wilson, 1988; Darling-Hammond & Wise, 1985; Herman & Golan, n.d.; Shepard & Dougherty, 1991). Moreover, the greater the consequences, the more likely such changes occurred (Corbett & Wilson, 1991). Recent growth in high-stakes testing has led to renewed concern about the influence of tests on school practices. The authors have been involved in a number of studies that have tried to quantify the degree to which practice has changed as a result of the introduction of test-based reform efforts at the state level (Koretz, Barron, Mitchell, & Stecher, 1996; Koretz, Stecher, Klein, & McCaffrey, 1994; Stecher & Barron, 1999; Stecher, Barron, Chun, Krop, & Ross, 2000; Stecher, Barron, Kaganoff, & Goodwin, 1998). The present work, which was conducted under the auspices of the National Center for Research on Evaluation, Standards and Student Testing (CRESST), continues this investigation.

There is heightened interest among U.S. policymakers in using content standards, standards-based assessments, and test-based accountability as levers to improve education. Early results from states that implemented reforms of this type (such as Kentucky and Texas) showed impressive gains in test scores. These results may have contributed to the race among states to implement educational reforms that follow this standards-based model. According to a national study (*Education Week*, January 13, 2000), 49 of the 50 states have adopted standards in at least one subject and 41 states have assessments aligned with the standards in at least one subject. According to the Council of Chief State School Officers (1998), 47 states publicly report test scores. A number of these states are either developing or implementing school accountability mechanisms for schools based on these assessments.

However, in their rush to implement standards-based, assessment-driven accountability systems, states may be overlooking other important evidence about the efficacy of such reforms. Recent research in Kentucky illustrates the importance of monitoring instructional practice in the context of statewide accountability. Kentucky's educational reform proponents hoped to drive instruction in particular directions by emphasizing students' ability to solve complex problems rather than multiple-choice questions via open-response questions and portfolios. The reform rewarded schools for improvements in test scores and intervened in schools whose scores declined. Researchers found that Kentucky's efforts had both positive and negative effects (AEL, 2000; Koretz et al., 1996; Wolf, Borko, Elliot, & McIver, 2000). On the positive side, the Kentucky education reform, which included standards and performance assessments (called the Kentucky Instructional Results Information System or KIRIS), influenced classroom practices in both elementary and middle schools (Borko & Elliott, 1999; McIver & Wolf, 1999).[1] Researchers found evidence of increased professional development related to the tests and the standards, increased coverage in the classroom of the subjects tested by KIRIS, and increased frequency of practices encouraged by the reform, such as problem solving and mathematical communication (Borko & Elliott, 1999; Stecher et al., 1998).

On the negative side, there was no evidence of associations between these changing practices and increased KIRIS scores (Stecher et al., 1998). In addition, teachers' instruction appeared to be influenced more by the tests than by the standards the tests were supposed to represent. One consequence of such "teaching to the test" was that curriculum coverage varied significantly from one grade to the next in parallel with the subject matter tested by KIRIS (Stecher & Barron, 1999). For example, Kentucky students in fourth and seventh grades received more instruction in reading, writing, and science (which were tested in fourth grade), while students in

[1]Researchers studied the KIRIS tests, which were in effect until 1998. The current assessment and accountability system is referred to as the Commonwealth Accountability Testing System (CATS).

fifth and eighth grades received more instruction in mathematics, social studies, and arts/humanities (which were tested in fifth grade). Similar shifts in emphasis occurred within specific subject areas. For example, the KIRIS writing test focused on short written pieces, and teachers focused on writing short passages at the expense of other types of writing.

Thus test score changes cannot be interpreted fully without direct evidence about changes in classroom practices. Better understanding of the influence of test-based accountability on classroom practices is essential to judge the effectiveness of standards-based, assessment-driven accountability systems.

WASHINGTON EDUCATION REFORM

This study focuses on changes that occurred at the school and classroom levels during the early years of standards-based assessment in Washington State. We use the term *school practice* to refer those actions and guidelines that affect all teachers, such as the assignment of teachers to grades and classes, scheduling the school day, school selection of curriculum and materials, and the provision of professional development. *Classroom practice*, by comparison, refers to those actions that are the responsibility of individual teachers, such as developing lessons, delivering instruction, assigning homework, and grading students. Washington's education reform, which was adopted by the state legislature in 1993, was designed to affect both school and classroom practices. It is similar to standards-based accountability systems in other states, such as Kentucky, Maryland, and Texas, in that it has three major components: a set of standards, measures of student performance, and a system of incentives for improvement (*Education Week*, 1997, 1999). Washington's system includes statewide standards for what students should know and be able to do—called the Essential Academic Learning Requirements (EALRs); tests to evaluate student knowledge and progress toward standards—called the Washington Assessment of Student Learning (WASL); and a mechanism to hold schools accountable for student performance (which is being developed during the 2000–2001 school year).

In 1995 and 1996, the state established standards in eight content areas: reading, writing, mathematics, listening/communication, science, social studies, health/fitness, and the arts. These EALRs describe desired student knowledge skills in each subject in general terms. For example, in writing the first standard is "The student writes clearly and effectively" (Washington State Commission on Student Learning, 1997, p. 29). There are three substandards, which provide somewhat more detail about this aspect of writing. For example, the second substandard is that students will "use style appropriate to the audience and purpose: use voice, word choice and sentence fluency for intended style and audience" (Washington State Commission on Student Learning, 1997, p. 29). Furthermore, in the three benchmark grades—4, 7, and 10—the EALRs delineate more detailed, grade-specific instructional goals. For example, for the substandard dealing with style for Grade 4, students are expected to be able to "communicate own perspective and ideas, demonstrate awareness of the audience, use patterns and vocabulary from literature and nonfiction, use figurative language and imagery, use words in more than one context and use a variety of sentence lengths and types" (Washington State Commission on Student Learning, 1997, p. 31). Currently, students are tested only in the benchmark grades.

The Washington Assessment of Student Learning (WASL) was developed to reflect these benchmark skills in Grades 4, 7, and 10. The fourth-grade WASL in reading, writing, mathematics, and listening was offered for the first time on a voluntary basis in 1996–1997, and it became mandatory the following year. For seventh-grade students, the assessments were voluntary in 1997–1998 and became mandatory beginning in the 2000–2001 school year. The tenth-grade WASL was administered on a voluntary basis in 1999–2000 and will be required of all tenth-grade students beginning in 2000–2001.[2] This study focuses on the impact of WASL testing in Grades 4 and 7, which were the only grades tested at the time of the study.

The third major component of Washington's education reform, an accountability system, is still in the development phase. Additionally, the educational reform also included professional development for teachers. Sixteen regional learning and assessment centers were established across the state to provide assistance to local schools and districts. Finally, the state developed supplemental print materials, including curriculum frameworks based on EALRs, Example Tests with items that mimicked WASL tests, and a CD-ROM with examples of student work scored using WASL rubrics.

This chapter focuses on the subject of writing. The WASL test in writing consists of two writing prompts of different genres. Each prompt is scored using two WASL-specific scoring rubrics, one that emphasizes content, organization and style, and one that emphasizes conventions. (The rubrics for scoring the WASL writing assessment are provided in Appendixes A & B.) The following is an example of a fourth-grade expository writing prompt: "Think about the area or community in which you live. Write several paragraphs *explaining*, to your teacher, what you like or dislike about the area or community and why" (Office of the Superintendent of Public Instruction,

---

[2]All testing is done in English. Students who are classified as English As a Second Language (ESL)/Bilingual may qualify for some testing accommodations if their level of English proficiency is sufficiently low. The only accommodations made for ESL/bilingual students are to "use a reader to read math assessment items **verbatim** in English" and to provide a dictionary "**only on the writing test**" (Bergeson, Wise, Fitton, Gill, & Arnold, 2000).

TABLE 4.1
Percent of Students Who Met Standard on the Washington Assessment of Student Learning in Writing

	Grade 4	*Grade 7*
1996–1997	42.8	–
1997–1998	36.7	31.3
1998–1999	32.6	37.1
1999–2000	39.4	42.6
2000–2001	43.3	48.5

Note. The fourth-grade WASL in reading, writing, mathematics, and listening was offered for the first time on a voluntary basis in 1996–1997, and it became mandatory the following year. For seventh-grade students, the assessments were voluntary in 1997–1998 and became mandatory beginning in the 2000–2001 school year.

2002, p. iv). Students are allowed to prewrite and write drafts; however, only the final drafts are scored. Students are provided up to four pages to write their final drafts.

Initial results from WASL showed that a minority of students was achieving the rigorous standards embodied in the state reforms.[3] Table 4.1 shows that fewer than one half of the students met the standards in reading or writing in 1997. Subsequent writing performance has been mixed; fourth-grade writing scores dropped in both 1998 and 1999, but there was slight improvement among seventh graders during the same period.

PROCEDURES

In spring 1999, we conducted two statewide surveys—of Washington principals and teachers—to study the impact of the Washington educational reform on school and classroom practice. We asked principals to report on school-level practices and teachers to report on classroom-level instructional practices. This chapter focuses on the results of the teacher survey, particularly teachers' reports about writing curriculum and instruction. We also draw on some data about school practices from the principal surveys when trying to model the impact of the reform on WASL scores. The research was conducted with the cooperation of the Office of the Superintendent of Public Instruction (OSPI) in Washington state.

[3]These test results are similar to early results in other states implementing challenging standards-based assessments. For example, during the first year of Maryland school performance assessment program in 1993, less than one-third of students tested "satisfactory" on the state reading test, and less than one-half met the standard in writing and mathematics.

Sampling

We selected a stratified random sample of elementary and middle schools based on the size of the community in which the school was located. The three strata (urban, urban fringe/large town, and small town/rural) reflected differences in character that are traditionally important in studying educational practice. The middle-school sample was limited to schools that administered WASL on a voluntary basis in spring 1999. For each of the survey populations (elementary schools and middle schools), 70 schools were selected.[4] Principal surveys were mailed to each school principal and teacher surveys were mailed to a sample of about 400 writing and mathematics teachers in the WASL-tested grades (fourth and seventh grades). In small schools, all teachers in the target grade levels (fourth and seventh grades) were included in the study. In large schools, it was necessary to sample teachers in order to use the available resources to collect data from a sizable number of schools.

The principal and teacher surveys covered a range of issues related to the Washington education reform. Teachers responded to questions about professional development, their familiarity with the education reform, and their opinions on the reform. They were also asked about current educational practices in their classrooms and about changes in practice that occurred in the last 2 years (since 1997–1998), including their allocation of time to different subjects, the topics they emphasized in mathematics and writing, and their teaching strategies. Teachers also rated the influence of different elements of the state reform on their classroom practices. Principals answered similar questions about professional development and their understanding of the education reform. They were also asked about school practices and about actions the district and school had taken in response to the reform.

A total of 277 teachers (69%) returned completed surveys. On average, the teachers who completed surveys had about a dozen years of experience and acquired one half of their teaching experience at their current school. About one half of the teachers had master's degrees, and the remainder had bachelor degrees. The teacher sample was similar to the population of teachers in the state with respect to these variables. One hundred eight principals (77%) returned completed surveys.

[4]The 70 elementary schools were selected from a population of 895 schools that included fourth grade (and that had at least 20 students). The middle schools were selected from a population of 400 schools that included seventh grade (and that had at least 20 students). The typical configuration in Washington is for elementary schools to include kindergarten through Grade 6, for middle schools to include Grades 7 through 9, and high schools to include Grades 10 through 12, but there is considerable variation among schools in grade range.

Data Analysis

Because we sampled teachers in the larger schools (rather than surveying all teachers), we weighted the teachers' responses to obtain results that reflected all Washington teachers in the three sampled groups (fourth-grade teachers, seventh-grade writing teachers and seventh-grade mathematics teachers). The data collection was designed to provide a large amount of information from a number of groups, rather than to maximize our power for making specific comparisons between groups. Thus, we do not focus much attention on testing the significance of differences between specific groups. In addition, regression techniques were used to explore the relationship between schools' WASL scores and combinations of school practices and classroom practices.

It should be noted that several factors limited the power of these analyses to detect relationships between test scores and practices at the school and classroom levels. First, the analyses were conducted at the school level, comparing average responses from teachers in each school to the aggregate scores of all students in that school. The analyses would have been more sensitive to relationships between classroom practices and WASL scores had we been able to link the responses of individual teachers to the scores of that teacher's own students. Second, in large schools the survey sample did not contain all teachers, so the average teacher responses to questions about classroom practices were based on incomplete data. Third, the school sample was relatively small, providing limited power to detect differences between WASL scores and school practices reported by principals or classroom practices reported by teachers. We pooled the data from elementary and middle schools to increase the power to find such relationships, but this may have clouded some associations if the relationships were different across school levels. For all these reasons, the analysis may have failed to detect some relationships between WASL scores and school and classroom practices that were actually present.

RESULTS

The major questions we investigated were how Washington's education reform affected school and classroom practices, which elements of the reform were most influential, and whether changes in practice were related to changes in scores. The second issue is particularly relevant to the theme of this book because the Washington education reform was multifaceted, involving new standards as well as new tests. The distinction between changes designed to promote broad mastery of the standards (EALRs) and changes designed to improve scores on the tests (WASL) is of crucial importance. Yet, it is difficult to determine the exact influences on teachers when they responded to the reform efforts. The survey included questions to try to disentangle teachers' reaction to the standards and their reactions to the tests. These questions asked separately about teachers' understanding of the EALRs and their understanding of the WASL, teachers' attitudes toward these two aspects of the reform, and teachers' perceptions of the influence of each component on practice. This information is reported first, followed by data on changes in curriculum and instruction and the association between practice and WASL scores. The surveys were too long to include in their entirety, so the relevant questions are reported along with the results.

Understanding of Reform Elements and Influence on Practice

The majority of teachers reported that they understood the elements of the reform, which we see as a precondition for making change.[5] Despite the fact that the EALRs were developed and circulated first, more teachers were knowledgeable about the WASL than the EALRs. Eighty percent or more of the teachers thought they understood the WASL well or very well, whereas 60% or more indicated they understood the EALRs and curriculum alignment well or very well.[6]

Teachers reported that most elements of the reform were having a positive effect on instruction and learning broadly construed.[7] Here too, a slightly greater percentage of teachers thought the WASL was influential than thought the EALRs were influential. In general, about two thirds of teachers said the EALRs and the short answer and extended response items contained in the WASL contributed either a moderate amount or a great deal to "better instruction and increased student learning." Seventh-grade writing teachers gave particularly high ratings to the influence of WASL extended response and short-answer items on instruction and learning. The percent of seventh-grade teachers who said those elements pro-

---

[5]How well do you understand each of the following aspects of Washington's education reform: Essential learnings and benchmarks (EALRs), Washington student assessments (WASL), Classroom-based assessments (e.g., Stiggins training), assessment Tool Kits, Aligning curriculum and instruction with EALRs? [Do not understand, Understand somewhat, Understand well, Understand very well]

[6]For the most part, we combined results from the top two response options when reporting results. We report disaggregated results when they suggest a different interpretation.

[7]To what extent have the following aspects of education reform promoted better instruction and increased student learning in your school: EALRs, WASL multiple choice items, WASL short answer items, District assessments, Classroom-based assessments (e.g., Stiggins training), assessment Tool Kits? [None, A small amount, A moderate amount, A great deal]

TABLE 4.2
Percent of Teachers Who Reported a Moderate Amount or Great Deal of Influence on Writing Lessons and Instruction

Aspect of Washington Education Reform[a]	*Grade 4*	*Grade 7*
WASL	75	76
In-service training or formal professional development on methods of teaching writing	66	66
Scores on WASL tests	64	73
Classroom-based assessments	65	60
EALRs	64	66
District standards	53	56
District assessments	45	53

[a]Question: To what extent did each of the following aspects of Washington's education reform contribute to changes in your writing lessons and instruction? [None, A small amount, A moderate amount, A great deal].

moted better instruction "a great deal" was 42% for WASL extended-response and 28% for WASL short-answer. The corresponding percentage for the EALRs was 15%. Fewer than 5% of the teachers believed that the WASL multiple-choice items, classroom-based assessments or district assessments promoted improved teaching and learning. In particular, less than one half of the seventh-grade writing teachers thought that WASL multiple-choice items or classroom-based assessments promoted better instruction.

Both the EALRs and the WASL were perceived by most teachers to have a strong influence on the teaching of writing. Table 4.2 summarizes teachers' reports of the perceived impact of aspects of the Washington education reform on the content and teaching of writing. The state-administered WASL test and the WASL scores appeared to be the influential for the largest percentage of teachers. About three fourths of writing teachers in both grade levels reported that WASL had a moderate or a great deal of influence on changes in their writing instruction. A similar proportion said that their schools' WASL scores contributed to making changes in their writing program. In fact, all components of the Washington education reform (including WASL, EALRs and classroom-based assessments) were reported to have a moderate amount of influence by more than one half of the teachers.

Allocation of Instructional Time Among Subjects

Fourth-grade teachers who teach all subjects reported increasing the instructional time devoted to subjects tested on WASL at the expense of untested subjects. Table 4.3 shows that teachers spent 63% of their instructional time on the tested subject areas of reading, mathematics, and writing. Teachers spent substantially less time on social studies, science, arts, and health and fitness, even though there are state standards for these subjects

TABLE 4.3
Fourth-Grade Teachers Who Reported Frequency
and Change in Instructional Emphases Across Subjects

	Hours per Week[a]		*Change in Hours*	
Content Areas	*Median*	*Percent of Total Hours*	*Percent of Teachers Indicating Decrease*	*Percent of Teachers Indicating Increase*
Reading	6	25	2	53
Writing	4	17	2	70
Mathematics	5	21	1	59
Communication/Listening	2	8	13	24
Social Studies	3	13	50	3
Science	2	8	55	8
Arts	1	4	52	4
Health and Fitness	1	4	46	1
Other	0	0	—	—
Total	25	—	5	21

[a]Question: In a typical 5-day week in your classroom, approximately how many hours are spent on instruction, in total, and how many hours are devoted to each subject?

and they all will be assessed in future years.[8] Moreover, many teachers increased the time they spent on tested subjects during the past 2 years and decreased the time they spent on the nontested subjects. In these ways, the allocation of instructional time appears to be influenced by the WASL testing program more than by the state standards. Teachers reported spending about 17% of their instructional time on writing; the median reported time spent on writing was 4 hours per week, exceeded only by reading (6 hours) and mathematics (5 hours). We can infer that less than 4 hours per week was spent on writing instruction in the past because 70% of the teachers reported increasing the time spent on the subject in the past 2 years.

Impact on the Teaching of Writing

Fourth- and seventh-grade writing teachers reported changes in the content of their writing lessons and their teaching methods during the period from 1997 to 1999.[9] In fourth grade, 42% of teachers changed their overall writing instruction a great deal, and 81% of teachers reported making at least a

[8]Teachers also reported less alignment of curriculum with the EALRs in the untested subjects compared to the tested subjects.

[9]Overall, how much change has occurred in the content of your writing lessons and the way you teach writing during the past two school years? [Not applicable (did not teach writing last year), None, A small amount, A moderate amount, A great deal].

moderate amount of change. By comparison, only 29% of seventh-grade writing teachers reported a great deal of change, and 55% reported at least a moderate amount of change in their writing program. Thus, changes were more widespread among fourth-grade teachers (in elementary schools) than among seventh-grade teachers (in middle schools). The structure of elementary schools (in which teachers teach all subjects to one class of students) and middle schools (in which teachers teach only one or two subjects to different groups of students) may, in part, explain the differences in these results. Also, at the time of the survey, fourth-grade teachers had administered the WASL in writing twice, whereas seventh-grade teachers had only given the test once.

Curriculum. The content of writing instruction was broadly reflective of the EALRs in both the fourth and seventh grades. For example, more than 40% of writing teachers reported that they covered 11 of the 14 writing behaviors specified in the EALRs at least once a week (see Table 4.4). However, teachers more frequently covered writing conventions (e.g., write complete sentences, use correct subject–verb agreement, use capitalization and punctuation accurately in the final draft, spell age-level words correctly in the final draft, indicate paragraphs consistently) and the writing process than the other elements of the standards. More than 80% of teachers indicated that they addressed the application of writing conventions at least weekly. All the stages of the writing process approach (prewrite, draft, revise, edit, publish) except publishing were covered at least weekly by more than two thirds of the fourth-grade teachers and more than one half of the seventh-grade writing teachers. (It is often the case that teachers do not have students formally "publish" all their written work in a public way, which is the last step in the writing process model. This extra step is often reserved for selected pieces.)

Teachers reported changing their emphasis on some of the writing topics. Roughly one half of the teachers reported increasing their emphasis on writing for different audiences, purposes, styles, and formats, whereas considerably fewer teachers increased their coverage of writing conventions and the writing process.

Pedagogy. Writing teachers also changed their instructional methods. Teachers were asked about the frequency with which they used 15 different instructional strategies, ranging from fairly traditional techniques (e.g., "read orally to students") to more innovative approaches (e.g., "write with students on the same assignment"; a strategy in which the teacher does the same writing assignment as the students). (See Table 4.5.) Most teachers reported that they read to students and taught language mechanics (grammar, spelling, punctuation, and syntax) at least once a week. More than one half of the teachers taught about word choice and helped students revise

TABLE 4.4
Writing Standards: Teachers' Reported Frequency of Coverage and Change in Frequency of Coverage

	Cover Aspect Weekly or Daily[a]		*Increased Coverage During Past 2 Years*[b]	
Aspects of Writing (from EALRs)	*Grade 4*	*Grade 7*	*Grade 4*	*Grade 7*
1.3 Application of writing conventions	86	83	37	46
3.2 Draft	73	65	34	35
3.4 Edit	68	57	36	32
3.1 Pre-write	67	67	35	38
3.3 Revise	66	56	44	35
4.2 Seek and offer feedback	54	50	38	51
4.1 Assessment of students' strengths and needs for improvement	46	43	44	43
1.1 Development of concept and design	44	45	48	49
1.2 Style appropriate to audience and purpose	42	32	51	60
2.2 Write for different purposes	42	44	51	49
3.5 Publish	42	41	31	23
2.3 Write in a variety of forms	38	43	46	45
2.1 Write for different audiences	28	22	43	53
2.4 Write for career applications	3	4	19	20

Note. Numbers in cells represent percent of teachers.

[a]Question: How frequently do you cover each of these aspects of writing during the current school year? [Never (zero times per year), 1–2 times per semester (about 1–5 times per year), 1–2 times per month (about 6–30 times per year), 1–2 times per week (about 31–80 times per year), almost daily (more than 80 times per year)].

[b]Question: How has the frequency changed during the past two school years? [Decreased, Stayed the same, Increased].

their work on a weekly or daily basis. Fewer teachers indicated that they regularly use writing from other content areas, hold conferences with students about their writing, or write with students on the same assignment. However, the greatest changes in writing instruction were increases in the use of rubric-based approaches (e.g., Six-Trait or WASL rubrics) and in commenting on student writing in different content areas.

Student Activities. Students were given regular writing assignments, but most of the writing assignments were short pieces, one to two paragraphs in length.[10] Eighty-five percent of fourth-grade teachers and 91% of seventh-

[10]How often do your students produce written pieces of the following lengths during the current school year (one to two paragraphs, one to two pages, three or more pages)? [Never (zero times per year), 1–2 times per semester (about 1–5 times per year), 1–2 times per month (about

TABLE 4.5
Writing Teaching Strategies: Teachers' Reported Frequency of Use and Change in Frequency of Use

	Use Strategy Weekly or Daily[a]		*Increased Use During Past 2 Years*[b]	
Teaching Strategy	*Grade 4*	*Grade 7*	*Grade 4*	*Grade 7*
Read orally to students	97	76	13	30
Explain correct usage of grammar, spelling, punctuation and syntax	90	86	20	46
Suggest revisions to student writing	62	61	32	37
Teach Six-Trait or other rubric-based approach to writing	64	41	56	61
Give examples of choosing appropriate words to describe objects or experiences	62	65	31	39
Use examples to discuss the craft of an author's writing	58	63	28	43
Provide time for unstructured ("free") writing	53	40	14	25
Demonstrate the use of prewriting	51	37	40	46
Provide a prompt to initiate student writing	44	45	30	39
Assess students' writing skills	45	50	29	35
Provide time for students to conference with each other about writing	38	29	31	44
Show examples of writing in different content areas	30	25	35	35
Comment on student writing in different content areas	30	31	62	69
Conference with students about their writing	31	15	27	25
Write with students on the same assignment	19	7	25	24

[a]Question: How frequently do you use each of these teaching strategies in writing during the current school year? [Never (zero times per year), 1–2 times per semester (about 1–5 times per year), 1–2 times per month (about 6–30 times per year), 1–2 times per week (about 31–80 times per year), almost daily (more than 80 times per year)].

[b]Question: How has the frequency changed during the past two school years? [Decreased, Stayed the same, Increased].

grade writing teachers reported that their students produced such short written works on a weekly or daily basis. This represented an increase in the frequency of short pieces for 45% of fourth-grade teachers and 41% of seventh-grade teachers. Most teachers assigned longer written pieces much less often.

WASL Preparation. Teachers also took many specific steps to help students perform well on the WASL tests in writing. In interpreting the survey

---

6–30 times per year), 1–2 times per week (about 31–80 times per year), almost daily (more than 80 times per year)] How has the frequency changed during the past two school years? [Decreased, Stayed the same, Increased]

TABLE 4.6
Teachers' Reported Frequency of Activities to Help Students Do Well on WASL Test in Writing

Activity	*Percent That Use Activity Weekly or Daily*[a] Grade 4	Grade 7
Teach Six-Trait or other rubric-based approach to writing	64	48
Use open-ended questions (short-answer and extended-response) in classroom work	59	77
Display scoring rubrics in classroom	39	42
Discuss responses to WASL or WASL-like items that demonstrate different levels of performance	29	30
Have students practice using items released from WASL	29	14
Have students score classroom work using rubrics	27	22
Use materials from assessment Tool Kits	24	9

[a]Question: How frequently do you engage in each of the following activities to help students do well on the WASL test in writing? [Never (zero times per year), 1–2 times per semester (about 1–5 times per year), 1–2 times per month (about 6–30 times per year), 1–2 times per week (about 31–80 times per year), almost daily (more than 80 times per year)].

responses it is important to distinguish activities that focus narrowly on the specific content and format that is used on the test from preparation that focuses on the broad domain of writing. Writing teachers indicated more frequent use of strategies that focused broadly on student writing than strategies that focused narrowly on the tests (see Table 4.6). In preparing students for the WASL test in writing, more than one half of teachers used two activities: Six-Trait or other rubric-based approaches to writing, and open-ended questions in classroom work. (See Appendixes A & B for the rubric used for scoring the WASL.) Most fourth-grade teachers and almost one half of the seventh-grade teachers adopted a rubric-based approach to teaching writing at least once a week. Three fourths of seventh-grade teachers and more than one half of fourth-grade teachers incorporated short-answer questions into classroom work once a week or more often.

Although explicit WASL-focused practice such as using WASL-related items was not as common, there was a noticeable amount of it in evidence. Teachers, especially at fourth grade, were more likely to report engaging in narrower practices on a monthly basis. For example, most fourth-grade teachers reported they had students practice with released items (60%), discuss responses to WASL items (63%), and use the rubrics to score classroom work (63%). Most fourth-grade teachers (64%) also reported they displayed the scoring rubrics in the classroom once a month or more. Fewer seventh-grade teachers reported they had students practice with released items (41%) or discuss responses to WASL items (52%) once a month or more.

On the survey, teachers were given an opportunity to describe in their own words other strategies they used to prepare students for WASL in writing.[11] They reported a wide range of activities. Some appeared to be narrowly focused on the test itself. For example, one teacher reported that she "spent far too much class time teaching to the test instead of teaching." Other activities were clearly designed to foster writing more broadly. For example, one teacher reported "giv[ing] them time to talk about writing with each other and with older students." Most teachers' comments fell between these two extremes. Typical of most was "I have recently incorporated WASL-like assessment in nearly every unit I teach throughout the year. These assessments include rubrics which imitate the WASL very closely." It is difficult to say, in isolation, whether this change would do more to help students improve their writing in general or to help them produce written pieces that were strong on the specific criteria used in the WASL.

School and Classroom Practices and WASL Scores

We selected a subset of school practices reported by principals and a subset of classroom practices reported by teachers and investigated their relationship with WASL scores using multiple regression analyses. The regression specifications and quantitative results are presented in other publications (Stecher et al., 2000; Stecher & Chun, 2002). For the most part we found no significant associations, but among the many relationships investigated there were a few features that were related to higher school scores after controlling for student demographic factors. The strongest effects were related to the alignment of curriculum with the EALRs and to the teachers' understanding of the reform. For two of the four subjects (reading and mathematics), WASL scores were higher in schools where teachers reported greater alignment between curriculum and the EALRs. Scores were also higher in schools where teachers reported that they understood the EALRs and WASL well (this difference was significant for mathematics and almost significant for reading). However, length of teaching experience was the only significant predictor of scores in writing. That is, students in schools with more experienced teachers tended to have higher scores in writing than students in schools whose teachers had less teaching experience.

DISCUSSION

There seems little doubt that Washington's education reform has widely influenced the content of the writing curriculum and the methods that are

[11]What other things have you done to prepare students for the WASL in writing?

used to teach writing. Teachers reported changes in their allocation of time to writing, the emphasis they placed on specific aspects of writing, their teaching methods, and their students' learning activities. In most cases, teachers indicated that they incorporated the processes and strategies into their existing teaching practice rather than displace familiar lessons and strategies. More generally speaking, fourth- and seventh-grade teachers appear to have made a variety of changes in classroom practices designed to promote the standards and raise scores on the state assessments.

What is more difficult to determine is the relative importance of the state standards and the state assessments in shaping teaching practices. Both elements were clearly influential, although there is some evidence that more teachers focused on the WASL content and format than the EALRs. Explicit test preparation for the writing exam (e.g., using released items from previous tests) was not widespread. However, a focus on tested content and format was evident in teachers' reports of classroom practice. To the extent that the tests broadly represent the domain of writing and the scoring rubrics broadly reflect the characteristics of effective written communication, a focus on the tests should not be substantially different than a focus on the standards. The WASL test in writing achieves these goals more than a multiple-choice test of writing would do, because students must produce an essay, not merely fill in blanks, identify mistakes, or complete other writing-related tasks that can be assessed using a multiple-choice format.

There are still, however, concerns about curriculum narrowing as a result of the WASL. In 1999, a state task force recommended a change to the WASL test in writing to eliminate uncertainty about which genre would be tested in each grade. Fourth grade was assigned narrative and expository writing, seventh grade was assigned persuasive writing and expository writing, and tenth grade was assigned persuasive and extended expository writing. The task force raised the concern about teachers' narrowing the writing curriculum to focus on these genres, "This action is in no way meant to limit classroom instruction or district and classroom-based assessments" (Elliott & Ensign, 1999, p. 1). This survey occurred before the change took effect, but such a revision could have significant repercussions for writing instruction. If teachers are attending to the test more than the standards, then teachers would spend more time on the tested genres over or in place of the untested genres.

Given the limited amount of class time available and the large number and breadth of the content standards, it is not surprising that teachers must look for a way to focus their instruction. Assessment plays a key role in signaling priorities among standards and in making student performance expectations concrete. The results of this survey suggest that the reform has created "winners" and "losers" among the subjects. The big "winner" to date is writing. According to the teachers, replacing or supplementing multiple-choice tests with more performance-based assessments has led to a dramatic increase in the amount of writing students do in school—both as part of language arts instruction and as part of instruction in other subjects.

The big "losers," at this point, are the untested subject areas. The most dramatic finding of the survey is the reallocation of instructional time from nontested subjects to tested subjects. This is strong evidence that the tests are driving change more than the standards. Washington adopted standards in eight content areas, but the survey shows increases in time for only those subjects that are tested. In elementary schools, the amount of time fourth-grade teachers spent on the four WASL-tested subjects (reading, writing, mathematics, listening/communication) has increased during the last 2 years. In middle schools, teachers generally are responsible for only one subject and class schedules are fixed, so teachers cannot reallocate time among subjects. Nevertheless, 55% of middle-school principals reported that their school implemented schedule changes to increase time for math, reading and/or writing.

It is unclear whether or not this emphasis on tested subjects over untested subjects is a short-term problem that will disappear once the WASL tests in the other subjects are implemented. In Kentucky, where testing occurs in some subjects at Grades 4 and 7 and in other subjects at Grades 5 and 8, instructional focus has been bent toward the subjects tested at that grade (Stecher & Barron, 1999). With the expected introduction of the WASL test in science at different grades (Grades 5, 8, & 10), Washington may face a similar situation. Although the standards-based, test-driven reform adopted in Washington has reduced the extent of the "washback" effect of testing on instruction, it has not eliminated the effect altogether.

APPENDIX A

WASL Writing Rubric for Content, Organization, and Style

Points	*Description*
4	• maintains consistent focus on the topic and has ample supporting details • has a logical organizational pattern and conveys a sense of completeness and wholeness • provides transitions which clearly serve to connect ideas • uses language effectively by exhibiting word choices that are engaging and appropriate for intended audience and purpose • includes sentences, or phrases where appropriate, of varied length and structure • allows the reader to sense the person behind the words
3	• maintains adequate focus on the topic and has adequate supporting details • has a logical organizational pattern and conveys a sense of wholeness and completeness, although some lapses occur • provides adequate transitions in an attempt to connect ideas • uses effective language and appropriate word choices for intended audience and purpose • includes sentences, or phrases where appropriate, that are somewhat varied in length and structure • provides the reader with some sense of the person behind the words
2	• demonstrates an inconsistent focus and includes some supporting details, but may include extraneous or loosely related material • shows an attempt at an organizational pattern, but exhibits little sense of wholeness and completeness • provides transitions which are weak or inconsistent • has a limited and predictable vocabulary which may not be appropriate for the intended audience and purpose • shows limited variety in sentence length and structure • attempts somewhat to give the reader a sense of the person behind the words
1	• demonstrates little or no focus and few supporting details which may be inconsistent or interfere with the meaning of the text • has little evidence of an organizational pattern or any sense of wholeness and completeness • provides transitions which are poorly utilized, or fails to provide transitions • has a limited or inappropriate vocabulary for the intended audience and purpose • has little or no variety in sentence length and structure • provides the reader with little or no sense of the person behind the words
0	• response is "I don't know"; response is a question mark (?); response is one word; response is only the title of the prompt; or the prompt is simply recopied

APPENDIX B

WASL Writing Rubric for Conventions

Points	*Description*
2	• consistently follows the rules of standard English for usage • consistently follows the rules of standard English for spelling of commonly used words • consistently follows the rules of standard English for capitalization and punctuation • consistently exhibits the use of complete sentences except where purposeful phrases or clauses are used for effect • indicates paragraphs consistently
1	• generally follows the rules of standard English for usage • generally follows the rules of standard English for spelling of commonly used words • generally follows the rules of standard English for capitalization and punctuation • generally exhibits the use of complete sentences except where purposeful phrases are used for effect • indicates paragraphs for the most part
0	• mostly does not follow the rules of standard English for usage • mostly does not follow the rules of standard English for spelling of commonly used words • mostly does not follow the rules of standard English for capitalization and punctuation • exhibits errors in sentence structure that impede communication • mostly does not indicate paragraphs • response is "I don't know"; response is a question mark (?); response is one word; response is only the title of the prompt; or the prompt is simply recopied

CHAPTER

5

The IELTS Impact Study: Investigating Washback on Teaching Materials

Nick Saville
Roger Hawkey
University of Cambridge ESOL Examinations

This chapter describes the development of data collection instruments for an impact study of the International English Language Testing System (IELTS). The IELTS is owned jointly by University of Cambridge Local Examinations Syndicate (UCLES), the British Council, and the International Development Program (IDP) Education, Australia. The test is currently taken by around 200,000 candidates a year at 224 centers in 105 countries, most candidates seeking admission to higher education in the UK, Australia, New Zealand, Canada, and the United States. The IELTS is a task-based testing system which assesses the language skills candidates need to study or train in the medium of English. It has four modules–listening, reading, writing, and speaking–all calling for candidates to process authentic text and discourse (for a summary of the format of IELTS, see Appendix A).

Following the most recent revision of IELTS in 1995, planning began for a study of ways in which the effects and the effectiveness of IELTS could be further evaluated. This project was coordinated by Nick Saville and Michael Milanovic at UCLES, working in conjunction with Charles Alderson at Lancaster University, who was commissioned to help design and develop instrumentation. Roger Hawkey, co-author of this chapter with Nick Saville, was invited to help with the validation and implementation of the IELTS Impact Study from 2000 on.

WASHBACK AND IMPACT

The concepts of washback and impact are discussed in some detail in chapter 1 of this volume. Beyond the learners and teachers affected by the washback of an examination like IELTS is a range of other stakeholders on whom the examination has impact, although they do not take the exam or teach for it. These stakeholders, for example, parents, employers, and others included in Fig. 5.1, form the language testing *constituency* within which UCLES, as an international examination board, is located. The IELTS Impact Study (IIS) is designed to help UCLES continue to understand the roles, responsibilities, and attitudes of the stakeholders in this constituency. The stakeholders with whom UCLES must have accountable relationships are represented in Fig. 5.1.

An examination board must be prepared to review and revise what it does in the light of findings on how its stakeholders use and feel about its exams, and it is test validation that is at the root of the UCLES IELTS Impact Study.

Messick (1989) insisted on the inclusion of the outside influences of a test in his "unified validity framework," in which "One facet is the source of justification of the testing, being based on appraisal of either evidence or consequence. The other facet is the function or outcome of the testing, being either interpretation or use" (p. 20). If this is so, test washback, limited

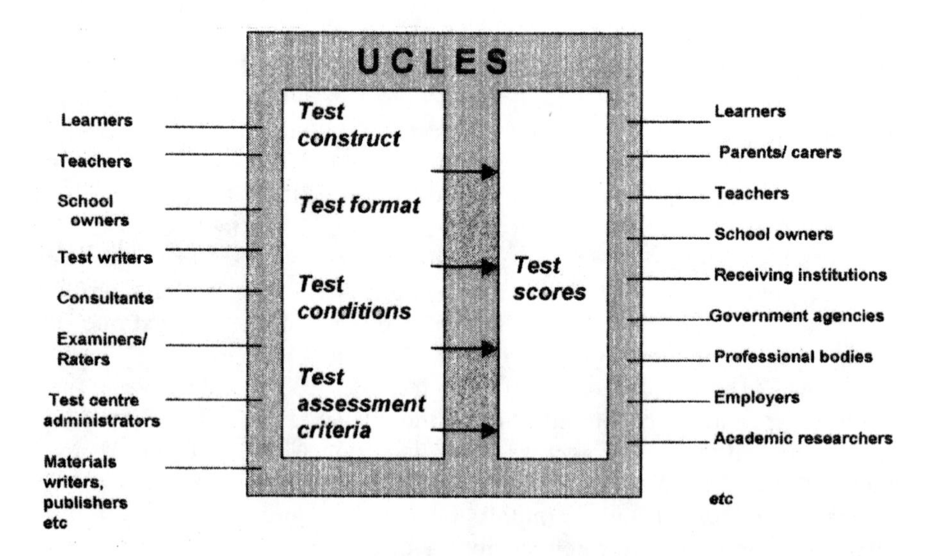

FIG. 5.1. Stakeholders in the testing community.

in scope to effects on teaching and learning, cannot really be substantiated without full consideration of the *social* consequences of test use, considered as *impact* in the earlier definitions. Thus, the IELTS Study is about impact in its broadest sense; the subproject examining the test's effect on textbooks, which is the focus of this chapter, is mainly about washback.

It is right, of course, that an impact study of an international proficiency test such as IELTS should concern itself with social consequences of test use. There is no doubt that tests are used increasingly to provide evidence of and targets for change. The implementation of new national curricula with regular national achievement tests, for example in the United Kingdom and New Zealand, provide examples of this at central government level. Hence, perhaps, the growing concern for ethical language testing (e.g., Association of Language Testers in Europe [ALTE], 1995; Davies, 1997). In tune with increasing individual and societal expectations of good value and accountability, testers are expected to adhere to codes of professionally and socially responsible practice. These codes should provide tighter guarantees of test development rigor and probity, as manifested by properly defined targets, appropriate and reliable evaluation criteria, comprehensive, transparent, and fair test interpretation and reporting systems, continuous validation processes, and a keener regard for the rights of candidates and other stakeholders (see the Association of Language Testers in Europe, 1998, and the IELTS Handbook, 1997–1998).

In other words, ethical language testing is feasible and test impact and washback studies can play an important role in ensuring this. Such studies can also help tests meet some of the even stronger demands of the *critical* language testing view. This tends to see tests as instruments of power and control, as, intentionally or not, biased, undemocratic, and unfair means of selecting or policy changing, their main impact being the imposition of constraints, the restriction of curricula, and the possible encouragement of boring, mechanical teaching approaches. For Shohamy (1999), for example, tests are "powerful because they lead to momentous decisions affecting individuals and programs. . . . They are conducted by authoritative and unquestioning judges or are backed by the language of science and numbers" (p. 711).

Learning from the impact/washback debate, the UCLES IELTS Study attempts to take sensitive account of a wide range of the factors involved. The study thus distinguishes between the effect of tests on language materials and on classroom activity; it also seeks information on and the views of: students preparing for IELTS, students who have taken IELTS, teachers preparing students for IELTS, IELTS administrators, admissions officers in receiving institutions, subject teachers, and teachers preparing students for academic study.

THE IELTS IMPACT STUDY: FOUR SUBPROJECTS AND THREE PHASES

The IELTS impact study can be seen as an example of the continuous, formative test consultation and validation program pursued by UCLES. In the 4 years leading to the 1996 revision of the First Certificate in English exam, for example, a user survey through questionnaires and structured group interviews, covered 25,000 students, 5,000 teachers and 1,200 oral examiners in the UK and around the world. One hundred and twenty receiving institutions in the UK were also canvassed for their perspective on the exam. As part of the recent revision of the UCLES Certificate of Proficiency in English (CPE) exam (see Weir, 2002), the revised draft test materials were trialed with nearly 3,000 candidates in 14 countries. In addition, consultative seminars and invitational meetings involved 650 participants in 11 countries throughout Europe and Latin America. Feedback from all stages of the process was reviewed constantly and informed subsequent stages of the revision program. The recommendations of the CPE revision program took effect in 2002 with the introduction of the revised examination (December 2002).

In 1995, when IELTS was introduced in its latest revised form, procedures were already being developed to monitor the impact of the test as part of the next review and revision cycle. The study was envisaged as comprising three phases: Phase One for the identification of areas to be targeted and development of data collection instrumentation; Phase Two for the validation and rationalization of these instruments, and Phase Three for the collection and analysis of impact data.

The initial development work for the Study was completed by researchers at Lancaster University (Banerjee, 1996; Herrington 1996; Horak, 1996; Winetroube 1997), under the guidance of Charles Alderson. During Phase Two, consultants commissioned by UCLES included Antony Kunnan and James Purpura (see below). UCLES also arranged data sharing with related studies, including the research by Belinda Hayes and John Read (see chap. 6, this volume), and the study by Tony Green at the University of Surrey, England, of the impact of IELTS-oriented and pre-sessional English language preparation programs.

The Lancaster team originally defined the following four subprojects for the IELTS Impact Study:

1. The content and *nature of classroom activity* in IELTS-related classes
2. The content and *nature of IELTS teaching materials* (*including textbooks*)
3. The *views and attitudes* of user groups toward IELTS
4. The IELTS *test-taking population* and the use of test results.

Project One, on the context and nature of classroom activity in IELTS classes, initially involved four draft instruments and associated procedures: an observation schedule for classroom activity; a procedure for producing summaries of classroom activity; a questionnaire for teachers after teaching an observed lesson; and a questionnaire for students who had just taken part in an observed lesson.

Early versions of these instruments were submitted for small-scale trial with staff and students at Lancaster University. More extensive feedback from individuals with a research interest in classroom observation was also analyzed, leading to the production of a final classroom observation and feedback instrument for use in 2002.

Project Three, on the attitudes of user groups to IELTS, originally involved seven questionnaires, developed to explore the views and attitudes of a wide population of IELTS users, namely:

1. students preparing for IELTS
2. teachers preparing students for IELTS
3. teachers preparing students for academic study (post-IELTS)
4. IELTS administrators
5. admissions officers in receiving institutions
6. students who have taken IELTS
7. academic subject teachers

Using proposals from a workshop led by Antony Kunnan in Spring 1999, pilot data and additional feedback from researchers, including Tony Green, working on related projects, Roger Hawkey revised and rationalized the user-group questionnaires. One of the revised instruments is a modular student characteristic and test attitudes questionnaire combining questionnaires 1 and 6 with the test-takers characteristics instrument from Project Four (see the following section). A second is a teacher questionnaire (combining 2 and 3 above), the third a rationalized questionnaire for receiving institutions (covering 4, 5, and 7 above).

Project Four: The IELTS Test-Taking Population

To supplement information collected routinely on IELTS candidates, an in-depth instrument was developed to elicit information on learner attitudes, motivation, and cognitive/meta-cognitive characteristics. In Phase Two of Project Four, this questionnaire was administered to a range of IELTS candidates and submitted to Structural Equation Modeling (SEM) for further validation (Purpura, 1999). Using additional insights from Kunnan (see Kunnan, 2000), Green's related instrumentation for IELTS-takers and EAP pre-ses-

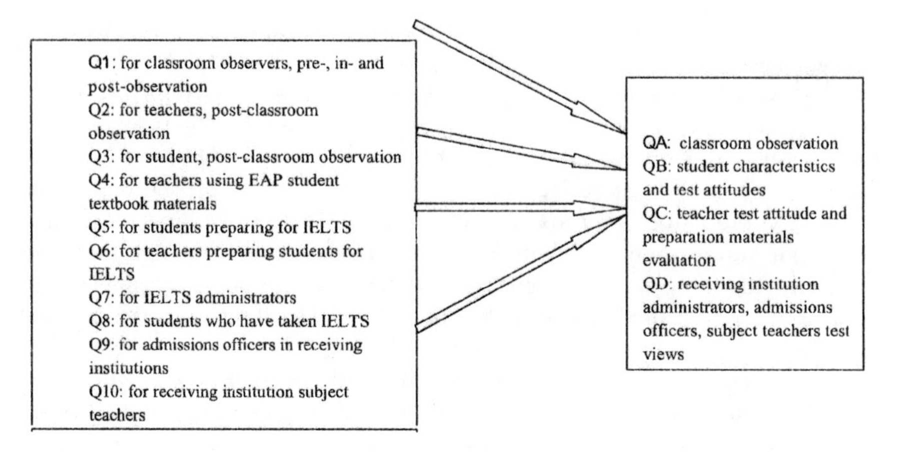

FIG. 5.2. Rationalization of original data collection instruments.

sional course participants, Roger Hawkey incorporated key elements of the language learner questionnaire into the modular student characteristic and test attitudes questionnaire referred to earlier.

In Phase Three of the Impact Study, revised questionnaires were used on a sample of IELTS stakeholders world-wide (results compiled in 2002). The process of validation and rationalization in Phase Two has led to the coverage of the 12 original questionnaires by four modular instruments, as conceptualized in Fig. 5.2.

THE IMPACT OF THE IELTS ON THE CONTENT AND NATURE OF IELTS-RELATED TEACHING MATERIALS

A data collection instrument for the analysis of teaching materials used in programs preparing students to take the IELTS is clearly germane to the focus of this volume on the influence of testing on teaching and learning. This section, then, describes the initial design of the draft pilot questionnaire, its validation through a first piloting, the analysis of data and first revision, and further validation through an interactive "mini-piloting" and second revision.

Initial Design of the Teaching Materials Evaluation Questionnaire

In Phase One of the Impact Study, the development of an instrument for the analysis of textbook materials (IATM) was part of the UCLES commission to Alderson and his team at Lancaster University. The initial pilot version of the IATM was developed by Bonkowski (1996), whose pilot instrument was a structured questionnaire in eight parts, four on the target textbook as a whole, four, respectively, on its listening, reading, writing, and speaking components.

The IATM development phase entailed a number of iterative cycles, including a literature review, section and item design in continuous cross-reference with the IELTS specifications, consultations between UCLES staff and researchers at Lancaster, drafting, trial, and revision (with, typically, six iterations at the drafting stage). A major validated source for the various classifications and lists included in the pilot textbook analysis instrument was the ALTE development and descriptive checklists for tasks and examinations (1995).

The IATM was intended to cover both the contents and the methodology of a textbook and related teaching materials, eliciting information from teachers using the book through open-ended comment, yes/no, multiple-choice, and four-point scale items. The items in the first version of the instrument were grouped under the following headings:

General information: baseline data on the textbook

Specific features of the textbook: items on organization, media, support materials, assessment; open general-comment section

General description of contents: items on topics, timings, texts, tasks, language system coverage, micro-skills development, test-taking strategies

Listening: sections headed: Input-texts; Speakers; Tasks; items on listening text length, authenticity, settings, topics, interaction, interrelationships, accent, turns, syntax, micro-skills and functions, test techniques and conditions; open comment section on listening activity content and methodology

Reading: sections headed: Input-texts; Speakers; Tasks; items on reading text length, source, authenticity, topics, micro-skills and functions, test techniques and conditions; open comment section on reading activity content and methodology

Writing: sections headed: Input; Task; Scoring Criteria; items on text length, topic, source, exercise task type and length, language system coverage, micro-skills, test techniques and conditions; open comment section on writing activity content and methodology

Speaking: subsections: Input; Task; Scoring Criteria; items on interaction, topics, prompt types, exercise tasks, register, exercise conditions, scoring criteria plus, open comment section on speaking activity content and methodology

Evaluation of textbook as a whole and summative evaluation: items on level, time pressure, task difficulty, test relationship to IELTS; open comment section on textbook: test relationship.

Piloting the Instrument, Analysis of Data and First Revision

In a paper commissioned by UCLES at the start of Phase Two of the Impact Study, Alderson and Banerjee (1996) noted that lack of validation is a feature of questionnaires in most fields. They also make a distinction between piloting–which is often carried out–and true validation as they understand it–which is rarely carried out. Many of Alderson and Banerjee's recommendations on the validation of instruments were followed, wholly or in part, in the development of the IATM, in particular, the use of both quantitative and qualitative validating methods.

Bonkowski's (1996) draft IATM was analyzed through the following pilot and trial data:

- author instructions for use of the IATM
- nine full trial IATM textbook rater analyses by trained and practicing teachers:

(a) four raters using the instrument to evaluate a current IELTS-oriented textbook;

(b) two raters using the IATM to evaluate a preparation textbook for another international proficiency test

(c) two raters evaluating a general textbook for upper-intermediate students;

(d) one rater evaluating a further IELTS-preparation textbook

- two IATM forms edited critically on format by ELT specialists
- four IATM data summaries by Yue Wu Wang, whose 1997 MA dissertation, supervised by Alderson, was a study of IELTS washback on textbooks
- a taped discussion between two raters who had used the IATM to evaluate textbooks (transcribed in Wang, 1997)
- a recorded interview (with written summary) of two authors discussing an IELTS-related textbook.

One IELTS preparation textbook was IATM-evaluated by four different raters. This proved useful for rater consistency analyses, an important part of instrument validation. Four textbooks were covered by one or more ratings, two of the books designed explicitly for IELTS students, one related to another proficiency exam (TOEFL), and one, a general text for upper-intermediate students of English, not intended specifically for international test preparation. This provided comparative data for the construct validation of the instrument in terms of convergent and divergent validity.

The discussion between raters of IATM results and their interpretations (included by Yue [1997] as an appendix to her dissertation) is a further validation exercise as recommended by Alderson and Banerjee (1996) to "provide insights into whether problems were caused by the instrument and raters' interpretations of wording or the raters' interpretation of the textbook" (p. 32). The recommendation that textbook writers should be contacted was also accepted. A 1998 paper by Saville "Predicting Impact on Language Learning and the Classroom" also informed the refinement of the IATM in phases two and three.

Perhaps the most revealing of the analyses of completed IATM forms were the returns of the four raters who used the IATM to evaluate one IELTS-oriented textbook. From these returns, five kinds of improvement to the IATM were made, through the exclusion, modification, merging, moving, and supplementing of items. The responses of the raters were consolidated on to a comparative analysis form containing all the draft IATM items (see Appendix B). The analyses suggested shortening the first version of IATM, for example, by the sampling of textbook units rather than covering all units, by rationalizing and merging checklists and classifications, and by strengthening the teaching/learning methodology coverage to include indirect as well as direct test impact on materials.

By common consent of all evaluating the IATM or using it to rate textbooks, the pilot instrument had been very long. Several of the users reduced their completion time by resorting to informal sampling procedures, for example, covering only a selection of the textbook units rather than all of them. Given that the purpose of the instrument is to evaluate relationships between textbook materials and tests in terms of construct, content, level, and methodology, it would seem unlikely that every text, activity, exercise, or test in every unit of a book needs to be analyzed. Rater comment, items left uncompleted by raters, and the wide disparities of views across raters on elements in the same textbook unit, all suggested some category and item redundancy. One Phase Two rater was "not convinced that an adequate description had been given," a dissatisfaction that appeared most strongly with some of the descriptive or explanatory checklists used in the IATM. Raters were not clear, for example, whether the term *task* used as a major subcategory in the items on listening, reading, writing, and speaking, referred to communicative assignments or questions to be answered. Raters anyway felt that the category "task" overlapped the various *micro-skills* also specified by the instrument. The explanation in the draft IATM instructions suggests perhaps too broad a conceptualization: "(Task) includes both the functional intent of the exercise or activity, the kind of instructions that are used, and the type of item or question that the students must answer or perform." The pilot IATM returns indicated that some of the references to "tasks" should be deleted because they overlapped with test exercises.

The development of linguistic classifications and taxonomies is, of course, an extremely delicate and complex undertaking. In the case of the draft IATM, significant rationalizations (and deletions) were indicated in the various lists and inventories. The aim after all is to evaluate textbook materials, a primary need thus to clarify and simplify to help ensure reliable and valid data, not to produce rigorous and elaborate socio- or psycholinguistic descriptions of textbooks. Rationalized and merged versions were thus developed for the IATM lists of: social or academic situations, reading microskills, speaker relationships, and communicative functions. These were now derived from more sources than exclusively the ALTE manual (1995), for example Munby (1978), Wilkins (1976), Bachman, Davidson, Ryan, and Choi (1993).

Some imbalance of coverage across the draft IATM sections covering the four skill sections was noted (i.e., listening: 130 items; reading: 91 items; writing: 69 items; speaking: 55 items). Given that dividing the instrument into these four main sections inevitably entailed significant item repetition it was felt that the separate listening, reading, writing, and speaking sections might eventually be merged, partially at least.

The analysis of items and of raters' comments also revealed somewhat limited coverage of a textbook's methodological approaches to the development of target language skills. Here was another case for review in the next validation step.

Rater comments were often insightful on test washback leading to test practice, as opposed to test washback leading to particular learning approaches. One rater distinguished between systematic skills development and the mere "replication of target behavior." Another noted an "obvious cross-over" of the skills developed in one of the books and the "so-called academic skills," meaning that students using the book concerned could respond well, perhaps "better than those using an IELTS prep book." Such revealing comments suggested that the revised IATM should seek more systematic information on textbook methods and approaches.

Because rater responses to the open-comment and summative evaluation sections in the IATM were interesting as elaborations of and checks on the more quantitative questionnaire data, it was agreed that space for evaluative comment would be retained in the revised version of the instrument.

The explicit reference to IELTS in the draft pilot IATM was questioned by some raters. Yue (1997) suggested that because some textbooks clearly focus on practicing skills and subskills that are demanded by IELTS, provide accurate information about the test, and increase students' test-taking knowledge, IELTS is producing positive washback on preparation materials. But the preferred logic would presumably be that the IATM revealed both direct relationships between textbook and test system (e.g., same formats, task types, dimensions, etc.) *and* indirect ones (e.g., opportunities to enhance performance of English-speaking culture-relevant micro-skills, functions, activities, in relevant settings, media modes, etc.). Both directly and indirectly test-relevant activities are likely to help users both prepare for a test *and* enhance their learning and future language performance, if the test has been developed to meet their real communication needs.

As would be expected, certain technical limitations emerged from the first piloting of the IATM. The extensive use of informal 1–4 rating scales was generally unsuccessful, producing improbably low agreements across raters even over relatively uncontroversial items. Several useful suggestions were also made by the raters themselves on the layout of the questionnaire, some of which were incorporated in the revised version.

At the end of Phase Two, a rationalized and shortened IATM was produced, based on detailed analyses of all ratings. The format was as follows:

1. *Baseline Information* (14 items for pre-completion)
2. *General Description of Textbook and Support Materials*: (12 items including final open-ended comment item, on textbook type, organization, components, skills, strategies, communicative activities, support materials, testing)
3. *Listening*: (18 items including final open-ended comment item, on teaching–testing relationship; components; text lengths, levels, media, dialects, types, situations, topics, relationships; skills; question techniques; tasks; tests)
4. *Reading*: (15 items including final open-ended comment item, on teaching–testing relationship; components; text levels, types, situations, topics; relationships; skills, question techniques, tasks, tests)
5. *Writing*: (15 items including final open-ended comment item, on teaching–testing relationship, components, text levels, contexts, types, media, situations, topics; relationships; functions and skills; question techniques; tasks; tests)
6. *Speaking*: (17 items including final open-ended comment item, on teaching–testing relationship; components; text levels, contexts, modes, types, situations, topics, relationships, dialects, media; functions and skills; question techniques; tasks; tests)

The revised IATM was 14 pages long, much shorter than the initial version, but still time-consuming to complete. The research team agreed, therefore, that the possible further shortening of the instrument should be a priority, though without losing data crucial to the impact study. It was agreed that space for evaluative comments should be retained in the revised version of the instrument.

Second Piloting and Second Revision

In tune with the iterative approach taken from the outset of the Study, it had always been planned to re-pilot the revised IATM. Given that feedback on the original version of the instrument had been largely in written form, and that the piloting had raised some fairly complex questions it was agreed that the second piloting should be in the form of a focus-group discussion.

The research team thus arranged for the revised IATM to be completed for two textbooks, one IELTS-oriented, one not specifically so, by two experienced, practicing EFL professionals. They would then meet the Impact Study coordinator for intensive discussion of their experience with the instrument, which he had re-designed.

This exercise proved very informative. The two raters had received the redesigned IATM with notes for users, re-stating its aims and characteristics. On arrival for the focus-group meeting with their completed questionnaires, they were given a background-and-remit note reiterating the purpose of the project, summarizing feedback from the previous phase and focusing the outcome of the exercise of the day, namely, "to discuss points that arise in order to provide further feedback (i.e., corrections, deletions, additions, mergings, reformattings, rewordings etc.) for a re-modification of the IATM. Especially welcome will be ideas on how to shorten the instrument without losing information useful for the impact assessment Project."

Suggested alterations to the instrument in the light of the written and oral feedback of the meeting were discussed on the spot. The most significant resultant reduction in the size of the instruments was the merging of the separate sections for the four skills, though still specifying items for them separately where there were intrinsic differences between the skills, and still requiring raters to comment separately on a book's overall treatment of each of the skills. The rationalized IATM format was thus a two-section questionnaire in place of the six-section first revised version.

Although the revised pilot, 14-page IATM had already attempted to rationalize and merge checklists such as social or academic situations, text types, micro-skills, speaker relationships, communicative functions, the rater-discussants considered there was room for further reductions. One of the discussants made the telling point that specifications of language micro-skills, however rigorous and comprehensive, were in practice very subjective and overlapping (cf. "retrieving factual information," "identifying main points," "identifying overall meaning," etc.). Similarly, even the reduced number of categorizations in the first revised questionnaire (text types, situations, topics, communicative relationships, micro-skills and question types) were felt to overlap and to invite redundant information.

The result of this feedback was a further rationalized re-categorization into skills; question task-setting techniques; communicative opportunities, and text types and topics. Given the usefulness of the open-ended comment sections in the first revised questionnaire, all topics in the second revised version were covered by open-ended as well as multichoice items.

While the checklists in the 14-page instrument had been derived from a range of reference sources rather than the one main ALTE source used in the draft pilot version, the coverage had not been checked against typical language teaching textbooks. As part of the second piloting and revision process, therefore, appropriate textbooks were analyzed to derive a checklist, to try to avoid major omissions in the revised instrument, including: pronunciation, grammatical structure, notions/functions, vocabulary, micro-skills, task types, topics, text types.

This rough guide was used as a final check for omissions in the third version of the IATM, and actually led to the explicit mention of *more* language components than in the previous, much longer pilot instruments. The very interactive and immediate nature of the focus group session suggested that some of the uncertainties likely in completing questionnaires at a distance could be avoided by including, within the instrument itself, a running metacommentary on the purpose of the exercise and its component parts. The comments thus inserted in the revised questionnaire were intended to encourage, explain and, where certain items are optional, redirect. It was also hoped that they render the instrument more user-friendly than its first two versions. For example:

(a) Questions Four, Five and Six ask whether the book teaches and/or tests particular *enabling or micro-skills*, using a variety of techniques and activities?
(b) Try checking Four, Five *and* Six before you comment, as skills, question/tasking and activities clearly overlap.

The intensive feedback session of the second IATM piloting also offered clarification of the question of direct reference to IELTS in the instrument. At least three categories of materials are used to prepare students for an international test such as IELTS. At one end of the continuum are books which are essentially *practice tests* (i.e., including specimen test materials only). Then there are *course books*, specifically dedicated to a particular examination. At the other end of the continuum are course books not directly linked to a test but whose content and level make them appropriate for use in test preparation programs. The revised IATM, which may be completed by teachers using all three types of materials, should reveal significant differences across these three categories and also, possibly, more subtle differences between materials within the categories. This could provide evidence for the convergent/divergent validation of the IELTS.

Emerging from the focus group discussion processes, the format of the revised IATM is as follows:

1. Teacher Background: items on the IATM user and experience of IELTS and similar tests
2. *Notes for Users*: guidelines on purpose, focus, baseline data and evaluative data sections
3. *Baseline Information* on the Textbook: objective features of the materials, to be pre-completed by UCLES
4. *Evaluative data* to be provided by raters: 18 items including open-ended overall evaluation at the end, on:
   - category of teaching/testing book
   - organizational units
   - breakdown of language components
   - enabling (or micro-) skills
   - question/tasking techniques
   - communicative opportunities
   - text types
   - text topics
   - authenticity
   - open-ended comment: listening, reading, writing, speaking
   - open-ended comment on the book as a whole
   - open-ended comment on the relationship between the book and test(s)

The revised instrument (see Appendix C) is seven pages long in its full-size format, half the length of the second pilot instrument, but still eliciting comprehensive information on and evaluation of textbook and support materials. The IATM is to be used to collect textbook and related washback information from a sample of teachers selected from IELTS-oriented teaching programs identified by a pre-survey administered mid-2001.

Early Washback and Impact Evidence

Work so far on an instrument for the analysis and evaluation of IELTS-relevant textbooks has been intended primarily to develop and validate the instrument rather than to collect or analyze data. Nevertheless, information and views have already been recorded by the pilot raters which underline the importance of washback and impact studies, and which may be useful for others constructing and validating instrumentation for their own studies.

The two types of textbooks analyzed in IATM piloting so far have been test practice books and language teaching course books. Raters tend to evaluate the test-related books in terms of how directly they reflect the content, level, and format of the test for which they are preparing learners, and to lament any absence of "language course" teaching material and activities. For example, a rater commenting on the listening practice in an IELTS-preparation textbook wrote: "Exercises only as per IELTS (demotivating?)"; a second rater of the same book wrote: "Each task closely related to topic of unit; learners have some input from the reading parts; clear sample answers; better to introduce grammar help before students attempt the tests? . . . Precious little skill building." Both comments suggest that the book should do something more than it sets out to do, but the second rater also implies positive washback from IELTS. Negative washback from a test, not in this case IELTS, is evidenced in this comment from a third rater: "The textbook is an inevitable product of a test that requires unrealistic target behavior."

The IELTS Impact Study must remain aware that a test may exert positive washback although textbook materials dedicated to it may still be unsuccessful. Shohamy (1999) discussed the point, wondering "whether a 'poor' test could conceivably have a 'good' effect if it made the learners and teachers do 'good' things by increasing learning" (p. 713). What re-emerges here is the complex nature of washback and the number of factors intervening between test and impact.

On the complicated matter of language skills and tasks (see earlier), there is some tentative evidence from the pilot data that the account taken by tests such as the IELTS of the communicative enabling or micro-skills needed in future academic or professional life, has beneficial washback potential. A rater commented that one of the IELTS textbooks provides "basic coverage of all components of IELTS" and is "good on types of task to be expected, strategies for difficulties, and timing," and that the book's "exam preps (are) OK, especially speed reading and time limits." Another rater felt that the same book "covers a broad range of topics and micro-skills." A further comment suggesting positive washback was that a non-test-related book used in the piloting "would be effective if supplemented with some IELTS type listening."

But the complex testing: teaching/learning relationship re-emerges, when a rater refers to the non-IELTS book's "obvious cross-over of the textbook skills and so-called academic skills; so students using this book could respond well if acquainted with IELTS writing; maybe better than those using an IELTS prep book."

There were also early indications that authenticity of texts, oral and written, is seen as a beneficial effect of the IELTS. One rater noted "realistic simulations of IELTS, texts fairly authentic"; a second: "readings all authentic texts, useful examples on tape, and in skills focus sections." But there is evidence again that raters want more learning and practice opportunities with the authentic discourse. One rater felt that "if (there is) some attention to reading speed, the (course book) is better than an exam prep textbook; challenging authentic texts, treats affective responses to reading."

It is encouraging for the future of the UCLES IELTS Impact Study that even the early pilot data from the IATM suggest that insights will be forthcoming that are subtle, revealing, and helpful to an understanding of test–textbook washback and the ultimate improvement of both.

APPENDIX A

IELTS Test Format

IELTS is a **task-based testing system** which assesses the real language skills candidates need to study or train in the medium of English.

In addition to a **band score** for overall language ability on a nine-band scale, IELTS provides a score, in the form of a **profile**, for each of the four skills (listening, reading, writing and speaking. (see IELTS Annual Review).

The first component of the IELTS assesses **Listening** skills in a test lasting 30–40 minutes with 40 items in four progressively more demanding sections, the first two focusing on social needs, the second two on educational or training topics.

The academic **Reading** test (60 minutes, 40 questions) includes three non-specialist, general-interest texts, lengths totaling 1500–2500 words, taken from magazines, journals, papers, books, on issues appropriate and accessible to under- or postgraduate participants.

IELTS academic **Writing** test is a 60-minute paper requiring the production of a text of 150 words and one of 250 words. Both academic writing tasks are intended for the assessment of candidates' responses in terms of register, rhetorical organization, style, and content appropriate to topics and contexts which appear similar to those in the Academic Reading Test.

The IELTS **Speaking** test is a face-to face oral test with a trained examiner. It assesses the candidate's ability to communicate with other English speakers using the range of language skills necessary to study through the medium of English.

APPENDIX B

UNIFIED RESPONSES RECORD FOR *PASSPORT TO IELTS* FROM FOUR RATERS (ref. 5,6,7,8), RATERS 5 AND 6 USING INSTRUMENT FOR ANALYSIS OF TEXTBOOK MATERIALS (IATM) 36-PAGE VERSION (V36), RATERS 7 AND 8 USING THE 24 PAGE VERSION (V24)

General Note: *The analysis of the use of the IATM by Raters 5,6,7,8 indicates the need for modifications of the IATM. Highlighting is used as follows to suggest such modifications:*

- Red highlight: items suggested for *deletion* from modified versions of the IATM
- Yellow highlight: items to be *modified* for future versions of the IATM.
- Green highlight: items suggested to be *added* to future versions of the IATM.
- Blue highlight: items to be *moved* from their original location in the IATM.
- Pink highlight: items suggested for *merging* in future versions of the IATM

A. Baseline Information on the Textbook

Title:	*Passport to IELTS*
Authors:	Diane Hopkins and Mark Nettle
Publisher:	Rater 5: Prentice-Hall; 6: Prentice-Hall Europe; 7: Phoenix ELT; 8: Macmillan
Year:	5: 1995; 6: 1993 (revised 1995); 7: 1995; 8: 1993, 1st edition
ISBN:	5: 0-13-405375-5 6: 0-13-405375-5 7: 0-13-405375-5 8: 0-333-58706-5

These materials are intended for:

(a) pre-1995 IELTS examination	8
(b) 1995 IELTS examination	5,6,7
(c) can't tell	

B. General Description of Contents

[*Future pilot version of the IATM will conflate the present Section B (Specific Features of textbook) and the present Section C (General Description of Contents) since they are not different in kind, and would benefit from rationalization]*

Rater ID: **Comment**	**5**	**6**	**7**	**8**	**Rater**
1. Is the textbook organized according to: a) subject/theme b) language skill c) language system d) test structure e) other (specify)	a	a	a	a	6: *mock tests, reading first for receptive–productive classroom ordering;;*
2. Is the textbook divided into a) units? b) sections? c) test components d) other units of organization (specify)	a	a	a	a	
3. How many units are there?	10	10	10	10	6: *final unit?*

Transferred items to be merged here on sample unit topics/titles/timing etc?					
4. Are there any review units?	N	Y	N	-	
5. Are there audiotape materials?	Y	Y	Y	N	
6. Are there audio tapescripts?	Y	Y	Y	Y	

APPENDIX C: INSTRUMENT FOR THE ANALYSIS OF TEXTBOOK MATERIALS

University of Cambridge Local Examinations Syndicate (UCLES) IATM

STUDY OF THE IMPACT OF THE INTERNATIONAL ENGLISH LANGUAGE TESTING (IELTS) ON TEXTBOOKS

Instrument for the Analysis of Textbook Materials (IATM)

A little about you *(please write, type, tick (✔) boxes ☐, leave blank as appropriate)*						
Your full name						
Form of address	Miss ☐	Mrs. ☐	Mr. ☐	Dr ☐	Other *(please specify)*	
Country where you were born						
Your first language						
Name and address of institution where you work						
Your position						
Your academic/ professional qualifications						
International English language test(s) with which you are familiar						
Your experience with this/these test(s) (*teaching test preparation courses, test administration, being trained as examiner etc*), if any	Test(s)	Experience				
Your brief opinion of this test/these tests (e.g., any comments on: *test components, levels, topics, skills, format, scoring, administration, reliability in predicting a student's English language competence and performance?)*	Test(s)	Comment(s)				

Notes on the use of the Instrument for the Analysis of Textbook Materials (IATM)

1. This questionnaire seeks your analysis and evaluation of the content, level and approaches of a textbook and its support materials.
2. We are especially interested in the relationships between textbooks and international tests for the certification of language performance.
3. The questionnaire invites:
   - objective analytic responses on features of the book (using a tick (✔) in the appropriate boxes ☐)
   - additional comment on most items and on relevant matters not covered, to be written in the appropriate spaces
   - your evaluation of the book's coverage of the four skills, and of the book as a whole, to be written in the spaces provided.

We are grateful for your help and look forward to reading your responses. Thank you.

INSTRUMENT FOR THE ANALYSIS OF TEXBOOK MATERIALS (IATM)

0. The textbook being analyzed:

Title:	*to be pre-completed*		
Author(s)			
Publishers			
Place of Publication		**Year of publication**	
What materials in addition to this book, if any, do you use when teaching students?			
Which students are you teaching using this book?			

O Questions on the kind of book this is, in general aim and organisation

1. What kind of book would you say this is?
(please tick (✔) the box ☐ where appropriate).

1.1 A language teaching book with no specific reference to international tests ☐	1.2 a book of practice tests only ☐	1.3 a language teaching book and an international test preparation book combined ☐
1.4 If it is a test-related book, for which test(s)?		
1.5 Any other comment on the type of book this is?		

- *If the book is a book of practice tests only, please go to Question 4.*
- *If the book contains teaching material as well as practice tests, please go to Question 2, about the way the book is organized.*

2. The book's units/chapters etc., seem to be organized mainly according to:
(please tick (✔) the box(es) ☐ where appropriate, more than one possible).

2.1 topics, themes ☐	2.2. language skills ☐	2.3 grammatical structures ☐	2.4 tests, tasks ☐	2.5 notions, functions ☐
2.6 other (please specify)				
2.7 Any further comment on the organization of the book?				

O *Now a question on whether the book tries to break the language down and teach the elements of the listening, reading, writing and speaking skills.*

3. Your analysis of the book's explicit practice of language features.
(Please tick (✔) appropriate boxes ☐.)

	A lot	A little	None		A lot	A little	None		A lot	A little	None
3.1 recognition of sounds	☐	☐	☐	3.2 pronunciation of sounds	☐	☐	☐	3.3 stress and intonation	☐	☐	☐
3.4 grammar	☐	☐	☐	3.5 sentence patterns	☐	☐	☐	3.6 notions, functions	☐	☐	☐
3.7 word formation	☐	☐	☐	3.8 connotation	☐	☐	☐	3.9 collocation	☐	☐	☐
3.10 idioms	☐	☐	☐	3.11 linking words, expressions	☐	☐	☐	3.12 punctuation	☐	☐	☐
3.13 Other language components or features given explicit practice:											
3.14 Related comments on how the book treats language features:											

O *Questions 4, 5 and 6 ask whether the book teaches and/or tests particular enabling or micro-skills, using a variety of techniques and activities?*

O *Try checking 4, 5 and 6 before you comment, as skills, question / tasking and activities clearly overlap.*

4. Enabling skills you think are covered in the book:
(please tick (✔) appropriate boxes ☐.)

4.1 understanding and conveying meaning through stress and intonation ☐	4.2 retrieving and stating factual information ☐	4.3 identifying main points ☐	4.4 drawing conclusions ☐
4.5 identifying overall meaning ☐	**4.6 predicting information** ☐	4.7 making inferences ☐	4.8 evaluating evidence ☐
4.9 distinguishing fact from opinion ☐	4.10 recognizing roles ☐	4.11 identifying attitudes ☐	4.12 planning and organizing information ☐
4.13 Other skills covered by the book (please specify):			
4.14 Further comment on skills covered or not covered by the book:			

5. Your summary of the use of question/tasking techniques in the book:
(please tick (✔) appropriate boxes ☐.)

	Frequent	A little	None		Frequent	A little	None
5.1 multiple/dual choice	☐	☐	☐	5.2 conversion	☐	☐	☐
5.3 true/false	☐	☐	☐	5.4 sequencing	☐	☐	☐
5.5 matching	☐	☐	☐	5.6 paraphrasing	☐	☐	☐
5.7 substitution	☐	☐	☐	5.8 open-ended questions	☐	☐	☐

5.9 linking/joining	☐	☐	☐	5.10 note taking/making	☐	☐	☐
5.11 expansion	☐	☐	☐	5.12 correcting/editing	☐	☐	☐
5.13 gap filling/completion	☐	☐	☐	5.14 summarizing	☐	☐	☐
5.15 Other techniques (please specify)							
5.16 Further comment on question and task techniques covered or not covered by the book							

6. Your evaluation of the extent to which the materials provide/encourage the following kinds of <u>communicative opportunities</u>. (Please tick (✔) appropriate boxes ☐.)

	A lot	Quite a lot	Very little	None		A lot	Quite a lot	Very little	None
6.1 pair communication	☐	☐	☐	☐	6.2 group discussions and debates	☐	☐	☐	☐
6.3 games, puzzles, quizzes	☐	☐	☐	☐	6.4 role play, simulations	☐	☐	☐	☐
6.5 surveys, other project work	☐	☐	☐	☐	6.6 report writing	☐	☐	☐	☐
6.7 review writing	☐	☐	☐	☐	6.8 essay writing	☐	☐	☐	☐
6.9 creative writing	☐	☐	☐	☐	6.10 IT e.g., telephone, fax, letters, email, web	☐	☐	☐	☐
6.11 listening, reading, viewing for personal interest	☐	☐	☐	☐	6.12 other communicative opportunities *(please specify)*:				
6.13 Further comment on the communicative opportunities offered by the book:									

○ ***Questions 7 and 8 ask for information on <u>text types and topics</u> to check the coverage of the books.***

7. How would you categorize the <u>text types</u> (heard, spoken, read, written) in the book?
(Please tick (✔) appropriate boxes ☐.)

7.1 public announcement ☐	7.2 lecture/talk ☐	7.3 press report ☐	7.4 textbook/ journal article ☐
7.5 correspondence ☐	7.6 fiction ☐	7.7 discussion ☐	7.8 face-to-face conversation ☐
7.9 radio/TV report ☐	7.10 manual/brochure ☐	7.11 advertising ☐	7.12 maps, charts, tables and graphs ☐
7.13 interview ☐	7.14 telephone ☐	7.15 email ☐	7.16 Internet ☐
7.17 other text type(s)? *(please specify)*			

8. And the book's text topics (heard, spoken, read, written)?
(Please tick (✔) appropriate boxes ☐.)

8.1 accommodation ☐	8.2 health ☐	8.3 physical environment ☐	8.4 leisure and sports ☐
8.5 daily routines ☐	8.6 education training ☐	8.7 science ☐	8.8 travel ☐
8.9 shopping ☐	8.10 world of work ☐	8.11 arts ☐	8.12 current affairs ☐
8.13 food and drink ☐	8.14 social environment ☐	8.15 customs ☐	8.16 moral issues ☐
8.17 Other topics: *(please specify)*:			
8.18 Any inappropriate topics: *(please exemplify and explain)*:			

- ***If the book has no recorded texts, please go to Question 11.***

○ ***Questions 9, 10, seek your views on the authenticity of the listening and reading texts and tasks.***

9. Authenticity of listening texts and tasks:
(Please tick (✔) appropriate boxes ☐.)

9.1 Do the listening text(s) appear:	scripted? ☐	authentic? ☐	some of each ☐
9.2 Do the recorded texts include redundancies such as:	repetition? ☐	rephrasing? ☐	hesitation? ☐
9.3 Please comment on the authenticity or realism of the listening tasks:			

10. Authenticity of reading texts and tasks: (please *tick (✔) the appropriate boxes* ☐)

10.1 Do the reading texts seem:	adapted or written for the book? ☐	authentic? ☐	some of each? ☐
10.2 Please comment on the authenticity or realism of the listening tasks:			

○ ***Most of the information you have been asked to provide so far has been relatively objective. Questions 11 and 12 here are very important as they request you to give your evaluation of how the book treats the main language skill areas, and of the book as a whole.***

11. Please give your comments on the book's treatment of the four language skills:

11.1 Listening	
11.2 Reading	
11.3 Writing	
11.4 Speaking	

12. Please now evaluate the whole textbook, preferably in terms of:

• type • level • contents • pedagogical approach • interest

13. Finally, please evaluate the book's relationship with the international test for which you use it to prepare your students.

How does the book help your students to cope with the international test you are preparing them for?

That is the end of the questionnaire. Thank you very much.

CHAPTER

6

IELTS Test Preparation in New Zealand: Preparing Students for the IELTS Academic Module

Belinda Hayes
Auckland University of Technology

John Read
Victoria University of Wellington

Changes to government policy in New Zealand in the late 1980s led to a rapidly increasing number of international students wishing to enroll in New Zealand polytechnics and universities. As a large proportion of these students did not have an English-speaking background, New Zealand tertiary institutions needed to ascertain that the applicants were proficient enough in English to undertake tertiary-level studies successfully. Most commonly, this involved setting a minimum score on a proficiency test like the International English Language Testing System (IELTS) or the Test of English as a Foreign Language (TOEFL). There has been a resulting growth in English language teaching programs in the adult/tertiary sector as prospective nonnative English-speaking students seek to meet the English language requirement in preparation for entry into tertiary study.

The potential for economic gains to New Zealand can be seen in the proliferation of private language schools as well as language centers at tertiary institutions, and in the increased numbers of international students being recruited by local secondary schools. Although many private schools offer a range of specific-purpose courses in addition to General English, preparing students for IELTS in particular has become an important part of their programs in recent years. However, despite the abundance of courses marketed as "IELTS Preparation," there is currently little research available to indicate what these courses consist of, or to what extent they show evidence of washback from the test.

THE TARGET TEST

IELTS is a preferred test of English for students intending to study in Australia and the United Kingdom, as well as in New Zealand. The test is jointly managed by the University of Cambridge Local Examinations Syndicate (UCLES), the British Council, and International Development Program (IDP) Education, Australia. It was introduced internationally in 1990 and 10 years later was available at 251 test centers in over 105 countries (UCLES, 2000).

IELTS consists of two forms, the Academic Module and the General Training Module. As the name suggests, the Academic Module is designed for those seeking admission to undergraduate and postgraduate courses, and so was chosen as the focus of the present study. This module assesses all four macro-skills through a variety of tasks that are designed to simulate genuine study tasks, within the constraints of a 3-hour test. Therefore, IELTS is intended to have a positive washback effect, in the sense of encouraging candidates to develop their language proficiency in ways that will assist their study through the medium of English. Individual performances in speaking and writing are rated according to a description of an acceptable performance at each level. The results of each of the skill areas are reported as band descriptors on a scale of 0–9 (*non-user* through *expert user*) and an overall band score is calculated (UCLES, 2000).

In New Zealand the IELTS test was introduced in 1991. In subsequent years the Academic Module has become the preferred measure of English language proficiency for admission to universities and polytechnics. Nine test centers operated throughout the country in 2000. A New Zealand-based item writing team was established in 2000 but, at the time of writing, all the Academic Module material was written in Britain and Australia.

METHOD

In 2000, we completed a study of the impact of the IELTS test on the way international students prepare for academic study in New Zealand. The research was a project of the IELTS Research Program 1999/2000, sponsored by IELTS Australia and the British Council. The two broad research questions were:

> What is the extent and nature of courses offered by language schools in New Zealand to prepare international students for the Academic Module of IELTS?
>
> What are the washback effects of the test, as revealed in a study of two classes taking preparation courses for the Academic Module?

The second question is the main focus of this chapter, but first we summarize the earlier part of the research. In Phase 1 of this research a survey of

96 language schools throughout New Zealand was conducted. A questionnaire was mailed out to collect information on whether schools offered an IELTS preparation course for the Academic Module and, if so, to obtain details of how the course was taught. With a response rate of 81%, the questionnaires showed that 60 (77%) of the responding schools offered IELTS preparation, as compared with 45 (58%) schools that taught English for Academic Purposes (EAP) or English for Further Study (EFS), and just 28 (36%) that prepared students for TOEFL.

As a follow-up to the questionnaire, 23 teachers engaged in preparing students for the IELTS Academic Module were interviewed to elicit more extended information about preparation courses. The teachers confirmed that there was a high level of demand for these courses from students who wanted to pass the test and qualify for admission to a university or polytechnic as soon as possible. The majority of the courses concentrated on preparation for the actual test tasks; relatively few of them incorporated to any great extent academic study skills that were not directly assessed in the test.

In Phase 2 of the research, a classroom study was conducted to compare two IELTS preparation courses—one clearly test-focused and the other with a stronger EAP orientation—which were offered in the language schools of two public institutions in a major New Zealand city. Including a comparative element is a common feature of washback studies (e.g., Alderson & Hamp-Lyons, 1996; Cheng, 1999; Shohamy, Donitsa-Schmidt, & Ferman, 1996; Wall & Alderson, 1993; Watanabe, 1996b). In this case, the purpose of the comparison was partly methodological: to explore various means of capturing the differences between the two courses. In addition, we wanted to seek possible evidence of test washback in the contrasting features of the two courses.

Thus, the classroom study focused on the following questions:

1. What are the significant activities in an IELTS preparation class, and how can they most usefully be recorded and classified?
2. What differences are there between a course which focuses very specifically on IELTS preparation and one that includes other learning objectives related to preparation for academic study?
3. How do the teacher's backgrounds and perceptions influence the way that the courses are delivered?
4. Is there evidence of student progress during the course towards greater proficiency in English for academic study?

Classroom observations, teacher interviews, teacher and student questionnaires, and pre- and posttesting of the students were employed to establish the nature of the two courses through a process of methodological triangulation.

The Schools and Courses

School A offered IELTS preparation as a separate course, whereas at School B the students took it as an elective within a full-time General English program. In both cases, the course was taught as a 4-week block. All of the actual class time (22 and 28 hours respectively) was observed during the same 1-month period in May–June, not long before the beginning of the second semester in July, when students could be admitted to an academic degree program. Although both courses were aimed at students preparing for the Academic Module of IELTS, each had different aims and structure. Table 6.1 summarizes the main features of the courses and the teachers.

The IELTS preparation course at School A, for which there was no entry test, was a 32-hour, part-time evening course. According to Teacher A, the aim of the course was to "prepare the students in terms of exam technique, not in terms of language level." The teacher at School A was responsible for deciding how the course was structured and which materials were used.

At School B, the IELTS preparation course was a 2-hour afternoon option available to mid-intermediate level students who were already taking a General English course at the school in the morning. Students could enroll for periods from 1 to 8 months (320 hours). Entry to the course was based on whether or not the students had reached the mid-intermediate level on the school's placement test. It was described as a skills development course rather than just a course to familiarize students with the test. It was topic-based and focused on developing general and academic English skills, as well as giving students practice with IELTS test tasks. Materials had been developed for each lesson of the course by the school, but the teacher was expected to adapt them as appropriate for individual groups.

For most of the lessons observed at School A, there were approximately 15 students in class; of these, however, only 9 were present for both the pre- and posttesting. Most of the students were aged between 18 and 25 and all were from Asia, which is the predominant source of students for New Zealand English language schools. They had previously studied English for periods ranging from less than a year to 9 years. Seven of the 9 students had not graduated from university before coming to New Zealand. Two thirds of them were also studying English at some other language school during the time that they took the IELTS course. Only one student had taken IELTS previously, but all intended to take the Academic Module, mostly within the following month, to meet the requirements for entry into a tertiary institution.

In her Phase 1 interview, Teacher A explained that, over the 4 weeks of the course, her approach was "to move from skills into practicing the test itself and practice three of the skills each time." On the first day she outlined the course and gave students a general overview of the IELTS test. She then gradually introduced possible question types found in the test and

TABLE 6.1
A Summary of Key Features of the Two IELTS Courses

Course Features	*School A*	*School B*
Focus	IELTS Academic Module	IELTS Academic Module
Length of complete course	32 hour, part-time evening course	320 hour (8-month course), part-time afternoon course
Length of Observation	22.10 hours	28.08 hours
IELTS Course Type	Independent course	Part of a General English course
Course Aims	To focus on skills needed in the exam and provide practice in various aspects of the exam	To develop general language and academic English skills, as well as familiarizing students with the test
Organization	Skills based	Topic based
Entry level	No entry test	Entry via placement test
Class size	Maximum class size–22 Average actual attendance–15	Maximum class size–12 Average actual attendance–8
Course Design	Designed by teacher, taken from IELTS preparation books	Designed by the school, taken from a range of sources and including material specifically written for the course
Room	Fixed seating–Tables in 'U' shape	Flexible seating–Desks in groups of 4
Students	Asian Aged between 18 and 25 Most students had not graduated from university One student had been studying English for less than a year, two for 1–3 years, two for 6–9 years and three for over 10 years One student had taken IELTS previously Interested in gaining entry to university	Asian Aged between 18 and 45 Most of the students had graduated from university Three students stated that they had been learning English for less than a year, but 4–9 years of language training was typical Half the class had taken IELTS once before Interested in gaining entry to university
Teachers	Teacher A–Female 30 years' teaching experience in secondary school (French, English, and TESOL) Trinity TESOL Certificate + enrolled in MA in Language Teaching 2 years' experience teaching IELTS preparation IELTS examiner	Teacher B–Male 7 years' teaching experience in ESL/EFL RSA Certificate in TEFLA + enrolled in MA in Language Teaching 3 years' experience teaching IELTS preparation Not IELTS examiner

gave students the opportunity to practice. Throughout the course the teacher regularly provided information about IELTS and tips on how to cope with the test tasks.

In the course at School B there were eight students, ranging in age from 18 to 45. As in School A, all of them were from Asia. Most had already graduated from university in their home country. Three of them had been learning English for less than a year but 4 to 9 years of language study was typical. Half the class had already taken IELTS once before. All students on this course were studying General English for 3 hours every morning in the same school and the majority of them had already taken the IELTS preparation course there the previous month. All of them planned to take the test, most within the following 4 weeks.

The course at School B was topic-based in the sense that it included a range of skills and tasks within the context of specific topics. The overall theme during the period of the observation was "Lifestyles" and it incorporated three subtopics. As the course proceeded, the students had numerous opportunities to encounter, and develop their knowledge of, key vocabulary items, grammatical structures, and concepts related to the theme. Each of the IELTS modules was practiced but the course also contained text types and tasks not included in the test. The teacher occasionally gave students test tips, but spent more time discussing the central topic and language issues.

DATA GATHERING PROCEDURES

Classroom Observation Instruments

The classroom events were first analyzed using the Communicative Orientation of Language Teaching Observation Scheme (COLT; Spada & Frohlich, 1995), which is a structured observation instrument originally developed by a team of Canadian researchers in the 1980s to investigate the extent to which different language classrooms exhibit the features of the communicative approach to language teaching. With Part A of COLT, the observer makes detailed notes in real time on the activities and episodes that occur during the lesson, including the time taken for each one. Part B records the linguistic features of classroom talk, based on a tape recording of the lesson. Because the language of the classroom was not a primary focus of our study, we used only Part A of COLT.

A second observation instrument was used to identify specific, test-related features of the courses, which was developed at Lancaster University as part of an ongoing series of projects undertaken by the University of

Cambridge Local Examinations Syndicate (UCLES) on the impact of IELTS (Alderson & Banerjee, 2001; Saville, 2000). The instrument contained lists of text-types and a range of task-types found in IELTS. It also identified test-related activities initiated by the teacher as well as grammar and vocabulary activities. Because Part 1 of the instrument largely duplicated Part A of COLT, only Part 2 was used in this study.

During the observation, it became clear that several significant activities were not specifically identified by either COLT or the UCLES instrument. These were recorded and analyzed separately, and included times when the teacher gave the students information about the test or discussed test-taking strategies. Instances of the teacher working with individuals or small groups, while the rest of the class continued with the main task, were also recorded. Additionally, the study required a more detailed analysis of classroom materials, including the amount and type of homework given. Finally, the instances of laughter in each of the lessons were recorded as an indication of the atmosphere in each lesson (cf. Alderson & Hamp-Lyons, 1996, pp. 288–289; Watanabe, 1996a, p. 230).

Teacher Interviews

Teachers A and B were among the 23 teachers who were interviewed during the earlier Phase 1 of the research project. In those interviews, which were based on a detailed interview schedule, the teachers discussed their own professional backgrounds, the organization of their courses, the teaching materials they used, and their opinions about the role of the test in preparing students for academic study. Once the observations were underway, the two teachers were interviewed weekly to (a) elicit their impressions of the class that week and (b) give them the opportunity to describe the materials they had used and the rationale behind their choices. All the interviews were recorded and transcribed.

Teacher and Student Questionnaires

At the beginning of the study, the students were asked to complete a pre-observation questionnaire to collect information about their background, English language training, their perceptions of IELTS, and their expectations of the IELTS preparation course. They were also given a questionnaire at the end of the course to record any changes in their perceptions of the test.

Once the observations were complete, each teacher completed a questionnaire designed to elicit their reflections on various aspects of the course they had just taught.

Pre- and Posttesting

In the first and last weeks of the courses the listening, reading, and writing tests of retired versions of the IELTS Academic Module were administered as pre- and posttests. The listening and reading modules were marked according to detailed marking schedules provided by IELTS. The writing scripts were double marked by experienced IELTS examiners using official IELTS criteria and band descriptors. The pretest essays from both schools were marked as one group and likewise the posttests. After completing each set of tests, the students completed questionnaires to report their perceptions of test difficulty.

SELECTED RESULTS

Structured Observation

Course Comparison Using COLT, Part A. The start time of each activity/episode was recorded to the nearest second. The duration of each episode was later calculated as a percentage of the total daily class time (length of lesson minus breaks) as a direct comparison of the lessons could not be made due to unequal class duration. The lessons were coded according to COLT. The results were calculated daily and also combined into weekly averages. The percentage of time spent on each of the categories under COLT's major features for School A and School B was compared. Analysis with COLT reflected substantial differences between the courses.

The most obvious difference was in who had control of the lessons. The teacher was the predominant focus of the classes at School A, almost three times as much as at School B. In terms of content, the main focus in both schools was on meaning, particularly of topics classified by COLT as "broad" (which includes the topic of IELTS itself). The teaching of language played a less significant role at School A, a fact acknowledged by the teacher and made clear to the students on the first day of the course. In contrast, a considerable part of the lessons at School B was spent focusing on language, in particular vocabulary, and vocabulary in combination with grammar. The expansion of the students' language knowledge was one of the main aims of Course B.

Listening, both alone and in combination with other skills, was the most common skill used by students at both schools. However, this pattern was much more obvious at School A, where the students were engaged just in listening for nearly half of the total class time, compared with less than 20% of the time at School B. In general, students at School B used a broader range of skills and covered the four skills more evenly. Because their course was less teacher-centered, they spent substantially more time on activities that involved speaking and writing than the students at School A.

The course at School A drew on a more restricted range of teaching materials, most of which came from published IELTS preparation books. This aspect of the courses is discussed in more detail next.

Course Comparison Using the UCLES Instrument. The UCLES instrument focused more on the attention that was given to the test in each course, and showed a difference in the amount of time the two teachers spent reviewing answers to tests. This activity took up 5% of Course A compared with 0.5% of Course B. Neither teacher gave any feedback to students in the form of IELTS band scores. The feedback consisted of more general comments about the strengths and weaknesses of the students' work.

In addition, the course at School A contained several text types not used at School B, in particular exercises focusing on selected IELTS task types and complete IELTS practice reading tests. Taking the practice tests was the most common reading task at School A, where it took up over 4% of the class time. In contrast, the practice test was completely absent at School B, where the students spent more time on general reading tasks. At School B there was a larger range of tasks that involved writing short answers, completing sentences or classifying information obtained from a text.

Both classes practiced all modules of the IELTS test; indeed the activities at School A were almost exclusively IELTS-like tasks, whereas Teacher B introduced a wider range of activities. For example, both classes practiced all phases of the IELTS speaking test, but it was the amount of time spent on other speaking tasks that clearly differentiated the two courses. At School A the predominant speaking activity involved student discussion of the answers to reading tasks, and although this happened at School B as well, it was for less than half the amount of time at School A. At School B students spent almost 9% of the total class time discussing issues related to the set topics and exchanging information. Overall, there was a particular focus on practice listening tests at School A, whereas the students at School B spent more time on different kinds of writing tasks.

Some of the key differences are presented in Table 6.2, which shows the percentage of class time that was devoted to particular test-related activities.

In every case, more class time was spent on such activities at School A compared with School B. The difference was particularly dramatic in the case of the first activity: giving tasks under test conditions.

Further Analysis. In addition to the variables included in the COLT and UCLES instruments, several others were observed during the courses. For instance, there were differences in the ways that the teachers referred to the IELTS test, both by providing the students with factual information

TABLE 6.2
Test-Related Activities as a Percentage of Total Class Time

Behavior Observed	*Average School A*	*Average School B*
Teacher gives the students tasks under test conditions	15.90	2.96
Teacher gives the students the test to do at home (self-timed)	1.02	0.00
Teacher gives feedback on student performance item by item	5.09	0.57
Teacher identifies answers in a text and explains	4.05	2.84
Teacher asks students to consider their strengths and weaknesses with respect to the test requirements	1.41	1.33
Teacher sets tasks under strict time pressure	4.00	2.62

about the test and giving them advice on test-taking strategies. As a percentage of the total class time, students at School A received twice as much information about the IELTS test than those at School B and spent 13 times more of the time receiving instructions about effective strategies to use in the test (13% vs. 1%). This finding explains, at least to some degree, why Teacher A was so often the focus of the class.

A second area of difference was the length of time that Teacher B spent assisting students both individually and in pairs or groups. This type of interaction, which typically focused on issues relating to task definition and language use, accounted for 15% of the total class time. Although Teacher A occasionally went around the class monitoring the students, there was little significant interaction of this kind in her class.

With regard to the source of classroom materials, published IELTS preparation texts were the predominant source at School A in activities representing almost 46% of the total class time. By comparison, at School B about 43% of the class time was spent on activities with materials developed by the school. These materials consisted of adaptations of authentic texts and of IELTS academic and general English textbooks, as well as supplementary exercises. Teachers A and B used their own materials for 6% and 4% of the total class time respectively.

Finally, keeping a record of the instances of laughter gave a general indication of the atmosphere in the classes. At School A, on average, one instance per day was recorded, compared to 11 at School B. While the specific causes of the laughter cannot easily be defined, it occurred most often during pair or group activities, the types of interaction that predominated at School B.

Teacher Interviews

Teacher A. In the preobservation interview, Teacher A explained that when planning her IELTS preparation course she moved from a focus on skills in the beginning of the course to more test practice as the course progressed.

She identified listening as causing many students considerable anxiety. However, she felt that in general, reading was the most problematic section of the IELTS test for the majority of her students, because of problems with vocabulary and unfamiliar concepts, coupled with time pressures.

In the weekly interviews, Teacher A expressed frustration that, although some of the students had quite good ideas and some idea of how to organize them, their grammar structures were still quite poor. She later mentioned that she observed a division in the class between those students who were genuinely motivated to take the course and those who were either having second thoughts about it or felt they would be able to just "sail through." As the course progressed, she felt that although the students had a better understanding of what test-taking strategies they should be using, they were not necessarily applying them. References to time constraints and lack of time were a common feature of the weekly interviews.

In the final weekly interview, Teacher A felt she had met her objectives for the course. The students had been acquainted with the format of the test, learned test-taking strategies, and had had enough practice to be able to approach the test with confidence. She felt that, because the course was so intensive, the content was completely directed toward coping with the test. The teacher expressed some frustration that the limited amount of classroom time, and the lack of a suitable classroom space, had not allowed her much opportunity to establish rapport with her students.

Teacher B. In the preobservation interview, Teacher B said that the school prescribed 90% of the course content and provided all the materials, but that there was considerable flexibility when it came to methodology. The materials were based on the set topics and gave particular attention to relevant vocabulary and grammatical features. IELTS reading and writing practice materials related to the topic were also used. In his experience, the students had more problems with the writing section than with the other parts of the test.

In the weekly interviews, Teacher B spoke of the importance of vocabulary learning. He used exercises such as peer teaching to make vocabulary study a more "communicative" activity. He said he would slowly move the students toward producing sentences and using the vocabulary introduced in class. He also indicated that error correction was a common feature of his classes as he wanted to encourage students to focus not only on fluency but also on accuracy. Teacher B felt the course was always "a bit rushed."

In the final interview Teacher B felt that he had met the objectives set for the course, but commented that time is always short in IELTS classes. He also observed that he had spent more time than normal on writing because of the needs of the students. Reflecting on the course in general, Teacher B stated that it gave the students knowledge of the language requirements of the test and provided practice under test conditions.

TABLE 6.3
Overall Band Scores in the Pre- and Posttests

Ss School A	*Pretest Overall*	*Posttest Overall*	*Ss School B*	*Pretest Overall*	*Posttest Overall*
1	4	4.5	1	4.5	6
2	6	6	2	6.5	6
3	5.5	5	3	5	6.5
4	5.5	6	4	5	5.5
5	5	6	5	5.5	6
6	5	5	6	5	5
7	4.5	5	7	6	6
8	5.5	6	8	6	6
9	6.5	6.5			

Pre- and Posttesting

Questionnaire responses from both groups of students suggested that they expected the preparation courses to boost their results. Teacher A felt that the course had met the needs of the students in terms of an improvement in band score. Teacher B agreed, although to a lesser extent. Thus the pre- and posttests were administered to assess whether the courses had a measurable effect on their IELTS performance.

The overall band scores for the students in each course—calculated as the mean of the individual scores on the Listening, Reading, and Writing test—are given in Table 6.3.

About half of the students in each class did increase their overall score by between 0.5 and 1.5. However, the difference in pre- and posttest mean scores for each class was not significant in either case. The only significant difference in the mean scores for the individual tests was found in Listening for the School A students ($t = -6.42$; two-tailed; $df = 8$; $p < .05$). This was perhaps not surprising, given the amount of listening test practice that these students received.

DISCUSSION

From a methodological perspective, observing every class hour of the two courses proved valuable, as it allowed a more accurate picture of the courses to emerge. A sampling approach would not have captured the continuous, and sometimes unpredictable, variations recorded by daily observations. Many of the classroom episodes lasted less than 2 minutes and occurred only once in a day or even just once in the entire period observed. For the same reason, observing alternate days would have resulted in significant episodes being missed. Tape-recording the classes might have been desirable but was not crucial for the purposes of this study, as the notes taken during the observation were detailed and provided an adequate record of classroom events. Interviewing the teachers before the study as well as on a weekly basis during the observations appeared to be adequate. However, a more structured form of weekly interview would have made comparisons easier.

Let us briefly revisit the four main research questions that were the focus of the classroom study and reflect on the methodology of this classroom study:

What are the significant activities in an IELTS preparation class, and how can they most usefully be recorded and classified?

COLT Part A provided a macroscopic description of the two classrooms, and this was complemented by the UCLES observation instrument, which looked at particular text- and task types used in the classroom, as well as test-related activities. However, to gain a more complete picture of IELTS preparation in these two courses, it was also necessary to record in more detail the test information and strategies offered by the teachers, patterns of secondary teacher–student interaction, the types of materials used, and instances of laughter in class time. Thus, neither of the structured instruments was entirely satisfactory for the purpose and a more comprehensive one would need to include information on: the test itself as the focus of classroom discussion; attention to test-taking strategies; patterns of class organization and teacher–student interaction; sources of teaching materials and the extent to which they are modified; and relevant learning activities carried out by the students outside of class during the course.

What differences are there between a course which focuses very specifically on IELTS preparation and one that includes other learning objectives related to preparation for academic study?

The teacher at School A aimed to familiarize students with the structure of the test and to teach them test-taking strategies. The course was organized around the practice of skills, particularly through test-related tasks. At School B, the goal was not only test familiarization, but also language development. Here, the course was topic-based, with a substantial emphasis on language forms as well as skills. It was not surprising, then, that the different objectives led the teachers to deliver the courses in rather different ways.

The teachers were asked if they perceived a mismatch between the IELTS test tasks and the students' academic study needs. Teacher A felt that her course differed in almost every way from an EAP course, as it was shorter and totally test-focused. She said the course did not prepare students for academic study, but only for the IELTS test. In contrast, Teacher B thought his course did help students prepare for university study. However, he acknowledged that, although there were many academic study skills included in the course at School B, a true EAP course should include skills such as referencing and extended academic assignments.

How do the teacher's background and perceptions influence the way that the course is delivered?

Teacher A, an experienced teacher and IELTS examiner, with extensive knowledge of the preparation books available, felt that the course was so intensive that the content was completely directed toward coping with the test. Therefore, there was little language component in the course. "It's basically IELTS exam technique and practice."

Teacher B, on the other hand, had no firsthand knowledge of the test and was less familiar with published materials. He taught one of a series of IELTS courses at his school and had a smaller class of students with a more homogenous level of language ability. He felt that the way he taught IELTS preparation was not significantly different from the way he taught General English. He thought that the content of the course was influenced by the IELTS test mainly because of the inclusion of IELTS practice test materials.

Teacher A had to depend more on her own resources and the published materials which were available to her as opposed to Teacher B, who had the advantage of being able to draw on a course design and a bank of materials that had been developed by a team of teachers at his school over several years.

Is there evidence of student progress during the course toward greater proficiency in English for academic study?

It was not expected that there would be any significant difference in the students' IELTS scores from the beginning to the end of these relatively short courses. It is generally recognized that students need an intensive and usually extended period of study to achieve any substantial increase in their score on a proficiency test like IELTS. The test results did not show any significant improvement, with the exception of the listening test at School A.

CONCLUSION

This study showed clear evidence of washback effects in the IELTS preparation course at School A. However, they did not seem to be the kind of positive effects envisaged at the outset of this study, in the sense that the teacher and students were narrowly focused on practice of the test tasks, rather than the development of academic language proficiency in a broader sense. By contrast, the course at School B appeared to address a wider range of academic study needs and to promote the students' general language development.

This comparison may be somewhat misleading, in two ways. First, what School A offered was very much an independent course which students took only once, whereas Course B was one of a whole sequence at School B which the students could follow for up to 8 months. This could be seen as taking some pressure off Teacher B to "deliver the goods" within the space of just 4 weeks, whereas Teacher A was considerably more constrained in this respect. Second, the majority of the students in Course A were also studying English in other language schools during the period of the research and thus it is possible that their broader language needs in the area of preparation for academic study were being met in this way. This suggests the need to take a comprehensive view of the English study programs of both groups of students, rather than simply focusing on courses designated as "IELTS preparation."

Both of the courses studied in this research were located in university language centers. However, Phase 1 of the study showed that the majority of IELTS preparation courses in New Zealand are offered by private language schools, and the evidence from our interviews with teachers was that these schools may come under greater pressure from students to coach them intensively to pass the test. It remains to be seen how the aims and structure of the IELTS courses in private schools compare with what we found in the present study. The commercial pressures on private schools may well create some more obvious washback effects of a negative kind. It would also be valuable to make a direct comparison of the various types of IELTS preparation course with university EAP programs, in terms of their relative effectiveness in preparing students for the language demands of academic study.

Language proficiency may be only one aspect contributing to the academic success of international students but, as long as the IELTS test is used as a gatekeeping device for entry into tertiary institutions, further investigation into the different forms of preparation for the test—their aims, methodology, and ultimately, their effectiveness—must be carried out. As the number of studies of IELTS preparation courses increases, we will gain a better understanding of the washback effects of the test in different classrooms and, more generally, its impact in this high-stakes environment.

CHAPTER

7

Washback in Classroom-Based Assessment: A Study of the Washback Effect in the Australian Adult Migrant English Program

Catherine Burrows
TAFE NSW

In Australia, English language tuition is provided to new adult immigrants under the Adult Migrant English Program (AMEP), funded through the Department of Immigration and Multicultural Affairs (DIMA). When this study was undertaken, between 1994 and 1998, the AMEP was delivered by an Adult Migrant English Service (AMES) in each state in Australia. Between the establishment of the AMEP in 1949 and this study, many different teaching methods had been used by AMEP teachers. Most commonly, teachers had employed a needs-based approach, largely based in communicative language teaching. Each teacher examined the needs of each group of students and designed a syllabus addressing those needs.

In 1993, the New South Wales Adult Migrant English Service (NSW AMES) implemented the *Certificate in Spoken and Written English* (CSWE) (Hagan et al., 1993). CSWE "is a competency-based curriculum framework structured around a social and functional theory of language . . ." (Hood, 1995, p. 22). During the following 2 years, CSWE was implemented across Australia, becoming the mandatory curriculum for the AMEP in 1998. CSWE consists of four *Certificate* levels, within which sits a series of modules, which focus on specific learning areas, including pronunciation and literacy. Within each module are a series of competencies, which are "descriptions of what a learner can do at the end of a course of study" (Hagan, 1994, p. 33). The curriculum specifies generic text types and lists the lexico-grammatical elements of which they are composed. These elements are then expressed as performance criteria, which, together with range statements outlining the parameters for the assessment, form the "test specification."

The implementation of CSWE entailed the introduction of formal, mandatory, competency-based assessment. Because it is classroom-based, the formality of the assessment is principally in its use for reporting student outcomes. The fact that the new curriculum is competency-based meant that it faced considerable criticism (Brindley, 1994; Grove, 1997; Quinn, 1993) although at the same time competency-based training was seen to hold great promise by others in Australia (Docking, 1993; Rumsey, 1993).

Before the introduction of CSWE, the most commonly used assessment tool in the AMEP was the Australian Second Language Proficiency Ratings (ASLPR; Ingram, 1984), although many teachers had devised their own classroom tests. The ASLPR was used to place students into classes and, in some instances, to report on student progress. When CSWE was introduced, it was accompanied by *Assessment Guidelines* (Burrows, 1993). These guidelines included model assessment tasks, which teachers were to use when designing their own classroom-based assessment. Subsequent editions of CSWE (New South Wales Adult Migrant English Service [NSW AMES], 1995; NSW AMES, 1997) include revised assessment tasks.

TESTING OR ASSESSMENT?

The difference between this assessment and many large-scale tests is that the assessment is explicitly tied to the curriculum. This relationship to the curriculum made the potential impact of the implementation different from that of large-scale tests such as TOEFL. The first difference concerns the notion of *teaching to the test* (Gipps, 1994; Morris, 1961). Because under CSWE, the teaching objectives (the competencies) are the assessment outcomes, teachers are expected to develop a syllabus, which teaches students to achieve specified competency outcomes, and are instructed to present items similar to the assessments tasks (Burrows, 1993, p. viii). This is seen as an essential part of CSWE's achievement assessment.

Goldstein (1989) described this difference between standardized testing and classroom-based assessment as:

> [a] basic distinction ... between assessment connected to learning and assessment separated from learning.... In the case of what I call *separate assessment*, its defining principle is its deliberate attempt to avoid connection with particular learning environments.... (p. 140)

Under this definition, CSWE is clearly an example of *connected assessment*.

Troman (1989) theorized a difference between assessment and testing, the former being democratic, diagnostic, school-based, professional-led, having a focus on process, and results which were hard to publish; the latter being authoritarian, nondiagnostic, centralized, bureaucrat-led, having a focus on product, and results which were easy to publish (p. 289). Under this model, the assessment of CSWE resembles both assessment and testing. It is both national, externally imposed on teachers and increasingly centralized; but it is designed to be diagnostic, professional-led, has a focus on process, and has results that are relatively hard to publish.

The implementation of CSWE and its assessment occurred when teachers felt they were experiencing great change in their profession (Robinson, 1993, p. 1). Teachers do not always perceive change as necessarily being of benefit to themselves or to their students, and this affects the degree to which change is adopted (Fullan with Stiegelbauer, 1991; Hargreaves, 1994, p. 12). Fullan and Park (1981) acknowledged the importance of the belief systems of those affected by change (pp. 7–8). Although the focus of this study was on washback and therefore on assessment, CSWE and its assessment are intrinsically interwoven through the competencies, resulting in an examination of assessment in the context of the curriculum and the classroom and, therefore, an examination of washback situated within the context of educational change.

THE RESEARCH METHODS ADOPTED FOR THE STUDY

By the time of this study, the era which saw quantitative and qualitative data techniques as representative of different paradigms had long passed. "Our position is that the transformation of such ideas into dichotomous choices is unnecessary, inaccurate, and ultimately counterproductive" (Goetz & LeCompte, 1984, p. 245). The study fell into three broad phases: a survey of 215 teachers, interviews with 30 teachers, and observations of four teachers. Because this study was undertaken as doctoral research, however, one essential element which must be recalled was that each section involved a process of learning for the researcher, such that the data collection and analysis techniques were chosen more wisely and used more proficiently as the research progressed.

THE SURVEY

The major issue facing this study was that the curriculum and its assessment had already been implemented before the study began. "The investigator arrives 'after the fact' . . . and tries to determine causal relationships"

(Merriam, 1988, p. 7). In order to manage this situation, it was necessary to find information from the past which could be compared to the present, and then to ask those involved in the present situation, and who had been involved in the past one, to comment on the differences. The aim of such strategies was to establish a baseline for comparison of the past and the present to form a valid basis for that section of the study, which was based in the present, the third phase.

The survey was designed to explore differences between past and current classroom practices, using the results of a survey of 131 teachers undertaken by Brindley in 1988 (Brindley, 1989). It was hoped that, should differences be found between the results of the two surveys, this could be analyzed in terms of washback. Brindley's survey was therefore replicated and the data compared using statistical techniques. In addition to this, a series of additional questions were added which asked the respondents to rate on a 5-point Likert scale their opinions of the implementation of the assessment. Provision was provided for comment after each question and the respondents were asked to give their names and indicate if they would take part in a later interview.

Despite trialing, the survey was flawed. The Likert scale questions performed poorly (Burrows, 1998, chap. 4) and efforts made to gain access to a random sample were unsuccessful, as a proportion of the respondents were self-selected. Such problems considerably lessened the usefulness of the statistical data gained. There was a marked similarity between the results of the 1988 and 1994 surveys (see Table 7.1 for an example). In question three, the respondents were asked to rate the importance of each of the stated possible functions of assessment.

Only one significant result was achieved for this question, whereas for question four, statistical tests could not be applied due to the addition of the new items (see Burrows, 2001, pp. 111–127 for a detailed discussion of the survey results). The results suggested that the populations were substantially the same, which supported the validity of a comparison between the teachers surveyed in 1989 and those surveyed in this study. In addition, many participants took the opportunity given in the survey to comment on the questions and their comments indicated that they felt change had occurred, although in different ways. The comments were used extensively in framing the interview questions.

THE INTERVIEWS

The interview questions (see Appendix) were designed to explore teacher beliefs: The interviews examined whether teachers believed that their teaching had been influenced by the introduction of the assessment; and

TABLE 7.1
Perceived Importance of Functions of Assessment

Function of Assessment	*MEAN 1988*	*S.D. 1988*	*MEAN 1994*	*S.D. 1994*	*RANK 1988*	*RANK 1994*	*df*	t_{obs}	*P* =
Place learners in class	4.296	1.059	4.472	0.826	1	1	344	1.607	n.s.
Provide feedback on progress	3.888	1.221	4.023	0.978	4	4	344	0.120	n.s.
Provide information on learners' strengths and weaknesses for course planning	4.137	1.129	4.074	1.056	2	3	344	–0.534	n.s.
Provide information to funding authorities for accountability purposes	2.482	1.512	2.733	1.567	6	6	344	1.476	n.s.
Encourage students to take responsibility for their own learning	3.957	1.268	4.117	1.021	3	2	344	1.231	n.s.
Provide students with a record of their achievement	3.207	1.393	3.825	1.131	5	5	344	4.296	<.001

whether they reported changes to their teaching practices as a result of the implementation of the assessment. These questions and those used for the observation phase of the study were based on three washback hypotheses taken from Alderson and Wall (1993): "A test will influence *what* teachers teach"; "A test will influence *how* teachers teach"; and "Tests will have washback effects for ... *some* [italics added] teachers, but not for others" (pp. 120–121).

After the survey, it was decided that it was not possible to find a random sample for the interviews: "Unfortunately, randomization almost always comes at the expense of representativeness. The controlled trial requires compliant agencies or volunteer subjects—both atypical" (Cronbach, 1982, p. 64). It was determined to use a convenience sample, composed of survey respondents who had indicated their willingness to be interviewed, with the addition of specific teachers to attempt to create a sample which approximately matched the teaching population (Burrows, 1998, pp. 154–155).

Analysis of the interviews led to a number of conclusions, which guided the observations through the development of specific hypotheses. Throughout the interviews, many respondents described changes they had experienced, regardless of the causes of these changes. The fifth question asked them whether those changes were directly related to the implementation of the assessment. Of those who agreed (all but six), nine respondents stated that the changes were directly related to the implementation of the assessment. The other respondents saw the changes they mentioned as being more related to other causes, particularly the implementation of the curriculum, because of the intrinsic relationship between the curriculum and its assessment.

To examine whether there was an important difference between these two groups, it was decided to compare the answers of these two groups to the questions concerning the *types* of changes they had experienced. This was undertaken in order to examine the question of causality, identified as a most important aspect of washback research by Messick (1996, p. 243). There was found to be a great similarity between the answers of the two groups. Both those who reported changes since the implementation of the assessment and those who listed changes caused by the implementation listed, *inter alia*:

- increased formality of assessment and detailed monitoring of student progress
- increased student motivation
- provision within course structuring to accommodate teaching and assessment of competencies
- the use of authentic teaching materials
- an increased concentration on teaching literacy

- increased use of meta-language and information given to students about assessment, competencies, and performance criteria.

Those who reported changes *caused* by the implementation of the assessment also listed increased accountability and responsibility for teachers; while those who reported changes *since* the implementation listed teaching new topics, particularly those related to competencies. These were the only areas in which the two groups differed. The great similarity reported by these two groups would seem to indicate that a distinction between the implementation of the assessment and the curriculum framework was not useful, perhaps because of the "connectedness" of the assessment and the curriculum.

The second major conclusion reached through examination of the interview data appeared to be that change had occurred for many teachers, but not for all, and to differing degrees. It also appeared that this change might differ with the passage of time as Shohamy, Donitsa-Schmidt, and Ferman (1996) have shown. This led to an examination of the comments of those who claimed not to have changed their teaching in order to attempt to discover the basis for this claim. In simple terms, these teachers had felt that the implementation was of benefit neither to themselves nor to their students and had, for this reason, resisted it (Clark, 1987). Teacher beliefs "are often critical to effective implementation. . . . They are also extremely difficult to change" (Fullan & Park, 1981, p. 7).

THE OBSERVATIONS

Taking into account all of the changes reported by the respondents, a series of hypotheses was proposed for the observation phase of the research, predicated on the underlying hypothesis that what the respondents had stated about their teaching and assessment practices would be observable in their actions. This is a concept supported by the findings of other studies undertaken at the same time (Alderson & Hamp-Lyons, 1996; Blewchamp, 1994; Watanabe, 1996b). These studies found that the washback effect of new tests and assessment systems were not clear cut but rather had varying effects depending on the teacher involved. This may go some way towards explaining why it is that data collected through interviews with teachers could be said to be inconsistent, additional to the problems of self-report data. Different people experience the same event, or series of events, differently, depending on such things as their political viewpoint, educational background, culture, and previous life experiences, what Woods (1996) referred to as their "beliefs, assumptions, and knowledge" (p. 195). In essence, the hypotheses assumed that the implementation of the assessment would have had an observable impact on the teaching of some, but not all, teachers.

A number of observation tools were examined before the decision was taken to employ the COLT Scheme (Spada & Fröhlich, 1995; see chapter 6 for the structure and purpose of the instrument). From the pre-analysis observations undertaken, it was felt that while COLT B might distinguish between one teacher and another, and thus provide evidence of difference, this difference would not in itself be informative, since the researcher wished to establish the extent to which the assessment system had been adopted and the effect of this on teaching. It was felt that this would not be shown in an examination of the extent to which one teacher allowed or encouraged, for example, sustained student speech to a greater or lesser extent than another. Therefore, only COLT A was employed.

Four teachers were purposively selected to represent different responses to the implementation, according to the content of their interviews. Teacher A did not believe the assessment was beneficial and stated that her teaching was unchanged. Teacher B stated that he had adopted useful aspects of the new system and had maintained useful aspects of the old. Teacher C stated that she had adopted the curriculum and its assessment wholeheartedly. Teacher D stated that she had adopted the assessment to some extent.

Analysis of the observation data led to the notion of "models of teacher assessment" (McCallum, Gipps, McAlister, & Brown, 1995, p. 57). This concept had been used in the field of educational change, and specifically curriculum innovation, for an extended period but had not been used in discussions of washback, although Wall (1996) had begun to explore the relationship between educational change and washback. Because of the intrinsic relationship between the assessment and the curriculum, it was felt that the area of curriculum innovation might be useful in this research. Markee (1997) cited Lambright and Flynn's (1980, as cited in Markee, 1997) use of the terms "adopters," "resisters," and "implementers," *inter alia* (pp. 43–44) and the different types of adopters on a "diffusion curve: *innovators*, *early adopters*, *early majority*, *late majority*, and *laggards* (Huberman 1973; Rogers 1983)" (Markee, 1997, p. 58). The four teachers chosen for observation might be placed on a similar continuum, ranging from the teacher who felt least affected by the change to the teacher who felt most deeply affected. Table 7.2 places the four teachers on a continuum, from least to most affected by the change, according to their stated behavior, attitudes, and beliefs.

Two 4-hour lessons were observed for each teacher: a total of 32 hours. The lessons were videotaped and analyzed using the COLT Scheme. The major findings were in three areas: the *Content*, summarized in Fig. 7.1; the *Form*, summarized in Fig. 7.2; and the use of *Texts*, summarized in Fig. 7.3. In each of these cases, the observations revealed marked differences between the four teachers, although not always as predicted. (Note: Teacher A = TA; Teacher B = TB; Teacher C = TC; Teacher D = TD.)

TABLE 7.2
Extent of Stated Changes for Observed Teachers, Teachers as Models

Teacher A *Resister*	*Teacher D* *Adopter (partial)*	*Teacher B* *Later Adopter*	*Teacher C* *Adopter*
• teaching was substantially unchanged; • had adopted the assessment only as required and where she felt it was relevant; • felt curriculum and assessment were interrelated; • did not find the implementation a confronting or exciting change	• teaching had changed in some respects; • had adopted the assessment; • now used competency-based syllabus and related outcomes to competencies, performance criteria and underlying skills; • liked the genre basis of the competencies; • had not found it a deep change	• teaching had changed with the passage of time; • used assessment all the time, subconsciously; • was accustomed to testing; • fitted competencies to teaching themes; • still used the same methods; • implementation allowed one to do virtually the same things if one could see how they fitted	• teaching had changed; • used assessment most of the time; • explained the performance criteria to her students; • understood the theoretical bases of the CSWE; • felt curriculum and assessment were inextricably linked; • had found it a deep change

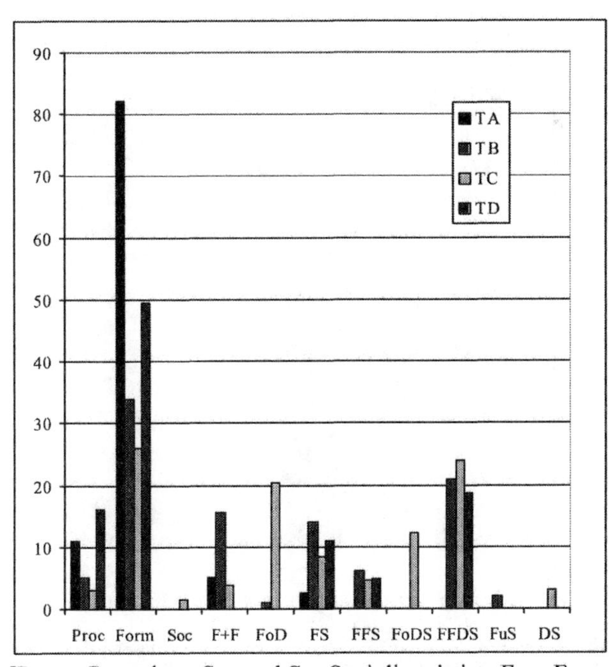

[Proc = Procedure; Soc and S = Sociolinguistics; Fo = Form; Fu = Function; FF = Form + Function; and D = Discourse.]

FIG. 7.1. All teachers: Lessons content combined %.

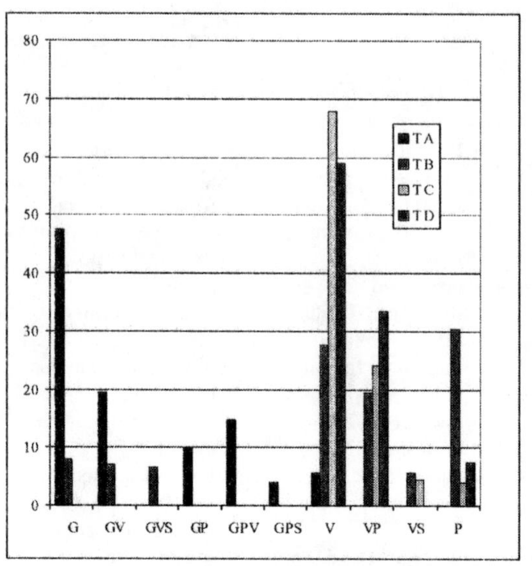

[G = Grammar; V = Vocabulary; S = Spelling; and P = Pronunciation]

FIG. 7.2. All teachers, subcategories of form only, lessons combined %.

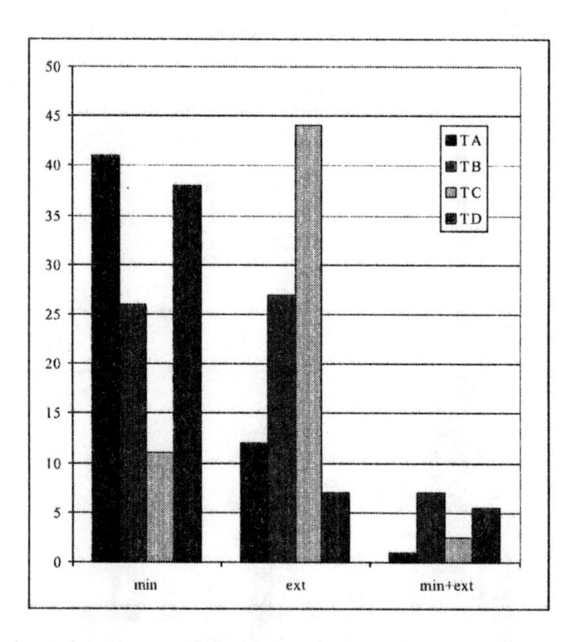

[min = minimal; ext = extended; min+ext = minimal + extended texts]

FIG. 7.3. All teachers, both lessons, minimal, extended and minimal + extended texts % of total lesson time.

COLT A provides for time-coding of lessons under a series of categories. The first is "Content" which includes *Procedure*; and *Language*, with the subcategories of *Form*, *Function*, *Discourse*, and *Sociolinguistics*. *Procedure* is used when a Teacher explains to the students what she or he wants them to do or how she or he wants them to do an activity.

Language is used to code the teaching of language itself, using the four subcategories listed earlier. *Form* is then divided further into the areas of Pronunciation, Spelling, Vocabulary, and Grammar, or any combination of these. Because of the importance placed on meta-language by the interview respondents, it was felt that this would be an important area for investigation. Consequently, for the purpose of this study, *Form*–Grammar was used to refer to traditional grammar. Examples of this were when a teacher explained the use of verbs in the past tense and how to form past tense questions. Meta-language seen as indicative of traditional grammar was the use of such terms as "noun," "verb," "adverb," and activities involving sentence level grammar. Meta-language seen as indicative of systemic-functional grammar and of genre was the use of such terms as "nominal groups," "participants," "processes," and activities involving the generic structure of texts. The participants' use of meta-language was not coded but was instead noted within the description of the appropriate episode.

Function was used to refer to the purpose of the language being taught, for example when the teacher explained that certain colloquial expressions were appropriate in some contexts but not in others, or when the teacher was relating the use of particular grammatical forms to specific text types. The teaching of the difference between spoken and written language was also included here.

Discourse was used to refer to cohesion, conjunction, and text structure. Examples of this were when the teacher had students undertake activities, which involved the construction or deconstruction of texts.

Sociolinguistics was used to refer to "forms or styles (spoken or written) appropriate to different contexts or genres" (Spada & Fröhlich, 1995, p. 48). This category was also used when the teacher described the social purposes for which language was used, for example, when Teacher B explained the socially cohesive purpose of casual conversation. There was a distinct association between *Function* and *Sociolinguistics*, and where a teacher was working with the student on a whole text, for example the joint construction of a cover letter for a job application, all four *Language* areas were considered to be being taught.

A second category within COLT A is Text, which includes *Type*, which in turn has the subsection Text (Minimal or Extended). Because the use of materials had been indicated by the interview respondents as an area of importance, this section of the COLT Scheme was used to measure the time spent on the use of different types of materials. The categories are described in COLT as *Minimal*–"Written text: captions, isolated sentences, word lists etc."—and *Extended*—"Written text: stories, dialogues, connected sentences, paragraphs etc." (Spada & Fröhlich, 1995, p. 19). Because of the interview comments and the nature of the *Certificate*, the category *Materials* was adapted to include texts other than written texts, such as video and audiotapes. For this same reason, the subcategory *Extended* was adapted to refer to whole texts, including models of the structure of whole texts. (For additional information about the use of COLT in this study, the reader is referred to Allwright & Bailey, 1991; Burrows, 1998.)

While generalizability is limited by the use of a purposive and very small sample, the results of the analysis of the four lessons using COLT A did reveal clear distinctions between the four teachers. In addition, there was a marked difference between the two lessons of Teacher B, described in detail elsewhere (Burrows, 1998). In essence, Teacher B used different materials and methods according to the topic he was teaching, just as he had said in his interview. As hypothesized, the *Content* of Teacher A's lessons differed from that of the other three teachers, with a far smaller percentage of teaching time spent in her lessons on *Function*, *Discourse*, and *Sociolinguistics* and a far higher concentration on *Form*. Teacher D fell between the two extremes, supporting her claim that she had adopted the implementation to some extent, but not entirely. When *Form* was broken down into its component parts, Teacher A was found to be most different from Teachers C and D in this respect, with Teacher B using the widest spread of topics within this category. The hypothesis that Teachers B, C, and D would spend more time using and teaching extended, generic texts than Teacher A was supported for Teachers B and C, while Teacher D's use of extended texts lay between these two. Teacher B used both kinds of texts.

When these results are examined in view of a washback hypothesis which states that the implementation of assessment will have an impact on teaching practice, it appears that the reality, at least in relation to classroom-based assessment, is more complex than this. As has been found in studies of curriculum innovation and in recent washback studies, the reaction of individual teachers to the implementation of CSWE assessment is itself individual. The observations undertaken here have revealed a cline from Teacher A, upon whose teaching the assessment would appear to have had no observable washback effect, to Teacher C, whose teaching demonstrates many of the changes spoken about by the interview subjects who stated that change had occurred. Between these two extremes lie Teachers B and D, upon whose teaching there would appear to have been a washback effect in some respects, but not in others.

Teacher D stated that she had adopted a more systemic functional approach. However, although she appears to have changed in respect of the *Content* of her lessons, where her teaching includes sociolinguistics and discourse, she has not adopted the teaching of whole texts. The results with regard to Teacher B were more complex still, as he would appear to have combined those aspects of his lessons that were still applicable in the new context, such as the teaching of traditional grammar, with those aspects which he had decided to adopt, such as the teaching of whole texts and their structures. The result of this in the analysis was a marked distinction between his two lessons and a wider spread across the different subcategories chosen for analysis. In terms of the inclusion of the assessment, Teacher B showed evidence of a marked washback effect.

These results call for a revision of the teacher models provided by Markee (1993, 1997), before further application to this context. The analysis supports the categorization of Teacher A as a resister, Teacher C as an adopter, and Teacher D as a partial adopter. Teacher B, however, would seem to be an "adaptor," one who takes from the new system as she or he chooses. What Teachers A and B would seem to demonstrate is an idea which has been absent from previous washback literature, that of choice. The literature on washback predating Alderson and Wall (1993) described the washback effect as an inevitability. Bearing in mind the limitations posed by the selection and extent of the data, and the complicating factor of the relationship of the assessment to the curriculum, the results here would appear to provide support for the notion that there is a degree of choice involved in washback, at least in the context of classroom-based assessment. This may be explained as follows. If it is possible to choose to resist the effect of an implementation upon one's teaching, then it is possible to choose whether the implementation of an assessment system or test will have a washback effect.

A NEW MODEL FOR WASHBACK

These findings lead to the proposal of a new model for washback (after Woods, 1996, p. 51), which takes into account teachers' belief systems and consequent responses to change. Three models of washback appear next: the traditional model, which predates Alderson and Wall (1993); a second model, which relates to much written about washback at the time of this study (e.g., Shohamy et al., 1996); and a proposed third model, which relates washback to curriculum innovation and teachers' beliefs, assumptions, and knowledge ("BAK"; Woods, 1996, p. 195).

This traditional view of washback predates Alderson and Wall (1993). It proposes that the introduction of any test would necessarily lead to a washback effect, a single and uniform response, which might be negative or positive and which depended on qualities of the test rather than on the teachers

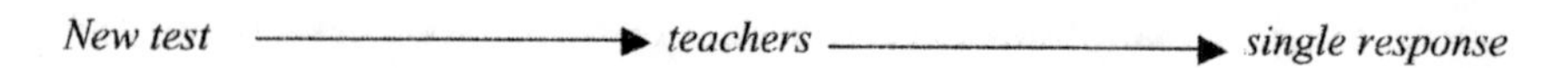

FIG. 7.4. Traditional washback theory: A stimulus-response model.

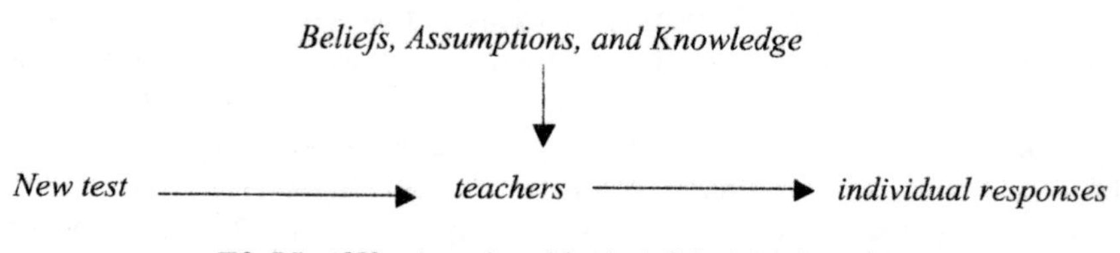

FIG. 7.5. 1990s view of washback: A "black box" model.

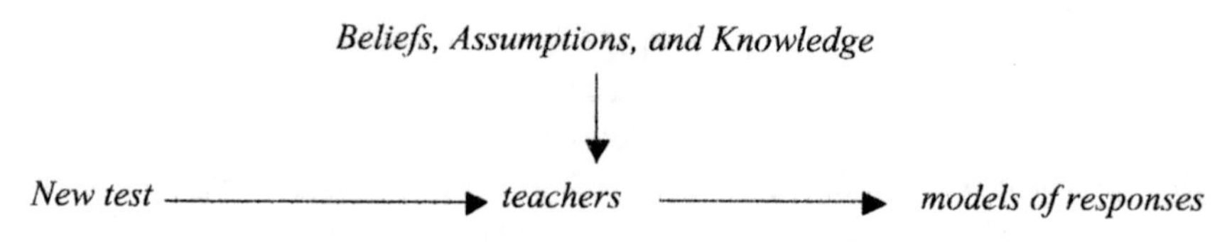

FIG. 7.6. Proposed view of washback: A curriculum innovation model.

involved, hence the consistency in response. From this view came the concept of washback validity (Morrow, 1986) and *working for washback* (Hughes, 1989; Swain, 1985). Observational and other evidence-based washback research were not characteristic of this traditional model of washback.

This "black box" model has been informed by objective data gathering, with observers gathering empirical evidence. Following the publication of Alderson and Wall's (1993) article, a series of evidence-based, observational washback studies were undertaken. In these studies, researchers collected empirical evidence for washback, primarily through classroom observation. The data collected indicate the existence of individual responses to the implementation of a variety of tests, taken further by Wall (1996). The discovery that the teachers involved in these studies did not all respond in the same way discounts the first model, since results indicate that a single washback response is not inevitable.

This curriculum innovation model embodies the view that a qualitative analysis of teachers' responses to the introduction of a new test or assessment system may reveal patterns in their responses. It derives from an analysis of individual teacher responses for patterns in behavior. It is grounded in the notion that washback is a form of educational change (Wall, 1996) and assumes that behavioral models proposed for other areas of educational change (Markee, 1997; McCallum et al., 1995) might be applicable to washback, since studies of washback and curriculum innovation have in common the examination of the impact of educational change on teaching.

Furthermore, this model proposes that these patterns may be similar to Markee's (1997) models of response to educational change and the models of teacher assessment proposed by McCallum et al. (1995). The issue here may best be summarized as follows: "a solely behavioral model is conceptually incomplete. It cannot account for predictable variations in teachers' behavior arising from differences in their goals, judgments, and decisions" (Shavelson & Stern, 1981, p. 455). This comment, which in the original related to teachers pedagogical intentions and behaviors, relates equally well to washback: Unless it were demonstrated otherwise through empirical evidence, it does not seem an acceptable proposition that washback should be different from all other types of educational change.

CONCLUSIONS

There are three principal conclusions to be drawn from this study. First, there would appear to be a link between washback and curriculum innovation, at least in terms of teacher response. Studies of curriculum innovation have traditionally explored the concept of an individual response to change, with proposed models of teacher behavior; washback research has traditionally been more concerned with the examination of large-scale responses to change. The outcomes of this study, although limited by its particular context and limitations, seem to indicate that it may be useful for test designers who wish to work for washback to take the teacher "variable" into account when designing implementation strategies for new tests.

Second is the importance of empirical research to washback. In recent years, washback research has begun to apply a rigor to its investigations, through the use of empirical data collection and analysis, which was previously lacking (Alderson & Wall, 1993; and the other studies reported in this volume), and this has led to rapid and exciting developments in refining and redefining washback. Even in a doctoral research, such as this, empirical methods of data collection can lead to promising discoveries within an established paradigm.

Above all, this study demonstrates the importance of complementary qualitative and quantitative data collection, as well as an acceptance that not all will go as planned. Flaws in the study and unexpected results led this researcher to analyze and re-analyze the data in an attempt to understand them. Thus, the comments from the survey became the basis of the interviews. The realization of the similarity between the groups of respondents to the interview question concerning the causality of change led to the hypotheses, which formed the basis of the observations. And the discovery of the patterns in the teacher responses led, finally, to the proposed new model for washback.

APPENDIX: THE INTERVIEW QUESTIONS

In all these questions, assessment of CSWE means the kind of assessment that teachers undertake within the framework of the CSWE, in order to inform their teaching and ultimately report on their students' achievement.

1. I want to ask you about the extent to which you use competency-based assessment of the CSWE in your classroom. Could you please describe your use of competency-based assessment of CSWE in your classroom? When you describe it, please think about the following questions. (a) How often do you use it? (b) In what ways do you use it?

2. Do you think the implementation of the assessment of CSWE has been positive or negative or both? In what ways?

3. Change has sometimes been described like this: "change can be very deep, striking at the core of learned skills and beliefs and conceptions of education, and creating doubts about purposes, sense of competence, and self-concept." (Fullan with Stiegelbauer 1991, p. 45) To what extent do you think this describes the implementation of the assessment of CSWE? Why?

4. Now I am going to ask you about some of the ways that some teachers said their teaching had changed since the implementation of the assessment of CSWE.

(a) In what ways have the structure and organization of your classroom changed since the implementation of assessment of CSWE?

(b) Has the implementation of assessment of CSWE led to your using any different teaching methods? (*If yes*) How are they different? Why did do you think this change happened? **or**

(*If no*) Why do you think your teaching methods did not change? [prompt repeated 4c–4e]

(c) Has the implementation of assessment of CSWE led to your using any different teaching materials?

(d) Have you observed any other changes in your own behavior as a teacher since the implementation of assessment of CSWE?

(e) Have you observed any changes in your students' behavior since the implementation of assessment of CSWE?

(f) Have you observed any (other) changes in your classroom, which you feel, have been brought about by the implementation of the assessment of the CSWE? (*If so*) could you please describe and explain them?

5. (*If yes to any of the above:*) Thinking back on the answers you have just given, do you think these changes are the direct result of the implementation of the assessment of CSWE?

6. Is there anything you would like to add?

CHAPTER

8

Teacher Factors Mediating Washback

Yoshinori Watanabe
Akita National University

The Japanese university entrance examination is an emotionally charged issue. Some people claim that it is a necessary evil only, useful for screening out the students, and if the system were to be eliminated, admission being given to all the students who wish to go to higher education, our education would become far better than it is now. Others argue that without the entrance examination, no students would study seriously. Indeed, a review of various opinions reported in the mass media in the past 10 years (Watanabe, 1997a) produced more than 500 claims, assertions, and anecdotes, the majority of which (approximately 80%) were concerned with negative aspects of the examination, with the only exception that the examination may motivate students (e.g., Ogawa, 1981; Vogel, 1979). In spite of this large number of claims, however, they may be summarized by referring to only a few common, underlying assumptions. First, it seems to be taken for granted that the university entrance examination drives students and teachers to do something undesirable, such as teaching of test-taking techniques, overreliance on grammar-translation, neglect of aural/oral aspects of English, a limited variety of classroom organization patterns, such as teacher-fronted or lock-step, etc. (e.g., Ministry of Education, Science and Culture, 1992; Nagano, 1984; Reischauer, Kobayashi, & Naya, 1989). An obvious corollary of this is the act of blaming the absence of particular skills in the examination for a particular skill being not taught in the classroom, with reference to listening in particular (JACET, 1993; Shiozawa, 1983), leading to underuse of English in aural/oral modes. The second assumption goes in a different direction from the first: One takes note of an undesirable educational practice, such as teaching with overemphasis on formal aspects of English rather than its use, and attributes its cause to the presence of the examination, in which, it is claimed, formal aspects are unduly emphasized.

However, the validity of these assumptions seems to have been rarely called into question. To date, a series of attempts have been made by the Ministry of Education to improve education through innovations in the university entrance examination system, but they seem to have not been as successful as might have been expected (Amano, 1990). One likely reason may be that those undertakings have been made capitalizing on sets of unproven assumptions. In this type of situation, the question to be asked is "Is the examination washback really so negative?" rather than "Does washback exist?" (Alderson & Wall, 1993).

Although a few studies have been undertaken to examine the washback of the entrance examination of various school subjects, they do not seem to provide us with a reliable set of information. Some of these studies were based only on the data showing what they say they are doing rather than what they are actually doing (Ariyoshi & Senba, 1983; Saito, Arita, & Nasu, 1984), whereas others examined the students after they had gone through the examinations rather than during the preparation process (Berwick & Ross, 1989; Takano, 1992). A notable exception is Rohlen (1983), who observed the classroom where the examination preparation is conducted. However, regrettably, as his research was not focused on the examination influence per se, it did not involve close analyses of the examination papers.

Based on a critique of these research studies, Watanabe (1996b) investigated the effect of the university entrance examination on the prevalent use of the grammar-translation method in Japan. His analyses of examinations of English in the past, classroom observations and interviews with teachers showed very little relationship between the test content and the use of this particular teaching methodology in the classroom. Rather, teacher factors, including personal beliefs, past education, and academic background, seemed to be more important in determining the methodology a teacher employs. This result is not uncommon in contexts other than Japan. The body of empirical research to date suggests that innovation in testing does not automatically bring about improvement in education. Among those findings relatively well-established are that "tests have impact on *what* teachers teach but not on *how* they teach" (Wall & Alderson, 1993, p. 68); the degree of washback varies over time in accordance with the status of the test (low or high stakes), the status of the language being tested, the purpose of the test, the format of the test, and skills tested (Shohamy, Donitsa-Schmidt, & Ferman, 1996); "the existence of a test by itself does not guarantee washback . . . tests will have different amounts and types of washback on some teachers and learners than on other teachers and learners" (Alderson & Hamp-Lyons, 1996, pp. 295–296); and, the examination does not influence teachers' fundamental beliefs and attitudes about teaching and learning, the role of teachers and students, and how teaching and learning should be carried out (Cheng, 1997, 1999). In summary, then, the examination may be only one of those factors that "affect how innovations succeed or fail and that influence teacher (and pupil) behaviors" (Wall & Alderson, 1993, p. 68), or a necessary but not a sufficient condition (Wall, 1999).

This chapter reports on the results of the research into the washback effect of the English language component of the Japanese university entrance examination on instruction. Part of this project has already been published elsewhere (Watanabe, 1996b, 1997a, 2000). This chapter is based on the results reported in Watanabe (1997a), but as the original was written in Japanese, it was felt to be important to present the study for a non-Japanese audience. The present chapter also expands on the previous report, in that it aims to identify a range of teacher factors that may be involved in the process of producing washback.

UNIVERSITY ENTRANCE EXAMINATIONS AND ELT IN JAPAN

The Japanese school year runs from April 1 to the end of March. The entrance examinations of most universities are administered during the period of January to February. There are more than 1,000 colleges and universities in Japan, approximately half of which are 2-year junior colleges, the other half being 4-year universities and colleges. Because there is no school-leaving exam, and because high school records are not given much weight, the entrance examinations are likely to be very high-stakes for the applicants.

There are three major types of university in Japan (i.e., national, local public, and private). National/local public universities on one hand and private universities on the other employ different screening procedures. National/local public universities require the applicants to go through two stages. First, they sit for the examination designed by the National Center for University Entrance Examinations (NCUEE), and at the second stage they take the test that each institution has created. Unlike national/local public universities, private institutions enjoy greater freedom in their screening procedures. Some institutions employ a two-stage screening system, whereas most of the others employ a "one-shot" examination system, in which they select students using their own examination. In addition to the variety of the selection procedures, most of the universities employ the recommendation system. In this system, the universities offer places to those students who have gained sufficient overall academic grades at high school. Such students used to be totally exempted from the examination, but as the number of the recommendees have increased, some form of screening examination is now required.

Each department of each university produces its own test and offers it on its own campus, except the NCUEE, which is employed as a first-stage examination for national/local public universities. The test dates of each university differ, so students have more than one opportunity to take the tests. It is common, then, that the students rank several universities, one as first-choice, another as second-choice, and so forth, according to the prestige of the institutions, and their difficulty levels. With only a few exceptions, virtually all universities require English or other foreign languages, such as German and French. However, the content and method of the examinations vary greatly among different universities. The NCUEE includes pronunciation, vocabulary, grammar, and reading, all of which consist of objective items. As if making up for the NCUEE, the second-stage examinations of national/local public universities consist of subjective items, including translation of English into Japanese, Japanese into English, writing, and so forth. The private university examinations exhibit even greater variety in their test contents and methods; some examinations include grammar, vocabulary, and reading, whereas others also include listening and writing. The items of these tests may consist of cloze, short-answer, multiple-choice, picture description, and a number of other varieties.

The information concerning the examination of any subject, such as scoring methods, weighting of each section, etc. is not made public except for the NCUEE, so the exam papers of past years become important sources of information for those who are preparing for the examinations. In addition to various private and public high schools, there are special exam preparatory schools, called *yobiko* and *juku*, and these schools not only prepare students for the examination, but provide the information which they obtain through meticulous analyses of the past exam papers.

The role of English is gradually changing in Japan. English is used to be a means of gaining access to high culture through the written language (Henrichsen, 1989), but now, in response to the need for international communication, there is a greater emphasis on active language use involving exchange of both spoken and written information. Nevertheless, the goal of EFL in the national curriculum does not seem to have been settled yet. In 1989, Henrichsen (1989) observed that "the debate between those who advocate the 'practical' objectives of oral English study and those who defend the traditional 'cultural' purpose of language study, which is more closely allied with the nature of the examinations, is a long standing one and has not yet been resolved" (p. 178). The debate is still going on. Given this greater emphasis on the teaching and learning of English as a genuine life skill, the EFL component of the university entrance examinations has been criticized for its lack of communicative content. There is a need for research into the washback effect of the English component of the examination in such a situation.

THE RESEARCH

Predictions

Based on the review of general public opinions presented at the beginning of this chapter, it was predicted that the lessons of high schools, their special exam preparatory courses in particular, would be characterized by the following "undesirable" teaching activities, indicating negative washback: frequent reference to the examinations; overreliance on grammar-translation methods; detailed explanations of formal structures of English rather than its use in actual communicative situations; little use of English aurally/orally; and a limited variety of classroom organization patterns (i.e., lockstep). There would be, however, an indication of the presence of positive washback in the form of students being motivated by the examinations.

Selection of the Participants

Classroom observations were conducted to examine the validity of the predictions. For this purpose, an attempt was made to find a type of senior high schools, from which a substantial number of students had been accepted to prestigious universities each year. Those schools that finally took part in the research widely varied in terms of their backgrounds (Table 8.1), but had in common that they all offered special exam preparatory courses.

Data Collection Procedures

From these schools, a total of five teachers took part in the study: Two teachers (Teachers A and B) were from High school A, one (Teacher C) from High school T, and two (Teachers E and F) from High school I. A total of 964 minutes of observations were carried out between June, 1994 and November, 1994. Prior to the observations, interviews were conducted with the teachers to gather information regarding their school backgrounds (Table 8.2). The teachers were informed of the purpose of the research in advance, but they were not asked about their attitudes toward the entrance examination, lest their awareness should unduly be raised, "polluting" their teaching. During the observations, various classroom events were recorded on a note-taking sheet, consisting of broad categories, such as "time," "material," "what teacher is saying/doing," "what students are saying/doing," "what is written on chalkboard," and "the observer's comments and ques-

TABLE 8.1
School Backgrounds

	High School A	High School T	High School I
Location			
	Rural	Rural	Urban
Total number of students			
	~1,400	~1,000	~700
Rate of students going to higher education			
	99%	95%	100%
Availability of yobiko nearby			
	A few	Very few	Quite a few
Target universities majority of students aiming at and having been accepted			
	National universities in the area and prestigious private universities in Tokyo area.	National universities in the area and middle-ranked private universities in Tokyo and Osaka areas.	Prestigious private universities in Tokyo area.
Academic ranking			
	High/Middle	Above average	Very high
Exam preparation class			
	Grades 2 and 3	Grades 2 and 3	Grade 3
Other			
	Typical co-educational Japanese high school; all students Japanese; three native speakers of English teachers	Holds annual English speech contest, international music contest; invites students from overseas; three native speakers of English teachers	~60% of students are returnees who graduated from overseas schools

Notes. ~ = approximately. Osaka = the second largest city in Japan. Yobiko = a special exam preparatory school.

tions" (see Appendix A). Also, the whole lesson was audio-recorded. Immediately after each observation, while the memory was still fresh, the field notes were completed by listening to the audio recording. The observer's impressions of the lesson were also written in the margins of the field note. Subsequently the field notes were summarized in the form of narrative vignettes, to remember the situations clearly and the flow of discourse at the stage of quantitative data analyses. Upon completion of each observation, each teacher was asked about his or her intentions behind a variety of classroom activities. Both pre- and postobservation discussions were conducted in Japanese, the transcriptions of which were subsequently summarized in English.

Data Analysis Procedures

The collected data sets subsequently served for frequency analyses. To this end, a special coding sheet was constructed. The sheet consisted of several categories, representing various aspects of classroom discourse, which

TABLE 8.2
Classroom Characteristics and Other Observations

School	*A*				*T*		*I*			
Teacher	*A*		*B*		*C*		*E*		*F*	
Age										
	Middle 30s		Early 40s		Early 50s		Middle 50s		Late 20s	
Purpose										
	R	E	R	E	R	E	R	E	R	E
Date of observation										
	June		June		June		September		November	
Class size										
	~45	~45	~45	5	~45	~45	~25	~20	~25	~20
Seat arrangement										
	IR	IR	IR	IR	HS	HS	HS	HS	HS	HS
Grade										
	3	3	2	2	3	3	2	3	3	2
Number of sessions observed										
	2	2	2	2	2	2	1	1	1	1
Total observation time recorded (in minutes)										
	79	79	56	77	98	80	47	47	50	48

Notes. R = Regular mainstream lesson. E = Special exam preparation lesson. ~ = approximately. HS = horse-shoe shape; IR = In rows.

emerged in the process of analyzing the field notes. These sets of categories were subsequently formulated into a form of coding sheet (Appendix B), modeled on the COLT observation scheme (Spada & Froehlich, 1995). Coding was carried out on the sheet by listening to the audio recording. To analyze the data to test predictions, one category was combined with another, deriving the following set:

(a) *Reference to examinations:* frequency of referring to test-taking techniques; frequency of predicting future test questions

(b) *Grammar-translation:* frequency of using metalanguage; frequency of translation at word, phrase, clause, and sentence levels

(c) *Focus on form:* frequency of teacher's feedback to students' utterances with focus on form; frequency of explanation of sentence structures

(d) *Aural/oral aspects of English:* length of time spent on formal listening practice; frequency of oral practice at word, phrase, clause, and sentence levels; frequency of utterances made in English to exchange genuine information (e.g., giving instructions, etc.) rather than mechanical oral practice (e.g., reading aloud from the text, etc.)

(e) *Request for information by students:* frequency of students' asking questions, asking for repetition, etc. (as observable evidence of students' motivation)

(f) *Classroom organization patterns:* length of time spent on lock-step (i.e., teacher-fronted), pair-work, group-work, oral presentation by students, and individual seat work.

Results

Results are provided in Tables 8.3 and 8.4. These tables show that indeed there were cases in which the predicted types of negative washback were present. For example, Teacher A referred to test-taking techniques 14 times in his exam preparatory lessons, while none in his regular lessons (Table 8.4). Aural/oral aspects of English seemed to have been neglected in his exam preparatory courses (Table 8.4). A similar tendency was also observed in Teacher B's classes. However, what may strike us most perhaps is that there were very few cases where the predicted types of negative washback were present. Closer analyses of the results indicate that even those cases where negative washback appeared to be present may actually not have been caused by the examination alone. For example, Table 8.3 shows that, overall, only a few types of classroom organization pattern were employed in exam classes, but this was also the case in regular lessons. This result may be interpreted as indicating that the regular lessons

TABLE 8.3
Classroom Organization Patterns

School	*A*		*T*	*I*		
Teacher	*A*	*B*	*C*	*E*	*F*	*Total*
Lock step						
Exam	51 (64%)	56 (84%)	26 (33%)	47 (100%)	28 (59%)	208 (65%)
Regular	57 (73%)	38 (67%)	73 (75%)	47 (100%)	24 (50%)	239 (72%)
Pair work						
Exam	1 (1%)	0 (0%)	3 (4%)	0 (0%)	0 (0%)	4 (1%)
Regular	12 (15%)	0 (0%)	5 (5%)	0 (0%)	2 (5%)	19 (6%)
Group work						
Exam	0 (0%)	0 (0%)	0 (0%)	0 (0%)	0 (0%)	0 (0%)
Regular	0 (0%)	0 (0%)	0 (0%)	0 (0%)	0 (0%)	0 (0%)
Oral presentation by students						
Exam	0 (0%)	0 (0%)	3 (4%)	0 (0%)	0 (0%)	3 (0%)
Regular	0 (0%)	0 (0%)	20 (20%)	0 (0%)	0 (0%)	20 (6%)
Individual seat work						
Exam	27 (34%)	11 (16%)	48 (60%)	0 (0%)	20 (42%)	106 (33%)
Regular	10 (13%)	19 (33%)	0 (0%)	0 (0%)	22 (46%)	51 (15%)
Total observation time recorded (in minutes)						
Exam	79	67	80	47	48	833
Regular	79	57	98	47	50	964

Note. The length of time is in minutes. The figures in parentheses indicate the total amount of time shared within the total lesson time. Adapted from Watanabe (1997b).

TABLE 8.4
Aspects of Classroom Discourse

School	*A*		*T*	*I*		*Total*
Teacher	*A*	*B*	*C*	*E*	*F*	
Frequency of reference to test taking techniques (frequency of utterance per minute)						
Exam	14 (.18)	2 (.03)	1 (.02)	1 (.02)	0 (.00)	18 (.06)
Regular	0 (.00)	1 (.02)	0 (.00)	0 (.00)	2 (.04)	3 (.01)
Grammar-translation (1) Frequency of using metalanguage (frequency per minute)						
Exam	8 (.10)	65 (.97)	5 (.06)	7 (.15)	5 (.10)	90 (.28)
Regular	22 (.22)	22 (.39)	0 (.00)	68 (1.45)	1 (.02)	113 (.34)
Grammar-translation (2) Frequency of translation at phrase, clause, sentence levels (per minute)						
Exam	47 (.59)	13 (.19)	15 (.19)	19 (.40)	3 (.06)	130 (.40)
Regular	53 (.67)	12 (.21)	0 (.00)	10 (.21)	9 (.18)	84 (.25)
Focus on form (1) Frequency of teacher feedback to student's utterance (frequency per minute)						
Exam	0 (.00)	2 (.03)	0 (.00)	1 (.02)	0 (.00)	3 (.01)
Regular	2 (.03)	1 (.02)	0 (.00)	0 (.00)	0 (.00)	3 (.01)
Focus on form (2) Frequency of explanation of structure of English (per minute)						
Exam	20 (.25)	39 (.58)	2 (.23)	8 (.17)	4 (.08)	73 (.23)
Regular	16 (.20)	24 (.42)	0 (.00)	43 (.91)	0 (.00)	83 (.25)
Aural/oral aspects of English (1) Length of listening practice expressed in minutes (percentage share of the time devoted to this practice within total lesson time)						
Exam	0 (0%)	0 (0%)	48 (60%)	0 (0%)	0 (0%)	48 (15%)
Regular	0 (0%)	0 (0%)	0 (0%)	0 (0%)	22 (46%)	22 (7%)
Aural/oral aspects of English (2) Mechanical oral practice; i.e., choral, reading aloud (per minute)						
Exam	43 (.54)	94 (1.40)	102 (1.28)	73 (1.55)	27 (.56)	339 (1.06)
Regular	93 (1.18)	123 (2.16)	182 (1.86)	90 (1.91)	39 (.78)	527 (1.59)
Language: Frequency of utterances made to exchange genuine information						
English (percentage of turns that were made in English within the total amount of turns)						
Exam	12 (10%)	15 (16%)	69 (88%)	31 (28%)	3 (7%)	130 (30%)
Regular	2 (2%)	27 (40%)	90 (100%)	36 (27%)	4 (10%)	159 (38%)
Japanese (percentage of turns that were made in Japanese within the total amount of turns)						
Exam	103 (90%)	76 (84%)	9 (12%)	79 (72%)	39 (93%)	306 (70%)
Regular	90 (98%)	40 (60%)	9 (0%)	97 (73%)	35 (90%)	262 (62%)
Frequency of request for information by students						
Exam	2 (.03)	0 (.00)	1 (.01)	12 (.26)	0 (.00)	15 (.05)
Regular	1 (.01)	1 (.02)	1 (.01)	14 (.30)	11 (.22)	28 (.08)
Total observation time recorded in minutes						
Exam	79	67	80	47	48	833
Regular	79	57	98	47	50	964

Note. Adapted from Watanabe (1997b).

were already negatively influenced by the examination. Indeed, there were several cases in Table 8.4 that appear to support this argument. For instance, the frequency of students' request for information was very low overall. There were also individual cases like the one of Teacher B, who explained structural aspects of English with almost equal frequency in both regular and exam lessons. It should also be noted that there were several categories in the lessons of some teachers in which even reverse tendencies were observed to the predictions. For instance, Teachers A and E used metalanguage more frequently in their regular than in their exam preparatory lessons, whereas Teacher F translated more frequently in his regular lessons than in exam lessons.

It should further be noted that there were cases where there was a diametrically opposite tendency to the one that had been predicted, which could be interpreted as indicating the presence of positive washback. Though there were very few lessons where listening practice was conducted, Teacher C was using a listening exercise in his exam class, devoting 60% of the total lesson time to this activity. This teacher was also using English to exchange authentic information with students very frequently. Although the frequency was lower in regular lessons than in exam lessons, the rate was still very high compared with other teachers' lessons. The frequency of aural/oral exercises also seems to have been very high overall, though the practice tended to be mechanical tasks, consisting of choral repetition and reading aloud from text.

It is interesting to note at this point that Teacher C, whose lessons seemed to be innovative compared with other teachers, was teaching at a school located in a rural area, where there were very few supporting private schools, such as *yobiko* (exam preparatory school), so "students placed total reliance upon the school for the exam preparation," according to the ESL coordinator of this high school. As Table 8.1 shows, however, this school held a variety of school activities, inviting overseas students, holding international concerts, and so forth. This type of school atmosphere may have positively influenced their exam classes as well.

It is certainly not possible to understand the complete complexity of these results. Nevertheless, it could be tentatively concluded that the presence of the entrance examination caused only some types of negative washback (in the sense expressed in a variety of public opinions) to only some aspects of some teachers' lessons. It may also be possible to add that there was some indication of the presence of positive washback in the way in which the teachers could make use of the exam preparation as a chance to improve their students' proficiency in English for authentic or actual language use situations. Despite the limited range of evidence, it would be possible to reformulate a part of the 15 Washback Hypotheses (Alderson & Wall, 1993, pp. 120–121) as "a test produces different types of washback to different teachers: it influences some teachers negatively while others positively." Inasmuch as the major purpose of washback research is to gather information to help show us how to make the best use of tests to engineer beneficial washback, the next question to be asked is why some aspects of some teachers' lessons were negatively influenced by the examination, whereas other aspects of other teachers' lessons were positively influenced.

INTERPRETATION OF THE RESULTS

It is certainly not possible to understand the whole range of teachers' intentions behind their teaching activities, partly because it took a long time to analyze the data to return to the teachers with the results for their reactions. Nevertheless, in-depth analyses of the information gained in pre- and postobservation interviews seem to indicate that several teacher factors were involved in the process of engineering washback, whether negative or positive.

The first factor is teachers' concerns for students' proficiency levels. Teacher B was using grammar exercises consisting of past examination questions, because he felt his students were "weak in this particular skill area." Teacher C, who was using listening exercises taken from the past exam papers in his exam classes, explained that he was "using them to improve students' test-taking skills as well as listening skills that are usable in real-life situations." As was noted at the beginning of this chapter, the number of the university examinations that included listening was limited, and the target examinations of this teacher's students were no exception. However, the number of such examinations seemed not to matter to this teacher, who was also innovative in his exam classes by employing pair-work, because he wanted to "give students chances to deepen their understanding of the English text by discussing their answers with other students." Teacher E was using grammar exercises of past exam papers, because he "felt that the returnee students, who graduated from overseas high schools, were lacking in the grammatical ability; I believe that the past exam grammar questions are helpful for them." Teacher F was using a listening exercise taken from a past exam paper, as he was "allowed to use any material in this class, and the Todai (the University of Tokyo) listening test is of an ideal level for my students." This teacher modified the original version of the listening test in his own way, making up a new exercise. During his lesson one student quipped, "I like your version better than the original exam paper." None of the teachers denied the importance of exam preparation, but the common concern shared among all the teachers was how to improve students' proficiency levels in exam classes. To engineer positive washback, then, it may be important to understand the students' levels of proficiency and set a classroom task at an appropriate level, so that the task may be slightly more challenging but not too challenging, to motivate students at an appropriate level (Csikszentmihalyi, 1992; Watanabe, 2001). For this purpose, it is important to monitor students' development on a regular basis. The schools would have students take practice tests regularly, but most of the teachers said that the purpose was to develop students' test-taking skills. The practice test should be constructed to measure students' proficiency as well.

Second, the teachers may be placing undue blame on the presence of the examination for what they are doing; blame which seems to be based on their perceptions, which might not accurately reflect the actual contents of the examinations. Teachers A and B claimed that teaching vocabulary, idioms, and structure is particularly important for exam preparation. These teachers said that they were preparing their students for the exams of prestigious private universities in metropolitan areas, such as Tokyo and Osaka, and those of prestigious national/local public universities in the area where each school was located. However, an analysis of the examinations of these universities revealed that only 25% included these skills in an independent section, at least in the 2 years prior to the research (i.e., 1992 & 1993; see Watanabe, 1997a for details). Thus, these teachers may have been overemphasizing these skills based on their biased perceptions. One difficulty with teaching exam classes certainly lies in the fact that the teaching should be effective for passing the examination as well as for developing language skills usable in real life situations. Vocabulary, idioms, and structures are certainly important for such authentic language use, so it does not seem to be justifiable to claim that these are only important for developing test taking abilities. Interestingly, Teacher F, who was not emphasizing formal aspects of English in his lessons, shared a similar view with Teachers A and B, who frequently referred to the structure of the language; that is, Teacher F claimed that "it is important to teach grammar in exam classes." Teacher F even went so far as to say that he felt guilty when teaching test-taking techniques. Also he regretted that he did not have "time enough to teach cultural contents in exam classes." But it may be that the cultural knowledge helps students to pass the examination as well as to improve their real life language use ability. Teachers seem to be holding various unproven assumptions, which may hinder the generation of beneficial washback.

Third, the degree of teachers' familiarity with a range of teaching methods might be a factor mediating the process of producing washback. For instance, Teacher A, who was using translation more frequently than other teachers, said that he was using this method "since it is a handy method to keep students' attention high." Teacher B said "if I were asked to teach listening for exam classes, I would get lost since I do not know much about teaching listening effectively." Teacher E claimed, "it's difficult to employ other methods than the one by which I was taught when I was a student." One school coordinator said, "teachers of this school are wondering what is the best way of teaching students for examinations as well as developing their English ability that can be used in actual life contexts," and added, "the number of students accepted to prestigious universities is important for the prestige of the school." It seems to be crucial then to identify empirically a range of effective teaching methods to improve authentic or real life language skills as well as to help students pass the examination.

To summarize the foregoing discussion:

1. What is reported in the mass media (as reviewed earlier is this paper) does not seem to be reflecting accurately what is actually happening in the classroom. The reality is far more complex. Indeed, the lessons of some teachers were characterized by the negative influence of the examinations (e.g., focus on formal aspects of English, reliance on the grammar-translation method, etc.), but others were not (e.g., using exam materials for developing students' authentic language ability that is usable in actual communicative situations).

2. Not surprisingly, there are various reasons behind what teachers are doing. Even when they are using exam-related materials, such as exercises taken from past exam papers, they may not necessarily have exam preparation in mind.

3. Teachers' psychological factors seem to be involved in mediating the process of washback coming into the classroom; for example, putting undue blame on the examination may be functioning as a debilitating factor, while familiarity with a wide range of teaching methods may be a facilitating factor.

4. School cultures may also be involved as a mediating factor. A positive school atmosphere which helps students improve their authentic foreign language skills may transfer to exam classes.

These results seem to imply that in order to induce beneficial washback from the university entrance examination, different types of problems need to be solved at individual, school and societal levels (Wall, 1999). However, the research into washback to date implies that an attempt to innovate in education could not be successful simply by changing the examination system. If this type of top-down approach does not work, then a more appropriate approach would be the one that starts at the level of individual teachers. As Fullan (1998) suggested in his innovation theory, "change is a highly personal psychological process" (p. 255). This may necessitate a type of teacher training, preservice or in-service, based on the idea of "action research," which is defined as "a form of *collective* self-reflective enquiry undertaken by participants in social situations in order to improve the rationality and justice of their own social or educational practices, as well as their understanding of these practices and the situations in which these practices are carried out" (Kemmis & McTaggart, 1988, p. 5).

Although what this type of teacher training should include remains to be explored, the present research suggests that it would need to incorporate a course in which teachers are provided with a variety of teaching methods involving various test tasks. However, since a range of psychological factors seem to be playing an important role in engineering beneficial washback, familiarity with teaching methods alone would not be sufficient. One important course that would need to be included in the teacher training may be a type of "re-attribution training." The importance of taking account of the attribution theory of motivation in the research into washback is suggested by Alderson and Wall (1993). This theory holds that people tend to refer to four main sets of attributions for their perceived successes and failures in life: (a) ability, (b) effort, (c) luck, (d) the perceived difficulty of the task with which they are faced" (Williams & Burden, 1997, p. 105). These attributions are placed on two dimensions: internal (ability and effort) or external (luck and task difficulty), and controllable (effort and difficulty) or uncontrollable (ability and luck). It is important to note that "individuals will vary in the way in which they personally view these attributions" (Williams & Burden, 1997, p. 105). Thus, different combination of these may lead to different action outcomes. One role of attribution training would then be to help teachers to change their tendency to attribute examinations, from being seen as "external" "uncontrollable" factors to being seen as "internal" "controllable" factors. Several constructive suggestions were made during the teacher interviews. For instance, Teacher A suggested that scoring methods and criteria of subjective tests be made public. If there is a system in which policymakers are able to respond to this type of request, and incorporate them in the development of the future test, it may help teachers to place the test on a controllable dimension rather than on an uncontrollable one. This is only one type of suggestion that has been made with respect to the Japanese university entrance examination system. Nevertheless, in principle, it would be applicable to any situation where tests are used to make important decisions.

In a context like this, the question the test developer needs to consider is "what would an examination have to look like to encourage teachers to change their way of teaching" (Wall, 1999, p. 724), also called "face validity by appearance" in the sense defined by Mosier (1947). He holds that in "the interests of the acceptability of the test to those most intimately concerned with its use, it is highly desirable that a test possess not only statistical validity, but also, as an added attribute, the appearance of practicality (*appearance*)"(Mosier, 1947, p. 205). In other words, when we come to think of washback, the important test quality may not only be the validity and reliability of the psychometric tradition, nor the notion of "consequential validity" (Messick, 1989), but a type of "face validity" understood from the viewpoint of the test users. It is in this sense that important insights may be gained from the study of authenticity or "the degree of correspondence of the characteristics of a given language test task to the features of a TLU [target language use] task" (Bachman & Palmer, 1996, p. 23). In this regard, Lewkowicz (2000) rightly asked the following question: "Will perceived authenticity impact on classroom practices and if so, in what way(s)?" (p. 52).

Much more research is needed to answer this type of question, so we can deepen our understanding of the nature of washback.

CONCLUSION

There is optimism that the entrance examination system in Japan could become obsolete in the near future, since a declining birth rate here will make it possible that all students will be accepted to universities. Meanwhile, there is an attempt by a group of policymakers to lobby for the elimination of the system. As if predicting the current situation of Japan, Glaser asserted that it "seems clear that we are over the threshold in the transition from education as a highly selective enterprise to one that is focused on developing an entire population of educated people. A selective system is no longer the prevalent educational demand" (Glaser, 1981, as cited in Johnston, 1989, p. 509). However, since the divisions between universities of different rank are regarded as being very important by people in Japan, and there is a widespread belief that entering renowned universities guarantees a better career after graduation, it is not very likely that the examinations will readily be discarded. What is needed in such a situation is rational argument based on empirical evidence indicating the actual power of the examinations, whether negative or positive. The present chapter is one attempt to cast light to this issue.

Author's note:

A set of bills to turn national universities into independent administrative institutions was approved at the Diet on July 9, 2003, when this paper was almost completed. The legislation will come into force on April 1, 2004. The Japanese national universities will be undergoing substantial changes in the years to come. However, very little argument has been made about the issue of innovation in the entrance examination system, except that an approval has also recently been made that the NCUEE will include a listening test as one of its components from 2006. Nevertheless, the system described in this chapter will hold as it is at least for the next several years to come.

Appendix A

OBSERVATION NOTE-TAKING SHEET

PAGE /

DATE / /

STARTS AT ____________

NAME OF SCHOOL ________________________

ENDS AT ____________

CLASS ID ______________________ GRADE __________

EXAM/ REGULAR/ PRIVATE/ NATIONAL

NO OF STUDENTS IN CLASS ______

LESSON ID ____________________

OTHER INFORMATION:

TIME	MATERIAL	TEACHER	STUDENT/S	ON BOARD	COMMENT/QUESTION

Appendix B

CODING SHEET A Version 2 8/10/1995 (c) Y.Watanabe

School: Teacher: Course:

Date of observation / /

Regular/Exam prep. Total time: minutes

Date of coding / /

Time	Organization patterns						Materials													Memo
										Reading										
	teacher-fronted	individual seat work	pair work	groups work	students presentation		Listening (direct)	Speaking (indirect)	Pronunciation (indreict)	Translation	Summary	Gap-filling	Multiple-choice	Visual response	Writing (translation)	Writing (direct)	Grammar/word usage	Vocabulary	

Appendix B

CODING SHEET B Version 2 8/10/1995 (c) Y.Watanabe

Total time: minutes Date of observation / / Date of coding / /

Teacher's turn																		Student/s' turn																				Topic				
Interaction								Levels			Activity							Interaction								Levels			Activity													
Request		Giving		React		Language								translation		summary		Request		Giving		React		Language								translation		summary				Language			Exam	
pseudo	genuine	predit	unpredict.	form	message	Japanese	English	ultra-minimal	minimal	extended discourse	choral	read aloud	paraphrase	E -> J	J -> E	in Japanese	in English	pseudo	genuine	predit	unpredict.	form	message	Japanese	English	ultra-minimal	minimal	extended discourse	choral	read aloud	paraphrase	E -> J	J -> E	in Japanese	in English	Listening	Writing	Form	Sociol/pragm	Coherence	Test-wiseness	Test-taking exp.

CHAPTER

9

The Washback Effect of a Public Examination Change on Teachers' Perceptions Toward Their Classroom Teaching

Liying Cheng
Queen's University

Changes in testing underpinned by a belief that assessment can leverage educational change have often led to top-down educational reforms designed to bring about changes in teaching and learning through changes in testing (Hong Kong Examinations Authority, 1994b; Noble & Smith, 1994a, 1994b; see also chaps. 1 and 3 in this volume). This chapter focuses on changes in one of many facets of teaching and learning, which could potentially be influenced by testing—teachers' perceptions on selected aspects of teaching derived from a large study in relation to washback (Cheng, 1998a). In particular, this chapter looks closely at the influence of a new examination on teachers' perceptions.

Over the past decade, an increasing number of research studies have been conducted particularly within the English as a second/foreign language (ESL/EFL) context to investigate the multifaceted nature and the mechanism of washback effects of language testing on aspects of teaching and learning. There is convincing evidence to suggest that examinations, especially high-stakes tests, have powerful washback effects on teaching and learning within different educational contexts (Andrews & Fullilove, 1997; Burrows, 1999; Cheng, 1998a; Lam, 1993; Scaramucci, 1999; Shohamy, Donitsa-Schmidt, & Ferman, 1996; Watanabe, 1997b).

However, these effects occur to a different extent in relation to different individuals and different aspects of teaching and learning within a specific educational context (Alderson & Hamp-Lyons, 1996). In particular, language tests are seen to have a more direct washback effect on teaching content rather than teaching methodology (Cheng, 1999; Wall & Alderson, 1993). In their study of washback on TOEFL preparation courses, Alderson and Hamp-Lyons (1996) found that the TOEFL affects both what and how teachers teach, but the effect is not to the same in degree or kind from teacher to teacher, and the simple difference of TOEFL versus non-TOEFL teaching did not explain why the teachers taught the way they did. It is undeniable that the actual teaching and learning situation is much more complicated than the linear ideas of bringing about changes in teaching and learning through changes in testing. As a result, washback studies have expanded to look at issues of context and research methodology in order to capture the complexity of washback. Specific educational contexts and testing cultures within which washback studies are carried out have also emerged as a significant factor in these studies (Bush, 1998; Read, 1999). Research methods for conducting washback studies have also been discussed more in the research literature (Bailey, 1999; Cheng, 2001; chap. 2, this volume).

In spite of the growing literature on washback, there is relatively little empirical research in this area. We still have little ability to predict the conditions under which various types of washback are most likely to be induced by testing within a particular educational context, and the ways in which context and washback co-construct each other. In order to further our understanding, we need to look at the phenomenon in a specific education setting by investigating in depth different aspects of teaching and learning. Only by putting the different pieces of investigation together can we fully understand the complex issues that shape the relationship between testing, teaching, and learning in a classroom setting.

The current study adopted the aforementioned approach within the context of the Hong Kong secondary school system, to investigate whether changes to an examination would actually change different aspects of teaching and learning—washback intensity—and to what extent the intended washback was realized. For the past two decades, the Hong Kong Examinations Authority (HKEA) has made consistent efforts to bring about positive washback effects on teaching and learning by means of major changes to public examinations. In particular, much thought has been given to how the examination process can be used to bring about positive and constructive change to the teaching and learning of English in the education system (Hong Kong Examinations Authority, 1994b). In Hong Kong, many of the major innovations in education in recent years have been designed with the expectation that changes to the examinations will help classroom teachers to maintain a better balance between teaching and skill-building on the one hand, and examination preparation on the other.

In Hong Kong, English language teaching is moving toward a target- and task-based approach to curriculum and assessment. In 1993, the HKEA introduced major changes to its existing English examination, the Hong Kong

Certificate Examinations in English (HKCEE). This examination is taken by secondary students at the end of the fifth year (Form 5) of secondary school. After that, students either proceed to further studies at the sixth form level or leave school and seek employment.

The major changes to the examination (the 1996 HKCEE[1]) were reflected in: (a) an integrated *Listening, Reading, and Writing* Paper requiring students to select from and make use of information they hear/or read to carry out a variety of short and extended tasks; and (b) an increase in the weighting of the *Oral* Paper from 10% on the old HKCEE to 18% on the new (Hong Kong Examinations Authority, 1993, 1994a; see Appendix A). The intention was to improve the current English language teaching and learning standards in Hong Kong secondary schools, which has been characterized as the three Ts' situation: test-centered, teacher-centered, and textbook-centered (Morris et al., 1996). The intended washback effect of this HKEA change to the public examination was to positively influence the teaching of English while moving toward a new philosophy of teaching and learning, from noninteractive, teacher dominated classrooms to more task-based teaching approaches.

Within the Hong Kong context, what is still not clear, however, is the nature and scope of the washback effects. This study specifically investigates what the changes to the HKCEE mean to classroom teachers and whether the changes have any impact on their perceptions, which is a key aspect of teaching and learning. This study aimed to determine whether changes to a high-stakes school leaving public examination in English toward more task-based assessment approaches actually changed Hong Kong's secondary school teachers' perceptions of English teaching and learning.

METHODOLOGY

A combined research framework, using multiple approaches, was employed in this study. Three research phases were designed together exploring the macro level (including the main parties within the Hong Kong educational context), then the micro level in schools (concerning different aspects of teaching and learning) in order to understand both the large and small pictures of the washback phenomena (Cheng, 2001; Fullan with Stiegelbauer, 1991). At the micro level, teachers' and students' perceptions and

[1]The process of HKEA modifying an existing examination takes approximately 18 months to complete, but because of the need to give 2 years' notice to schools, it has to begin at least 3½ years before candidates write the examination affected by such modifications. The HKCEE was revised in 1993. The official syllabus was introduced to schools in the 1994–95 school year. The first cohort of students took the revised HKCEE in 1996, which is referred to here as the 1996 HKCEE.

attitudes toward the new HKCEE and their classroom behaviors were studied, focusing on one such essential aspect at the micro level—teachers' perceptions. It is important to note that this focus is not because this is regarded as the sole aspect of teaching that could be influenced within this context, but rather to illustrate one example of the many complex aspects of washback within the Hong Kong context.

What was the nature and scope of the washback effect on teachers' perceptions of aspects of teaching toward the new HKCEE?

Teachers' perceptions are operationally defined as teachers' comprehension and understanding of aspects of classroom teaching in relation to the 1996 HKCEE. Aspects of teaching discussed here include the following:

- Teachers' perceptions of (a) the reasons for the examination change; (b) the new test formats; (c) possible extra work and pressure; (d) possible change of teaching methods; and (e) possible difficulties in teaching
- Teachers' reactions to the new 1996 HKCEE
- Classroom behaviors within the context of the new 1996 HKCEE

Design

This research was conducted between January 1994 and November 1996, aiming to capture the changes when the 1996 HKCEE was first introduced into teaching in 1994 until the first cohort of students took the new HKCEE in 1996. During the time of the research, teachers[2] at the F4 (Form 4) and F5 (Form 5) level were teaching two cohorts of F5 students who were studying English with the *same* teaching syllabus (Curriculum Development Council, 1982), but who were required to take *different* HKCEE examinations at the end of their F5 year (Hong Kong Examinations Authority, 1993). Teachers prepared one group of students for the old HKCEE in 1995 and another group for the new HKCEE in 1996. Therefore, a teacher questionnaire was designed, which was administered twice to compare the differences in teachers' perceptions when the new 1996 HKCEE came into place for the initial two years (see Appendix B).

The Teacher Questionnaire (TQ) consisted of three parts, and was designed and administered in English. Part One consisted of eight categories of teachers' personal details. Part Two consisted of 12 categories and 95 items altogether (TQ2.1[3] to 2.12). All of them were designed on a 5-point

---

[2]Teachers in Hong Kong secondary schools are usually scheduled to teach at F1–F3 and/or F4–F5 levels.

[3]TQ 2.1 refers to the Teachers' Questionnaire Part Two, Category One, which consists of 10 items.

Likert scale of agreement, where 5 = *Strongly Agree*, 4 = *Agree*, 3 = *Undecided*, 2 = *Disagree*, and 1 = *Strongly Disagree*, regarding teachers' perceptions of selected aspects of teaching, learning and assessment, and evaluation.[4] Part Three consisted of 10 categories, which dealt with teachers' reactions to the new examination and aspects of classroom teaching and learning activities. Categories 1 to 6 (TQ3.1 to 3.6) were designed for teachers to select answers according to their own classroom situations. Categories 7 to 10 (TQ3.7 to 3.10) were designed on a 5-point Likert scale of frequency, where 5 = *Always*, 4 = *Often*, 3 = *Sometimes*, 2 = *Seldom*, and 1 = *Never*.

In terms of the questionnaire development, qualitative input and piloting procedures were employed to ensure the validity and reliability of the questionnaire items (Erickson, 1986; Low, 1988). Whereas qualitative input ensures the content validity, piloting procedures ensure the construct validity. Qualitative input consisted of: (a) theoretical sources from related research conducted in Hong Kong; (b) interviews with members of the HKEA English Subject Committee; interviews with school principals, panel chairs, teachers, and students; and (c) regular school visits. This procedure allowed the researcher to go into the field (schools and classrooms) to watch what was happening in the classroom, and to get a "feel" for what was in teachers' minds in terms of the research problem in context (Alderson & Scott, 1992; Arnove, Altback, & Kelly, 1992) so that the content and format of the questionnaire could best capture teachers' perceptions of such an examination change. Two pilot studies[5] were carried out to ensure that questionnaire items and formats would be interpreted consistently in the same way by all survey respondents (Cohen, 1976; Cohen & Manion, 1989; Jaeger, 1988). Both pilots were conducted in the presence of the researcher, so that questions regarding the questionnaire scales and items could be taken into consideration before its administration.

Participants

There were, at the time, about 448 day secondary schools in Hong Kong in 19 districts (Hong Kong Government, 1993). The survey focused on 323 aided schools among 388 Anglo-Chinese[6] schools. Teachers of English from

---

[4]TQ 2.6 to TQ 2.12 in relations to teachers' perceptions of learning, assessment and evaluation are not discussed here. This discussion focuses on teachers' perceptions of selected aspects of teaching.

[5]Two major pilot studies for the survey were carried out. The first pilot was carried out on April 16, 1994 with 48 teachers, four months before they began teaching toward the new 1996 HKCEE for the first cohort of F4 students in September 1994. The second was carried out on October 18, 1994 with 31 teachers. This was at the time when the revised examination was being implemented to prepare the first cohort of F5 students for the new 1996 HKCEE.

[6]Anglo-Chinese schools refer to schools whose medium of instruction is English, that is, all courses are delivered in English, except Chinese and Chinese history.

60 such secondary schools were surveyed in 1994 and in 1995. These 60 schools make up 19% of the foregoing school population (i.e., 60 out of 323). F5 students from 35 of the 60 such secondary schools were also surveyed (see Cheng, 1998a). Teachers who taught those students from the 35 schools were included in the teachers' survey in both years.

In 1994, 350 teachers were sampled with a return rate of 40% (140 out of 350 questionnaires issued that year). In 1995, 200 teachers were sampled, with a return rate of 47% (94 out of 200 questionnaires issued). The 1995 sampling was smaller compared to that in 1994, the rationale being that the second year sampling served as a focus study.

Data Collection and Analysis Procedures

The comparative nature of the survey required the questionnaire to be issued twice. SPSS (DOS version in 1994) was used for the data analysis. First, frequency distributions were calculated for all the questionnaire items, and missing values of each item—missing completely at random (MCAR)—were replaced by the items' mean value. All percentages were reported as valid percentages with missing data excluded.

The surveys explored the differences between findings over the 2-year period. The differences were tested for statistical significance using the chi-square test and the independent sample t test. A probability of less than .05 was taken as statistically significant for the survey. The chi-square test was performed to find the similarities between the two groups of teachers according to the survey demographic information. This test was used to evaluate the discrepancy (the degree of relativity) between the two years' samples. A significance level ($p < .05$) from the chi-square statistical analysis provided a valid basis for further sample mean comparison using the independent t test. The findings showed that the two years' teacher samples were very similar, even though they were not the same groups of teachers (see Table 9.1). It should be noted that the possibility of error increases with the number of chi-square tests and t tests being carried out (Woods, Fletcher, & Hughes, 1986, p. 149). A complementary multiple-method design and a method triangulation were employed in this study to guard against errors arising from the data collection and analysis.

The following report focuses on those findings showing a significant difference in the two-year samples on different aspects of teaching. This, however, does not indicate there was or would be no washback in those aspects of teaching not showing any significant difference. There might be changes (differences), which emerged later on, or there might be changes that could not be observed by the survey alone.

RESULTS AND DISCUSSION

Teachers' Characteristics and Their Teaching Contexts

Eight teachers' characteristics were studied (see Table 9.1). Two thirds of the teacher participants were male, one third female, between 20 and 40 years of age. More than 40% of the teachers had 1 to 6 years of teaching experience, and half of them had more than 10. The majority of the teachers (around 75%) taught between 22 to 33 periods[7] per week. The sampled teachers came from schools of various banding[8] in Hong Kong.

This sample of teachers was better qualified both academically (more than 69% with a bachelor's degree) and professionally (more than 80% with a teacher's certificate) when compared with the general population of teachers of English in Hong Kong secondary schools, only 18.9% of whom are subject trained and only 14.2% of whom are both subject and professionally trained (Falvey, 1995). There are also teachers of English in Hong Kong secondary schools who have a bachelor's degree, but are not subject trained in English. They could have a degree in any subject, but still teach English. In most of the cases, their bachelor degrees are obtained from overseas, English-medium universities.

Teachers' Perceptions of and Reactions to the 1996 HKCEE

There are six categories in this section, five of which refer to the teachers' perceptions—TQ 2.1 to 2.5, and are scaled from 5 = *Strongly Agree* to 1 = *Strongly Disagree*. One category referring to the teachers' reactions (TQ 3.1) is designed on a 4-point scale.

Five categories are related to the teachers' perceptions of:

- the reasons for the new 1996 HKCEE
- the new exam formats of the 1996 HKCEE
- possible extra work and pressure under the new 1996 HKCEE
- possible teaching methods teachers would like to adopt to prepare for the new 1996 HKCEE
- possible difficulties in teaching the new 1996 HKCEE

[7]The duration of a lesson period in Hong Kong secondary schools is usually from 35 minutes to 45 minutes.

[8]Banding is based on the Secondary School Places Allocation (SSPA) in Hong Kong. The SSPA is the process by which primary students are allocated to secondary schools. Band 1 schools have the students with the highest scores and Band 5 the lowest. However, banding is not an absolute scale. The level of students is also related to the geographical locations of the schools.

TABLE 9.1
Characteristics of the Respondents and Chi-Square Test of Significant Difference in 1994 and 1995

Items	*Variables*	*1994 (%)*	*1995 (%)*	*Chi-Square Significance*
Gender	Male	69.1	63.4	.373
	Female	30.9	36.6	
Age	20–30	38.1	36.6	.667
	31–40	36.0	37.6	
	41–50	20.9	17.2	
	Above 50	5.0	8.6	
Academic qualifications	B.A.	59.0	66.3	.182
	B.Sc.	10.8	3.3	
	Master's	12.9	10.9	
	Others	17.3	19.6	
Professional qualifications	Teacher's Cert.	38.2	32.4	.224
	P.C. Ed/Dip. Ed	48.0	62.0	
	Advanced Dip.	8.8	2.8	
	R.S.A	2.0	0	
	M.Ed.	2.9	2.8	
Years of teaching	1–3	26.9	22.3	.493
	4–6	17.9	20.2	
	7–9	8.2	13.8	
	10 & Above 10	47.0	43.6	
Major forms currently taught	F1–F3	35.1	40.4	.000
	F4–F5	35.1	52.1	
	F6–F7	29.8	7.4	
Teaching periods per week	16–21	19.8	25.8	.181
	22–27	35.9	38.7	
	28–33	40.5	35.5	
	Above 33	3.8		
School band	Band 1	28.1	35.9	.189
	Band 2	26.6	22.8	
	Band 3	26.6	15.2	
	Band 4	10.9	13.0	
	Band 5	7.8	13.0	

Perceived Reasons for the Change of the HKCEE (TQ 2.1)

When teachers were asked *what they see as the 10 major reasons for the HKEA to change the present exam syllabus* over the 2 years, teachers' perceptions of four reasons changed significantly over the 2-year period (see Table 9.2). Teachers' perceptions of the reasons "*to prepare students for their future careers*" and "*to motivate students to use integrated skills*" changed in an

TABLE 9.2
Differences in Teachers' Perceptions of the Reasons for the 1996 HKCEE

Variables	*Year*	*Cases*	*Mean*	*SD*	*T-Value*	*df*	*2-Tail Probability*
To prepare students for their	1994	120	3.56	1.00	−2.31	211	.022
future careers	1995	93	3.85	.78			
To widen the gap between the	1994	118	2.97	1.05	2.29	209	.023
top and low students	1995	93	2.62	1.12			
To motivate students to use in-	1994	120	3.73	.86	−2.24	211	.026
tegrated skills	1995	93	3.99	.79			
To encourage more good text-	1994	121	4.04	.91	11.71	211	.000
books	1995	92	2.52	.98			

increasing direction.[9] This might suggest that the teachers seemed to agree with the major principles of the HKEA intended washback effect. The agreement might also indicate that teachers became more aware of the rationale behind the new HKCEE over the two years.

However, teachers' perceptions of the reasons "*to widen the gap between the top and low students*" and "*to encourage more good textbooks*" decreased, especially with regard to textbooks. In 1994, teachers perceived "*to encourage more good textbooks*" as one of the main reasons behind the 1996 HKCEE, but fewer teachers held this view in 1995. The reason for this decrease might be the actual quality of the revised textbooks produced. On the one hand, it was the intention of the HKEA to have teaching material support from the textbook publishers for the change to the examination. On the other hand, teachers also expected to have something to rely on in the case of such an exam change. However, this might not necessarily lead to good textbooks. Indeed, teachers have different points of view of good textbooks (Andrews & Fullilove, 1994; Hivela & Law, 1991). Textbooks catering for an examination syllabus are not necessarily good.

The New Exam Formats of the 1996 HKCEE (TQ 2.2)

In this section, teachers were asked "*what are the major changes that you have perceived in the exam papers of the 1996 HKCEE?*" The teachers' responses show that they were aware of the changes made in the 1996 HKCEE. Four out of eight aspects (see Table 9.3) were found to have changed significantly over the 2-year period.

[9]The use of *increase* (or in an increasing direction) or *decrease* (or in a decreasing direction) in reporting of the findings refers solely to the increase or decrease in the mean score comparison over the 2-year period for the independent *t*-test.

TABLE 9.3
Differences in Teachers' Perceptions of Changes Made in the 1996 HKCEE

Variables	*Year*	*Cases*	*Mean*	*SD*	*T-Value*	*df*	*2-Tail Probability*
More integrated and task-based approaches	1994	119	3.82	.81	−3.71	208	.000
	1995	91	4.18	.51			
More practical and closer to real life	1994	119	3.56	.89	−2.31	208	.022
	1995	91	3.85	.86			
Closer to the Use of English in the oral paper	1994	118	3.89	.94	−2.41	206	.017
	1995	90	4.20	.89			
More role play and group discussion	1994	116	3.97	.89	−2.37	205	.019
	1995	91	4.25	.77			

As a result of such changes, the teachers' perceptions matched more closely with the intended washback effect (i.e., to bring about positive change in teaching and enable students to perform "real-life" tasks and use their language skills integratively). All four aspects were related to communicative language skill building suggesting that teachers' perceptions of the changes in the new HKCEE were compatible with the HKEA intended washback effect. Teachers' perceptions of the other four items in this category remained relatively unchanged. A possible reason for this might be that they were less explicitly matched with the format changes of the exam (see Appendix A).

Extra Work or Pressure Involved in Teaching Toward the 1996 HKCEE (TQ 2.3)

Teachers were asked what kind of extra work or pressure (if any) they thought the 1996 HKCEE would create in their teaching. Only one out of eight aspects of their teaching—*preparing more materials for students*—was found to have changed significantly, and in a decreasing direction, from a mean of 4.06 in 1994 to 3.77 in 1995 (see Table 9.4). The results suggest that teachers initially thought, in 1994, that the change of the HKCEE would create extra work for them. However, their attitudes changed in 1995, and there seemed to be less worry or tension regarding extra material preparation as a result of the 1996 HKCEE.

Teaching Methods the Teachers Would Change Due to the 1996 HKCEE (TQ 2.4)

There are eight items in this section regarding the changes the teachers would like to make in their teaching because of the 1996 HKCEE. Two items differed significantly (see Table 9.4). Teachers were clearly aware of the in-

TABLE 9.4
Differences in Teachers' Perceptions of the Extra Work or Pressure the 1996 HKCEE Puts on Their Teaching

Variables	*Year*	*Cases*	*Mean*	*SD*	*T-Value*	*df*	*2-Tail Probability*
Preparing more materials for students	1994	121	4.06	.83	2.35	212	.020
	1995	93	3.77	.93			
Differences in Teachers' Perceptions of Changes They Would Like to Make							
More oral and listening tasks	1994	121	4.02	.65	−2.91	211	.004
	1995	92	4.26	.55			
More real-life tasks	1994	121	4.11	.67	2.03	211	.043
	1995	92	3.91	.72			
Differences in Teachers' Perceptions of the Difficulties in Teaching the 1996 HKCEE							
Inadequate textbooks	1994	120	3.94	.95	2.62	211	.010
	1995	93	3.57	1.13			
Noisy learning environment	1994	119	3.49	.98	4.99	210	.000
	1995	93	2.78	1.06			
Lack of teaching and learning resources	1994	119	3.86	.83	3.64	210	.000
	1995	93	3.40	1.01			
Inadequate time for students to practice	1994	118	4.12	.85	−4.78	209	.000
	1995	93	4.61	.59			
Students' current English levels	1994	119	3.96	1.00	−3.90	210	.000
	1995	93	4.44	.73			

crease in weighting for both the oral and listening components, and their perceptions in this respect changed in an increasing direction. This matched with one of the assumptions made by the HKEA, which was that if the weighting of certain components in the examination were increased, there would be an increased emphasis on teaching those components. This indicates possible washback effects of this examination change in the weighting of the oral and listening components on teachers' perceptions.

However, the other item that showed a significant difference was teachers' attitudes toward *employing more real-life language tasks*. Teachers initially thought they would put more emphasis on real-life tasks as specified in the new examination, but their attitudes changed over the following year. It is interesting to notice the discrepancy between this statement and teachers' perceptions of the format changes made in the examination, where there was a significantly increased difference in teachers' attitudes toward the 1996 HKCEE being *more practical and closer to real life* (see Table 9.3). However, when teachers were asked whether they would like to *employ more real-life language tasks*, their attitudes changed in a decreasing direction in 1995. This discrepancy might demonstrate the gap between the teachers' attitudes and the teachers' actions in the classrooms. What the teachers think they would like to embrace in terms of the new exam and what they can actually do in teaching might not necessarily match.

Difficulties in Teaching Toward the 1996 HKCEE (TQ 2.5)

Teachers were asked that *what do you find the most difficult aspects of teaching the 1996 HKCEE syllabus*? Five out of the seven aspects are seen to have significantly changed (see Table 9.4). Teachers' attitudes toward aspects such as *inadequate textbooks*, *noisy learning environment*, and *lack of teaching and learning resources* were seen to change, but in a decreasing direction. This indicates that there were fewer tensions and worries regarding those aspects. These foregoing three aspects were teachers' main concerns when the change to the HKCEE was first made known to them. However, it seemed that, as time went by, these external or environmental worries lessened, especially in relation to textbooks and teaching resources. Two aspects–*inadequate time for students to practice* and *students' current English level*–showed significant differences, and in an increasing direction, which were the two major worries that the teachers most frequently mentioned and identified as problems in teaching in 1995. Even in the later interviews with the teachers after the first cohort of F5 students had taken the new 1996 examination, teachers still considered students' current English levels as the main obstacle in teaching toward the new examination (see Cheng 1999).

Teachers' Reactions to the New 1996 HKCEE (TQ 3.1)

When teachers were asked about their *reactions to the 1996 HKCEE*, there was a significant difference in their reactions. There was an increase in the number of teachers who *welcome the change*, from 30.4% in 1994 to 42.7% in 1995, and a decrease in teachers who were *skeptical about the change*, from 38.4% in 1994 to 20.2% in 1995. Teachers who *enthusiastically endorse the change* also increased from 1.6% to 4.6%. This increase suggests positive teachers' attitudes toward the new HKCEE from 1994 to 1995.

Teachers in Hong Kong tend to have a positive and supportive attitude toward change in general (Morris, 1990). It is only when they come across problems and difficulties in actual teaching that they confront the pressure of change. The resistance to actual changes and taking actions that would lead to change might be due to the practical aspects of teaching in the case of this examination change. It is only to be expected that teachers would modify what they have been doing to prepare their students for the new

HKCEE, as it is high stakes for both students and teachers (Morris, 1995). However, even if the survey showed a positive attitudinal change, this does not necessarily mean that teachers were going to change their behaviors (see Cheng, 1998a).

Exploring this section on teachers' perceptions of and reactions to the new 1996 HKCEE, it can be seen that washback on actual aspects of teaching in the context of the examination change was very complex as perceived by the teachers. Their overall perceptions of the teaching and learning activities (i.e., the *what*) changed in an increasing direction from 1994 to 1995. However, teachers' perceptions of the teaching methodology (i.e., the *how*) required by the examination change seemed to have remained relatively unchanged, even though part of the findings showed that teachers did perceive the HKEA reasons for the changes made in the 1996 HKCEE. This might suggest a reluctance to make the actual changes in their teaching at the level of teaching *methods*, rather than at the level of teaching *activities*.

Another aspect of the findings was that initial tensions and worries over the new teaching materials and textbooks in relation to the 1996 HKCEE decreased over the two years. Instead, the students' current English level and inadequate student practice time emerged as the major concern over the two years. It needs to be pointed out here that the actual impact of the examination change on teachers' attitudes could not be fully determined from the survey results alone, and were further explored from classroom observations in Phase III of the study (see Cheng, 1999).

In addition, it can be seen from the survey findings discussed earlier that teachers tended to have a more positive reaction to the new HKCEE in 1995 compared to 1994. Moreover, their perceptions of the reasons behind the changes and the changes actually made in the HKCEE matched the HKEA intended washback. The agreement between teachers' perceptions and the policymakers' might suggest a positive attitude toward the new HKCEE. However, whether teachers actually changed their teaching according to the intended washback could not be answered by the survey alone, and probably not in the initial two years.

Washback on Classroom Teaching Behaviors (TQ 3.2 to 3.4; 3.7 to 3.9)

Six categories were designed in this part to explore whether the introduction of the 1996 HKCEE influenced the teachers' perceptions of their day-to-day teaching activities. The first three categories (TQ 3.2, 3.3, and 3.4) were in a multiple-choice format. The next three categories (TQ 3.7, 3.8, and 3.9) were designed on a 5-point Likert scale of frequency, where 5 = *Always* and

1 = *Never*. Both groups of categories are related to aspects of teacher classroom behaviors.

Teaching Planning and Medium of Instruction (TQ 3.2, 3.3, and 3.4)

There are three categories in this section. Only one category regarding *how teachers arrange their teaching in schools* (TQ3.4) showed a significant change (see Table 9.5). The greatest difference among these items was seen in *Scheme of Work* in Hong Kong secondary schools, which is the overall teaching plan. In 1994, the teachers arranged their teaching more according to the *Scheme of Work*, but in 1995 there was a sharp decrease in this arrangement, from 56.6% to 39%. In addition, in 1995 the teachers seemed to arrange their lessons much more according to *separate skills* (an increase from 9.2% to 24.4%) and *contents to be taught* (from 11% to 17.1%). The other two choices, *textbooks* and *language activities/tasks*, remained relatively unchanged.

The remaining two categories (TQ3.2 and TQ3.3) did not show significant difference. However, the item regarding *medium of instruction* showed an interesting pattern. There were more teachers in 1995 that used *English supplemented with occasional Chinese explanation* as their medium of instruction than in 1994, and there was a decrease in teachers' use of *English only* in 1995. This seems to indicate that teachers tended to use *English with occasional Chinese* more often, with one possible reason for this being their concerns and worries over their current students' English levels. Teachers focused on the meaning of the language so that students could pass the exam, which was frequently mentioned by many teachers in all phases of the study. No significant differences among these aspects of teaching might suggest that no washback effect of the 1996 HKCEE was observed on general teaching planning and preparation.

TABLE 9.5
Teaching Planning and Medium of Instruction

Items	*Variables*	*1994 (%)*	*1995 (%)*	*Chi-Square Significance*
How do teachers arrange their teaching in schools?	According to textbooks	18.3	17.1	.01593
	According to Scheme of Work	59.6	39.0	
	According to separate skills	9.2	24.4	
	According to the contents	11.0	17.1	
	According to language activities	1.9	2.4	
What is the medium of instruction?	English only	37.8	24.4	.05198
	English supplemented with occasional Chinese explanation	48.9	63.3	
	Half English and Chinese	12.6	8.9	
	Mainly Chinese	.7	3.4	

Lesson Planning, Teacher Talk, and Teaching Activities in English Lessons (TQ 3.7 to 3.9)

These three aspects of teaching were placed on a Likert scale of frequency, where 5 = *Always* and 1 = *Never*.

Teachers were asked how often they considered seven specific aspects when they prepared their lessons. Two aspects of teaching were found to have changed significantly (see Table 9.6). In 1995, the teachers seemed to pay more attention to *contents of teaching* and *homework to give to students* in their lesson preparations. This result matched the earlier results concerning teachers' attitudes to their general teaching, planning, and preparation. Other aspects such as *tasks to be performed in teaching* and *the skills to be taught* received the same attention in teaching.

The fact that teachers paid more attention to the homework given to their students in 1995 might suggest that this examination change could redirect the teachers' attention toward developing their students' abilities to work autonomously by doing more work at home. In addition, giving more homework to students indicated the pressure of the new examination.

Regarding teacher talk, teachers were asked about their teaching mode. The four teacher talk modes remained more or less the same, apparently unaffected by the examination change. For the great majority of the time, teachers talked to *the whole class*, and much less *to groups* and *to individuals*. The mean score of teachers' *keeping silent* for both years, in 1994 and 1995, was at 2 out of 5 on the Likert scale, indicating that teachers were talking most of the time in class (see Table 9.7). These results suggest that teachers dominated and controlled the classroom talk for most of the lesson time—an area on which the examination change did not seem to have any impact.

Ten teaching activities are included under this category, which was designed to explore how often teachers carried out those activities in class. None of the teaching activities were found to change significantly. Activity four—*explain specific language items, such as words or sentences*—was carried out most often by teachers, closely followed by *explain the meaning of the text*, together with activities such as *explain textbook exercise* and *explain homework*. All these activities are types of explaining, which related to the reasons why the teachers spent most of the time talking to the whole class.

TABLE 9.6
Aspects of Teaching to Be Considered While Preparing Lessons

Variables	*Year*	*Cases*	*Mean*	*SD*	*T-Value*	*df*	*2-Tail Probability*
Contents of teaching	1994	133	4.28	.63	−2.36	222	.019
	1995	91	4.47	.57			
Homework to give to students	1994	133	3.46	.78	−2.95	222	.003
	1995	91	3.79	.89			

TABLE 9.7
Self-Reported Teacher Talk in English Lessons

Variables	*Year*	*Cases*	*Mean*	*SD*	*T-Value*	*df*	*2-Tail Probability*
Talk to the whole class	1994	133	4.44	.633	.80	222	.425
	1995	91	4.37	.661			
Talk to groups of students	1994	133	3.38	.831	1.12	222	.263
	1995	91	3.25	.769			
Talk to individual students	1994	132	3.08	.768	.72	221	.471
	1995	91	3.00	.775			
Keep silent	1994	131	2.03	.952	.24	218	.814
	1995	89	2.00	.929			

This finding was also supported by later classroom observations, when teachers were seen to spend a great deal of time explaining language points and the meanings of a text to their students in class. Some teachers[10] felt they would not have done their job well if they failed to give students the required language knowledge.

Summarizing the findings in washback on classroom teaching behaviors (TQ 3.2 to 3.4; 3.7 to 3.9), there appears to have been little indication of washback on those behaviors. Teachers' general ways of teaching, such as teachers' talk, the nature of teaching, and delivery modes, remained unchanged in relation to the examination change. However, some changes were observed. There was a tendency in 1995 for teachers to pay more attention to the content and skills to be taught and homework to be given to students. The medium of instruction was also seen to change from using English only to using English occasionally with Chinese explanations in 1995. These changes, however, might not be directly related to the examination change. The medium of instruction, according to follow-up interviews with the teachers, might be due to the teachers' perceptions of their current students' English proficiency levels.

CONCLUSION

The findings from the teacher survey illustrate further the complex nature of washback effects. First, in exploring teachers' perceptions of, and reactions to, the new HKCEE, teachers reacted positively to this examination change. There seemed to be a match between the teachers' perceptions and those of the HKEA policymakers', suggesting certain washback effects on those aspects within the Hong Kong educational context. In this sense,

[10]The data was obtained from interviews carried out on January 5, 1994 with some senior teachers in one secondary school–Phase I of the study.

there was a relatively small gap between the policy of the exam change and perceptions of the teachers within the Hong Kong context.

Second, when aspects of daily teaching activities were explored in the context of the new examination, the situation was less clearly perceived by the teachers. The teachers' perceptions of what was expected of their teaching changed toward the requirements of the new HKCEE. However, teachers' daily teaching activities and their perceptions of the underlying teaching methodology associated with the new HKCEE remained relatively unchanged, which suggests a reluctance to make the necessary changes that the teachers need to undertake in their own teaching. What is not clear, though, is why there was such reluctance, which may be an area for future study.

Third, teachers' initial concerns or worries over new teaching textbooks in the context of the exam change shifted to their students' current English levels, suggesting a washback effect on the teaching materials within the Hong Kong education context. The HKEA informed the textbook publishers of the examination change immediately after the decision was made. Textbook publishers then reacted quickly and produced new textbooks. This indicates that within the Hong Kong educational system there seemed to be some part of the system that worked efficiently to provide teachers with new materials to deal with the examination change. Teaching materials support was not one of the difficulties that teachers were initially concerned about. However, when the use of the teaching materials was explored in teaching, no clear evidence of changes was observed. Teachers' reliance on textbooks remained unchanged. This shift from teaching materials to students' language level of proficiency may also suggest that washback effects can manifest themselves in different places at different times.

The changes produced by the new examination, nevertheless, were shown to be superficial rather than substantial, based on the earlier results. Although teachers might have had a positive attitude and might have been willing to change their classroom activities on the surface in accordance with the examination change, substantial changes in their teaching methodology were not seen from the survey, not over the initial two years, even when the new HKCEE was the most significant change being made in Hong Kong schools at that time. This lack of change, however, may have been partly due to the length of time this study was conducted. Furthermore, the design of exam-related textbooks was based on information from the HKEA related to an instructional reform, but the final product might not have been molded according to the HKEA's view of what is desirable in terms of teaching, but rather according to the publishers' view of what will sell. In the Hong Kong context, at least, this unfortunately tends to lead to the rapid production of materials which are very examination-specific with a limited focus for teachers and students, rather than a broadening of horizons (see Andrews & Fullilove, 1994). The findings of this study further suggest the limited function of such an instructional reform by changing the examination, at least within the Hong Kong context.

It appears that changing the examination is likely to change the *kind* of exam practice, but not the *fact* of the examination practice. Changing the examination formats might not lend to a change in the degree of emphasis on the examinations. It might even re-focus teachers' attention on the exam, as in the case of assigning more homework to students. Changing the HKCEE to more integrated and task-based approaches could possibly change some aspects of teaching pedagogy. However, from the findings discussed earlier, the most important aspects that governed teachers' daily teaching in Hong Kong secondary schools remained relatively unchanged. Teachers were examination-oriented, and teaching was content-based and highly controlled.

Washback is an educational phenomenon in which change is central. It was intended by the HKEA to bring about changes in teaching and learning through changes in testing. Therefore, washback for teachers in this context means change that they feel "obliged" to make in their teaching for the new HKCEE. Change can also be a highly personal experience—"each and every one of the teachers who will be affected by the change must have the opportunity to work through this experience" (Fullan with Stiegelbauer, 1991, p. 117). Furthermore, change involves learning how to do something new. From the point of view of the HKEA, the new examination was designed to bring about positive washback effects on teaching and learning in schools—consequential validity of test design (Messick, 1989, 1992, 1994, 1996). Senior HKEA officials claimed they had successfully changed the *what* in teaching and learning (Hong Kong Examinations Authority, 1994b). However, the extent to which this new examination has changed the *how* of teaching and learning was limited. The change of the HKCEE toward an integrated and task-based approach showed teachers the possibility of something new, but it did not automatically enable teachers to teach something new.

What has been occurring here is the fact of the examination. What is being seen is the importance of this public examination in the Hong Kong education system. The high-stakes nature of public examinations drives teaching and learning, a fact that is very well documented in general education (Linn, 2000), and which can be traced back to imperial examinations in ancient China (Latham, 1877; Spolsky, 1995a). However, examinations drive teaching in the direction of coaching and drilling for what is required in the examination. Examples can be seen in this study of an increasing number of activities similar to exam activities being carried out in classroom teaching. Such a driving force of the public examination could be the same in other educational contexts in which the public examination function is similar. Areas of washback intensity,[11] however, are unlikely to be the same as different educational contexts are based on different political, social, economic, and cultural traditions (see other chapters in Part II of this book). What does seem clear is that a change in the examination syllabus itself alone is highly unlikely to realize the intended goal (see also Shohamy et al., 1996; Wall & Alderson, 1993).

APPENDIX A: COMPARISON OF THE OLD AND NEW HKCEE EXAM FORMATS

OLD HKCEE (from 1983 to 1996)		*NEW HKCEE (from 1996 onwards)*	
Paper I—Composition, Comprehension and Usage	25%	**Paper I**—Writing	26%
Paper II—Comprehension and Usage	20%	**Paper II**—Reading Comprehension and Usage	24%
Paper III—Listening Comprehension Section A—Short Items Section B—Extended Listening	15%	**Paper III**—Integrated Listening, Reading and Writing Part A—Short Tasks Part B—Extended Tasks	32%
Paper IV—Oral English Section A—Reading and Dialogue Section B—Conversation	10%	**Paper IV**—Oral Part A—Role Play Part B—Group Interaction	18%
Paper V—Summary, Directed Writing and Comprehension	30%		

APPENDIX B: TEACHERS' QUESTIONNAIRE

Teachers' Perceptions of Public Examinations in Hong Kong Secondary Schools

PART ONE [omitted due to the length of the book, see description in the chapter]

PART TWO Please grade the following on a 5-point scale format where 1 = Strongly disagree, 2 = Disagree, 3 = Undecided, 4 = Agree, 5 = Strongly agree. Put 1, 2, 3, 4 or 5 in the brackets provided.

[11]Washback intensity refers to the degree of washback effect in an area or a number of areas of teaching and learning affected by an examination (see Cheng, 1997, p. 43).

(1) What do you see as the major reasons for the HKEA (Hong Kong Examination Authority) to change the present HKCEE in English?

1[ ] To meet the demands of tertiary education
2[ ] To prepare students for their future career
3[ ] To refine testing methods
4[ ] To narrow the gap between HKCEE and UE
5[ ] To cope with the present decline in English standards
6[ ] To widen the gap between the top and low ability students
7[ ] To motivate students to use integrated skills
8[ ] To encourage students to play an active role in learning
9[ ] To enable students to communicate more with others
10[ ] To encourage more good textbooks

(2) What are the major changes that you have perceived in the exam papers of the 1996 HKCEE in English?

1[ ] More related to Target Orientated Curriculum principles
2[ ] More integrated and task-based approaches
3[ ] More practical and closer to real life
4[ ] Closer to the Use of English in the oral paper
5[ ] More role play and group discussion
6[ ] More emphasis on oral activities
7[ ] More emphasis on listening
8[ ] Less emphasis on grammatical usage

(3) What kind of extra work or pressure if any do you think the 1996 HKCEE in English will put on you in your teaching?

1[ ] Following a new syllabus
2[ ] Doing more lesson preparation
3[ ] Preparing more materials for students
4[ ] Revising the existing materials
5[ ] Employing new teaching methods
6[ ] Setting up new teaching objectives
7[ ] Meeting new challenges in teaching
8[ ] Organizing more exam practices

(4) What are the major changes you are likely to make in your teaching in the context of the 1996 new HKCEE?

1[ ] To teach according to the new test formats
2[ ] To adopt new teaching methods
3[ ] To use a more communicative approach in teaching
4[ ] To put more stress on role play and group discussion
5[ ] To put more emphasis on the oral and listening components
6[ ] To put more emphasis on the integration of skills
7[ ] To employ more real life language tasks
8[ ] To encourage more students' participation in class

(5) What do you find the most difficult aspects of teaching the 1996 HKCEE in English, if any?
1[ ] Students' current English level
2[ ] Class size
3[ ] Inadequate textbooks and other available teaching resources
4[ ] Noisy learning environment
5[ ] The lack of teaching and learning aids and facilities
6[ ] Too heavy work load
7[ ] Inadequate time for students' practice of English outside the language classroom

(6) What are the learning strategies you would recommend to your students in the context of the new HKCEE?
1[ ] To learn to jot down better notes
2[ ] To expose themselves to various English media
3[ ] To learn to express their opinions in class
4[ ] To put more emphasis on listening and speaking
5[ ] To learn to initiate questions
6[ ] To be more active in classroom participation
7[ ] To use English more in their daily life
8[ ] To change from passive learning to active learning
9[ ] To communicate more in English

(7) What types of activities do you think should be involved with language learning?
1[ ] Task-oriented activities
2[ ] Language games
3[ ] Role play and group discussion
4[ ] Exposure to various English media
5[ ] Authentic materials
6[ ] Training in basic language knowledge
7[ ] Extracurricular activities

(8) What do you think are the major aims for learning English in Hong Kong?
1[ ] To pursue further studies
2[ ] To pass examinations
3[ ] To obtain jobs
4[ ] To satisfy school requirements
5[ ] To satisfy parents' requirements

(9) In what ways do you think you would like to motivate your students to learn English?
1[ ] To do more mock exam papers
2[ ] To use more authentic materials
3[ ] To organize real life language activities

4[ ] To do more interesting language games
5[ ] To give students more encouragement to learn
6[ ] To create a positive attitude toward language learning
7[ ] To provide students with effective language learning strategies
8[ ] To have better classroom discipline

(10) What do you think are the basic functions of mock tests in school?
1[ ] To give feedback to teachers
2[ ] To assess students' learning difficulties
3[ ] To motivate students
4[ ] To direct students' learning
5[ ] To prepare students for public examinations
6[ ] To identify areas of re-teaching

(11) How is your teaching assessed in your school?
1[ ] Your own reflections on teaching
2[ ] The performance of your students in tests and public exams
3[ ] The overall inspection of your students' work by your school
4[ ] The overall completion of the subject contents
5[ ] Anonymous student evaluation of teaching
6[ ] Evaluation by colleagues
7[ ] Evaluation by principal or school inspectors

(12) The factors that most influence your teaching are?
1[ ] Professional training
2[ ] Academic seminars or workshops
3[ ] Teaching experience and belief
4[ ] Teaching syllabus
5[ ] Past experience as a language learner
6[ ] The need to obtain satisfaction in teaching
7[ ] Textbooks
8[ ] Public examinations
9[ ] Learners' expectations
10[ ] Peers' expectations
11[ ] Principal's expectations
12[ ] Social expectations

PART THREE Please tick the appropriate answer or provide written answers.

(1) What is your ***current*** reaction to the 1996 HKCEE in English?
1[ ] skeptical about the change
2[ ] neutral
3[ ] welcome the change
4[ ] enthusiastically endorse the change

(2) What is the medium of instruction you use when you teach English in the classroom?
1[ ] English only
2[ ] English supplemented with occasional Chinese explanation
3[ ] Half English and half Chinese
4[ ] Mainly Chinese

(3) Who generally makes the decisions on the arrangement of lessons?
1[ ] Principal 2[ ] Panel chair
3[ ] English teachers together 4[ ] Yourself

(4) How do you arrange your teaching in your school?
1[ ] According to textbooks
2[ ] According to the school Scheme of Work
3[ ] According to separate skills such as reading or listening
4[ ] According to the contents to be taught
5[ ] According to language activities/tasks

(5) Who makes the major decision on the choice of textbooks?
1[ ] Principal 2[ ] Panel chair
3[ ] English teachers together 4[ ] Yourself

(6) What are the primary functions of textbooks in teaching?
1[ ] To provide practical activities
2[ ] To provide a structured language program to follow
3[ ] To provide language models
4[ ] To provide information about the language

Please grade the following on a 5-point scale where 1 = never, 2 = seldom, 3 = sometimes, 4 = often, 5 = always and put 1, 2, 3, 4 or 5 in the brackets provided.

(7) How often do you consider the following aspects when you prepare your lessons?
1[ ] The methods of teaching
2[ ] The contents of teaching
3[ ] The tasks to be performed in teaching
4[ ] The skills to be taught
5[ ] Any supplementary materials to be used
6[ ] How to motivate students to learn
7[ ] Homework to give to students

(8) How often do you do the following in class?
1[ ] Talk to the whole class
2[ ] Talk to groups of students
3[ ] Talk to individual students
4[ ] Keep silent

(9) How often do you do the following activities in class?
1[ ] Tell the students the aims of each lesson
2[ ] Demonstrate how to do particular language activities
3[ ] Explain the meaning of the text
4[ ] Explain specific language items such as words or sentences
5[ ] Explain textbook exercises
6[ ] Explain homework
7[ ] Explain mock exams
8[ ] Organize language games
9[ ] Organize group work or discussion
10[ ] Organize integrated language tasks

(10) How often do you use the following teaching and learning aids in your teaching?
1[ ] Textbooks
2[ ] Supplementary materials
3[ ] Television/Radio
4[ ] Newspapers
5[ ] Language laboratory
6[ ] Pictures and/or cards
7[ ] Teaching syllabus
8[ ] Examination syllabus
9[ ] Overall lesson plan (scheme of work)

— End of Questionnaire —

Thank you very much for your help

CHAPTER

10

Has a High-Stakes Test Produced the Intended Changes?

Luxia Qi
Guangdong University of Foreign Studies

This chapter reports on a study of the intended washback effects of a high-stakes test, the National Matriculation English Test (NMET) in China, with a view to improving our understanding of the washback phenomenon through new empirical evidence, which is much needed for in-depth understanding of this issue. Pragmatically, the present study, which is part of an on-going washback project, aims to inform policymakers and test constructors of how successful the NMET has been in achieving one of its major goals, that is, to produce changes in English teaching and learning in secondary schools in China.

The chapter begins with a brief description of the Chinese educational system and the NMET as background information about the study. The research purpose, methodology, and results are then discussed, followed by conclusions and implications for using tests as levers for pedagogical change in China.

BACKGROUND

The Educational System in China

The Chinese educational system provides for 9 years of compulsory education: 6 years in primary school and 3 years in junior secondary school (Liu, 1992). Almost all children go to primary school at the age of six or seven.

But at the end of junior secondary school, only a small portion of them continue their formal education in senior secondary schools for another 3 years and then at universities for 4 years. The majority either enter the job market or attend career-oriented schools, like technical schools and vocational schools (Han, 1997).

A uniform curriculum and the same set of textbooks are used for senior secondary schools, which cover such subjects as Chinese, mathematics, English, history, geography, politics, physics, chemistry, biology, physical education, music, and art. The responsibility for designing the curriculum and compiling and publishing textbooks rests with the Curriculum and Teaching Materials Research Unit of the People's Education Press (Liu, 1992).[1]

Normally, almost all senior secondary school graduates wish to seek tertiary education, but only about half of them eventually attain their goal. According to the Educational Statistics Yearbook of China (Han, 1997), the enrollment of regular universities and colleges in 1997 amounted to 1,000,400 students, which constituted approximately 45% of the total number of senior secondary school graduates. There were 14,633,000 junior secondary school graduates that year, but only 7,536,000 were admitted into senior secondary schools, which made up 51.5% of the total. These figures show that China adopts a highly selective educational system, with fewer students at the higher end of the educational ladder. Students who have succeeded in climbing high on the ladder are those who have passed various competitive examinations, such as the NMET.

The Role of Examinations

Examinations play a crucial role in the Chinese educational system. Students are faced with numerous examinations as soon as they start their schooling. The two most important examinations are the one for senior secondary school entrance at the municipal level, and the other for university entrance at the national level. The latter tests nine subjects dictated by the national curriculum. A student has to take five or six tests depending on the requirements of the type of university for which he or she applies. Chinese, mathematics, and English are three compulsory subjects for all candidates regardless of their choice of university. Only those candidates whose scores rank high in the results of these norm-referenced tests have any chance of enrolling at a university. In the present study, I have chosen the National Matriculation English Test (NMET) as the research focus, as this is

[1]Most recently, it was decided that under the centralized curriculum, local education departments and schools are allowed to compile or select their own textbooks.

one of the three compulsory tests in the university entrance examination battery in China.

The National Matriculation English Test

The NMET is a standardized norm-referenced proficiency test, introduced in 1985 as a replacement for the old national university entrance English examination (Li, 1990). Apart from its major function of selection, the NMET aims to produce a positive washback effect on school teaching and learning (Ministry of Education, 1999). Similar to the situation elsewhere in the world (e.g., Cooley, 1991; Smith, 1991b), test results here have been used by society to evaluate schools, and by schools, parents, and students to evaluate teachers. Undoubtedly, this test can be rated as a high-stakes test; the type of test that is supposed to exert a profound influence on teaching and learning (Madaus, 1988).

PURPOSE OF THE STUDY

Researchers who are interested in the influence of tests have studied this issue from different perspectives. Some have taken tests as "given" and focused only on what is happening in the school system during a certain period of time, assuming that tests were the most important, if not the only, cause of what happened in the classroom. Some investigations along this line have shown that the effects of tests on teaching and learning are negative (e.g., Herman & Golan, 1993; Paris, Lawton, Turner, & Roth, 1991). However, one drawback of these studies is that insufficient attention has been paid to the purpose and structure of a test and other factors, which might have interacted with the test to shape school practice.

Other researchers (Cheng, 1998a; Wall & Alderson, 1993), in my view, have adopted a more fruitful approach. They have started from the expected washback effect in relation to the test designers' intentions, then compared classroom practice prior to the introduction of a test with what occurred in school after the use of the test, and finally established a relationship between the test and the teaching/learning. One difficulty for researchers conducting these studies was that due to time constraints they could only observe school practice shortly after the adoption of the relevant test. One reason for the apparent absence of some of the intended effects might be that not enough time had passed to allow the effects to become evident (Wall, 1996). It might be more revealing, therefore, to study the washback effect of a test that has been in operation for several years, which is the case for the NMET.

The problem of studying a test that has been in use for years, however, is the lack of baseline data to capture the situation before the test was introduced. One approach to the problem is to make a close comparison between test constructors' intentions and teaching practice at school (Andrews, 1995). The present study adopts this approach with the aim of investigating whether the NMET affects teaching in the way intended by the test constructors. The investigation involves three steps. First, test constructors' intentions are established and the structure of the test under study is analyzed, to see if the test expresses the constructors' intentions. Second, relevant school practices are investigated to find out what and how teachers teach. Third, intentions and school practices are compared to identify matches and mismatches between the two. The results thus obtained hopefully throw light on the intended and actual washback effects.

METHODOLOGY

Participants

Participants in the study were: (a) eight test constructors; (b) ten Senior III secondary school teachers from both city and county (rural) schools; (c) three English inspectors with many years of experience teaching Senior III students. Altogether there were 21 participants involved in the washback project at this stage.

Senior III teachers, rather than teachers from other grades, were selected for the study on the grounds that, because they have to help their students prepare for the NMET to be taken at the end of the school year, they would have been more concerned with and have a better knowledge of the philosophy of the test than teachers teaching the other grades. Therefore, Senior III seemed the most suitable grade to start with. Investigation into the influence of the NMET on other grades is also desirable, but would be the focus of a different study.

The English inspectors were chosen because they were responsible for assisting Senior III teachers in the preparation for the NMET. For example, it is the inspectors' job to organize teachers' meetings to give guidance in test preparation. English inspectors, who are normally selected from experienced teachers, are staff members in the education departments at various levels.

Data Collection

The data collection procedures in the present study are based on in-depth interviews and follow-up contacts. As a point of departure, unstructured interviews were conducted with the English inspectors to gain initial understanding of the test influence. This also served as a pilot study, paving the way for designing the guidelines for the semistructured individual interviews. Notes taken in these unstructured interviews were included in the data analysis.

The major interviews consisted of semistructured individual interviews and a group interview. The individual interviews were conducted face-to-face with test constructors and teachers between June and October 1999, using the interview guidelines (see Appendix) to ensure that the same topics were covered in all the interviews. Each individual interview lasted between 23 and 75 minutes. The group interview was conducted with test constructors after the first round of data analysis. A summary of results of the individual interviews was used to elicit the test constructors' comments on the researcher's interpretations. In addition, follow-up contact was made with test constructors, teachers, and inspectors, either in person or by phone during and after data collection, to invite them to clarify unclear points and confirm or disconfirm some findings.

All the interviews were conducted in Chinese and audiorecorded. The recordings were transcribed and translated into English[2] by the present author. The group interview was audiorecorded but not transcribed and notes were kept of the follow-up contacts.

Data Analysis

Using WinMax (Kuckartz, 1998), a software for qualitative data analysis, the individual interview data was analyzed to explore and clarify the test constructors' intentions and the schools' practices. The data was initially coded with a "start list" (Miles & Huberman, 1994, p. 58). For example, from previous conceptualization, a code of *pragmatic and sociolinguistic knowledge* was included on the list. When, in the interview, a test constructor said, for example, "They [test items] should be socially acceptable and appropriate," this was coded with the *pragmatic and sociolinguistic knowledge* label. New codes were added to accommodate for data that could not be covered by the existing start list. For instance, when a test constructor said, "Some teachers still think it [the NMET] is a test of grammar," the code *teachers' perception of the NMET* was added to the list. Memos were also written to record insights occurring during data analysis. Glaser (as cited in Miles & Huberman, 1994) defined a memo as "the theorizing write-up of ideas about codes and their relationships as they strike the analyst while coding . . ." (p.

[2]I combined the transcribing and translation processes. Specifically, I listened to the recordings and wrote down, in English, what I heard. The reasons are: (a) it would be too time consuming to transcribe all the data in Chinese and then translate them into English and (b) translation is necessary because the software (WinMax) used for data analysis has problems processing data in Chinese.

72). In WinMax, memos can be attached to the code or text and retrieved for use later.

The patterns emerging from the data were confirmed or disconfirmed by the participants through the group interview and follow-up contacts. NMET-related documents and teaching materials, such as testing syllabi, past papers, textbooks, and commercial test preparation materials, were scrutinized to verify participants' declared intentions and actions. Finally, the test constructors' intentions and school practices regarding the Senior III English course were compared to locate matches and mismatches.

Based on the coded data concerning practices in the Senior III English course, further analysis was carried out using Woods' (1996) concept of dual structuring of a course. Thus, a brief description of this concept is necessary at this point.

Woods (1996) posed that a course has two types of structure: a chronological (calendar/clock) structure and a conceptual structure. The chronological structure is a formal schedule in terms of the calendar and the clock. Within this time frame, there are a certain number of lessons or classes as shown in Fig. 10.1.

The conceptual structure, on the other hand, is made up of conceptual units or elements at different levels of abstraction which can be looked at as contents, as goals, or as methods. This structure is also hierarchical. At the top of the conceptual structure of a course there is the overall conceptual goal or goals. At the next level there are subgoals in terms of themes or

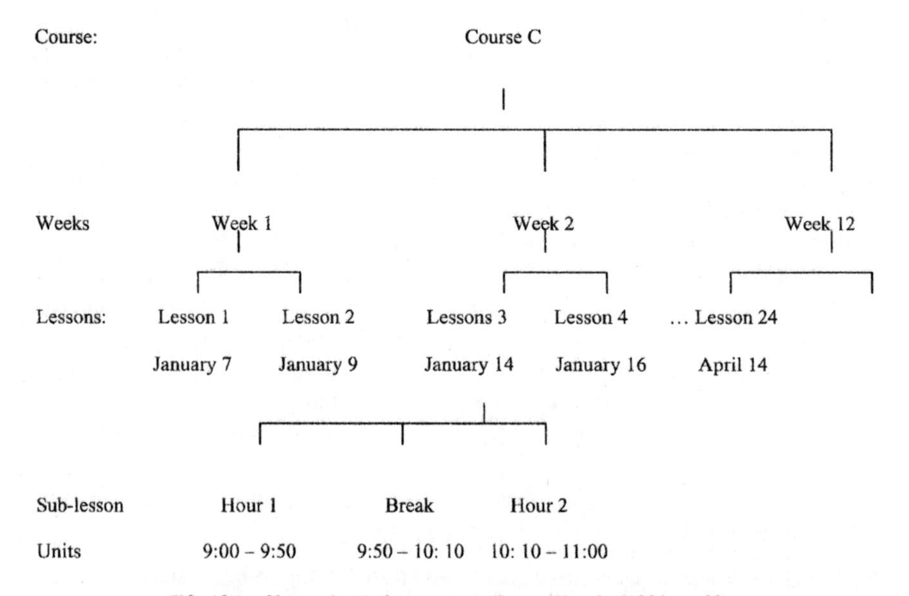

FIG. 10.1. Chronological structure. From Woods (1996, p. 89).

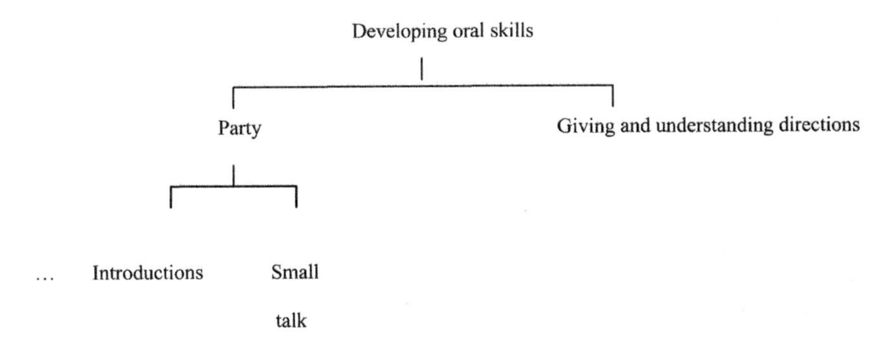

FIG. 10.2. Organization of major conceptual components. From Woods (1996, p. 95).

topics to be covered in the course, which can comprise intermediate conceptual units in terms of activities carried out to accomplish one of the conceptual goals at the higher level of the structure. Figure 10.2 is an example of this structure.

In the present study, the Senior III English course was analyzed from both the chronological and the conceptual structure.

Considerations for Trustworthiness

Lincoln and Guba (1985) discussed the concept of trustworthiness in relation to the quality of qualitative studies. Specifically, they placed emphasis on four criteria: credibility, transferability, dependability, and confirmability. These criteria are roughly equivalent to internal validity, external validity, reliability, and objectivity in quantitative research. To establish these qualities in a study, various measures have been proposed, such as member checking, thick description, inquiry auditing, and triangulation (Brown, 2001; Davis, 1992, 1995; Lincoln & Guba, 1985).

Member checking involves having participants confirm or disconfirm data, analysis, and conclusions. Thick description requires a detailed description of the study context, so that readers can determine for themselves whether the results are applicable to another similar setting or context. Inquiry auditing requires the creation of an audit trail consisting of raw data, data reduction, analysis products, etc., which is examined by another person (or persons) to confirm the findings or interpretations. A single audit, according to Lincoln and Guba (1985), "can be used to determine dependability and confirmability simultaneously" (p. 318). Triangulation refers to the study of data from multiple perspectives. Different types of triangulation have been suggested, such as data triangulation, methodological triangulation, theory triangulation, and so on (Brown, 2001).

In the present study some of the earlier measures were taken. First, member checking was done through a group interview and follow-up contacts (see the sections on data collection and data analysis). Second, tape recordings, field notes, codes, memos, analysis sheets, etc., were kept to create an audit trail. Although it was not done because of practical constraints, it is possible for another person to check and determine the confirmability and dependability of this study. According to Brown (2001), "whether or not it is actually done, it must be possible for another person to confirm the results or interpretations" (p. 227). Third, method triangulation was carried out. Information obtained from interviews was cross-checked by scrutinizing NMET related documents and teaching materials (see the section on data analysis).

Owing to constraints on time and resources, however, other useful techniques such as data triangulation, investigator triangulation, and prolonged engagement were not adopted, although these techniques would have helped to enhance the trustworthiness of the study if they could have been used. Due to space limitations, thick description is not possible in the present chapter. Therefore, lack of transferability might be a limitation of the study. Nevertheless, as mentioned previously, this chapter is based on the results of the first stage of an on-going washback project. In the later stages, more techniques were employed to enhance the trustworthiness of the study, the results of which will be reported elsewhere.

RESULTS AND DISCUSSION

To maintain confidentiality, the participants are identified by their professions. Thus CA stands for test constructor A, TA for teacher A, IA for inspector A, and so forth. When participants are quoted, the corresponding line number of the extract from the transcribed interview data is given, and quotations without a line number are from the field notes. If the participants' publications are quoted, the source is given in the reference list.

In this part of the chapter the general intention of the test constructors is discussed first, followed by a discussion of the foci of the Senior III English course. Then, a comparison is made between the two to identify possible matches and mismatches.

Test Constructors' General Intention and a Chief Measure Taken to Realize It

The interview data and the NMET-related documents demonstrate that the positive washback effect the test constructors anticipated in English Language Teaching (ELT) at secondary schools in China was to bring about "a

TABLE 10.1
The National Matriculation English Test

1985			*1999 (Guangdong Version)*[1]		
Content	*Item Type*	*Weighting (%)*	*Content*	*Item Type*	*Weighting (%)*
Paper One			Paper One		
I. Pronunciation		7	I. Listening		20
II. Cloze		13	II. Grammar/ Vocabulary	MC	10
			Cloze		20
III. Grammar/ Vocabulary	MC	20	III. Reading		27
IV. Reading		34			
V. Aptitude[2]		13			
Paper Two			Paper Two		
I. Writing	Guided writing	13	I. Proofreading	Error Correction	6.5
			II. Writing	Guided writing	16.5
Total		100			100

[1]In 1999, this version was used in Guangdong province as a pilot version for the whole country. It is scheduled to replace the national version in the year 2002.

[2]The aptitude component was removed in 1988 because its reliability and validity were greatly undermined due to excessive drilling at schools, according to the test constructors (Li et al., 1990).

shift from formal linguistic knowledge to practice and use of the language" (Li, 1990, p. 402). This general intention arose from the belief that ELT in schools focused on linguistic knowledge and neglected language use (Gui, Li, & Li, 1988; Li, 1988; Li, Gui, & Li, 1990). To quote one of the test constructors, "ELT in schools was, and still mainly is, a matter of teaching the form of English as knowledge" (Li, 1990, p. 396). As another test constructor put it, "We always want our test to show the teachers and students that they should develop the ability to use English" (CC, L.542), more specifically, "the ability to use the language appropriately in real communication" (Li, 1984, p. 83).[3] To encourage the development of these abilities via the NMET, the test constructors have taken a number of steps, such as building communicative elements into all sections of the NMET at the design stage. One important step is to gradually reduce the knowledge component and gradually increase the use component of the test. This process has been going on since 1988. The NMET structure in 1985 and that in 1999 are presented in Table 10.1 to illustrate the results of this process.

[3]The NMET designers favored the communicative approach. For a detailed account of their intentions the reader is referred to a paper by Li (1984).

The NMET consists of two papers. Paper I comprises multiple-choice items only and Paper II is a guided writing task in the 1985 version, and a guided writing task plus a proofreading task in the 1999 version.

Table 10.1 shows that the weighting of discrete-point items testing linguistic knowledge (pronunciation, vocabulary, and grammar) decreased from 27% in 1985 to 10% in 1999, whereas the weighting of the items testing language use, namely, listening, reading, and writing, increased from 47% in 1985 to 63.5% in 1999.

According to two test constructors (CA and CC), the gradual move toward greater emphasis on language use was a strategy intended to ensure public acceptance of the test before thought was given to positive washback. The implicit assumption that a steady reduction of the linguistic knowledge component in the test would encourage teachers and learners to spend less effort and class time on discrete linguistic forms and more on use through listening, reading, and writing activities is summarized in Fig. 10.3.

Although the multiple-choice format is adopted in the NMET for the sake of reliability (Gui et al., 1988), the test constructors did not support its use in teaching. To quote one of them, "But as practice, you don't need MC questions, just open questions to check their [students'] comprehension. . . . They [teachers] can ask the students to draw a diagram according to what they hear" (CA, L.295). Another test constructor said, "They [students] read and do mc questions. . . . They should read and do other exercises. For example, they can read a long story and discuss it" (CE, L.297). These two test constructors seem to believe that despite the format of the NMET, various types of activities should be carried out to develop language use ability. With the "right" abilities developed, test performance would take care of itself.

A reasonable question to ask at this point is: As the NMET has been in operation for 15 years, with a gradual decrease in its linguistic knowledge component, has ELT at school shifted its focus from formal linguistic knowledge to language use? Possible answers to this question can be sought by analyzing ELT practices in Senior III of secondary schools (rea-

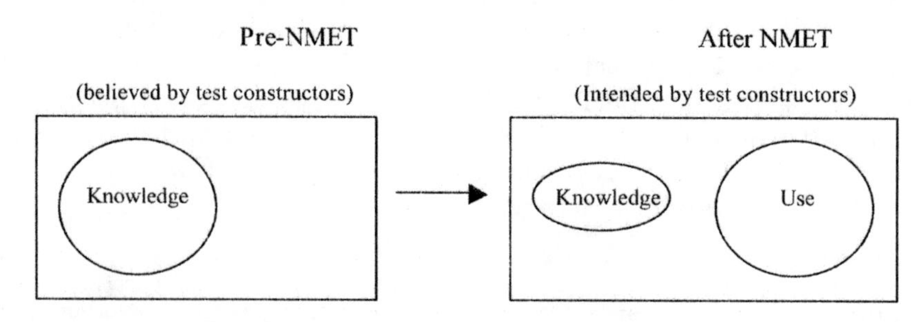

FIG. 10.3. Test constructors' intended change.

sons for choosing this grade for investigation are given in the section on participants).

The Foci of the Senior III English Course

As was mentioned previously, the Senior III English course was analyzed both in terms of their chronological and conceptual structure. The chronological structure is presented in Table 10.2.

Table 10.2 shows the time, name, and content of the Senior III English course based on the descriptions of the teachers and inspectors. The practice of Phase 1 demonstrates de-contextualized learning of formal linguistic knowledge of English, that is, drilling in grammatical rules and isolated words. This practice runs counter to the test constructors' intention to discourage the teaching of isolated linguistic knowledge. Phase 2 appears to be a typical example of teaching to the test. Some specialists consider such a practice counterproductive (Bracey, 1987; Haladyna, Nolen, & Haas, 1991).

TABLE 10.2
The Chronological Structure of Senior III English Course

Time	*Phase 1* *August–January*	*Phase 2* *February–May*	*Phase 3* *June–July*[1]
Name	*Revision*	*Individual Section Training*	*Comprehensive Training*
Content described by the teachers & inspectors	The students go over the lessons in the English textbooks they learned in Senior I and Senior II, concentrating on grammar rules and vocabulary. They usually do this before coming to class. In class we lecture on the relevant rules and words before making our students drill in them. We want to help them reinforce the linguistic knowledge they learned in the previous years.	Students are trained to do different sections in the NMET, one by one. For instance, they will practice the grammar items for a few days, then the cloze for another few days. We discuss some test-taking strategies and the characteristics of these sections.	Students are engaged in doing mock tests, one test a day. For example, on Monday, they have a test on math, Tuesday on Chinese, Wednesday on NMET and so forth. We're busy marking papers and locating our students' weaknesses so that we can help them improve.

[1]The length of each phase varies from school to school depending on the beginning of the revision work. The earliest occurs in August and the latest around October. July 9th was the date for the NMET every year. But, it is changed to June 8th starting from 2003.

Others believe it is capable of bringing about beneficial results if, as Hughes (1988) put it, "teaching for the test becomes teaching towards the proper objectives of the course" (p. 145). One of the test constructors shares Hughes' view. When discussing the writing task, she said, "I think it's important that our items are well designed so that the students will really learn how to write when they practice our test" (CA, L.75). What happens in Phase 3 is repeated rehearsal that prepares students for the real test.

It is important here to note that the types of activities listed under each phase are not limited to that phase alone. For example, one of the teachers interviewed said:

> A mock test is usually given at the beginning of the whole course in order to find out where our students' weaknesses lie and where the focus of our teaching should be in the revision. We have a mock test every month at our school besides the mock tests administered by both the district and the municipal education department. (TH)

Therefore, the types of activities attributed to each phase are just the main activities for that phase.

This chronological structure of the Senior III course seems to suggest that linguistic knowledge is still the focus. The other focus of the course appears to be the NMET. An analysis of the conceptual structure confirms the impression given by the chronological structure. Further, the conceptual structure provides a clearer picture of the foci of the course because, in the opinion of this researcher, the goals or subgoals inherent in a course are a better indicator of its focuses (see Fig. 10.4).

The overall goal of the course, according to inspector A and teacher F is to raise the students' scores in the coming NMET, because the students entered a senior secondary school, not a vocational school, for the sole purpose of competing for a place at a higher learning institute. To quote the teacher, "The students come here [to the school] to achieve their goal, that is, to enter a university" (TF, L.132).

This overall goal can be broken down into two subgoals. The first is to reinforce the students' linguistic knowledge or strengthen the "language foundation" (TF, L.62). This goal manifests itself in the teachers' description of the activities involved mainly in the first phase (see Table 10.2). The second subgoal is to develop the students' NMET skills[4] by familiarizing them with the test format and content. This goal can be detected in the second and third phase of the course called "individual section training" and "comprehensive training" respectively (see Table 10.2). Overall, the two sub-

---

[4]By "NMET skills" I refer to the teaching of skills restricted to and in the format of the NMET. No teacher has mentioned teaching of speaking, a skill that is not tested in the NMET. And according to the teachers, listening, reading and writing activities are all modeled on the NMET format.

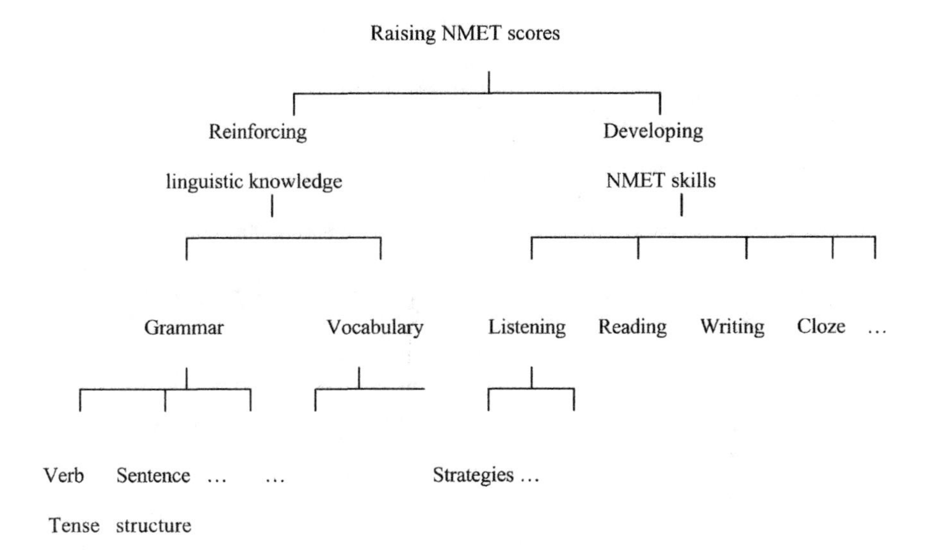

FIG. 10.4. The conceptual structure of Senior III English course.

goals are conducive to achieving the overall goal of raising the students' scores in the NMET.

The subgoals can be further divided into some intermediate conceptual units. Under the goal of reinforcing linguistic knowledge we find the components of grammar learning and vocabulary learning. One teacher (TJ) described how grammar was reviewed:

> We'll review the grammar with the students systematically and make them do a lot of exercises. . . . We'll surely review the important grammar points such as the attributive clauses, the inverted sentences, the agreement between the verb and the subject, the infinitive, and so on. . . . But we spend less time on some simple grammar points such as the nouns. We'll only lecture on the plural form, some words with unusual plural forms. (TJ, L.218; L.245)

Therefore, teachers lecturing on language points and students doing grammar exercises are two ways to reinforce the linguistic knowledge. Another means to reinforce the students' linguistic knowledge is to use quizzes. In an interview, one teacher described the kind of vocabulary quizzes used in his school:

> I used last year's NMET syllabus to print out the vocabulary list.[5] There're more than ten pages. I give them [students] a page every other day. There're

[5]In the NMET testing syllabus, there is a vocabulary list of about 2,300 words, taken from the National Teaching Syllabus (1990, 1996). Any word that is outside the vocabulary list should not be used in the NMET unless its meaning is given in Chinese in brackets.

> about 200 words in it. I ask them to write these words by themselves. They write out the meanings for each word in Chinese. Following repeated practice, we sample some words to test my students. We test about 200 words in one class. . . . Given 100 English words, they have to write out their Chinese equivalents. Given 100 Chinese words, they have to write out their English equivalents. Those who fail to get 80% right will have to take the same quiz again. Those who have got 80% right will have to get 90% next time. This practice makes the students learn words by heart. (TE, L.837)

This response supports the view that decontextualized linguistic knowledge continues to occupy a central place in the Senior III English course. The question is why teachers still adhere to teaching formal linguistic knowledge at the expense of communicative meanings and contexts despite reduction of the weighting on linguistic knowledge in the NMET over the past decade. Is it because the students are too weak in their linguistic knowledge, as the teachers believe (TD, L.417; TE, L.304; TJ, L.46; TF, L.486)? Or does it mean that teaching language form is an effective way to raise test scores? If so, we need to find out what the NMET really measures—linguistic knowledge or language use?

It is possible, and not unusual, that a language test or subtest taps the knowledge or capacity it is not intended to. For example, Alderson (1990) conducted a study to investigate the role of grammar in a reading subtest created by the English Language Testing Service, and found a high overlap between the grammar test and the reading test. He concluded that "the test probably measured a fairly generalized, if not general, grammatical ability" (Alderson, 1990, p. 217). Is it likely that, although grammar items constitute only 10% of the present NMET, some of its other sections—like reading, cloze, and proofreading—actually measure "the generalized grammatical ability" and this ability can be developed by repeated exposure to lists of words and language points? Answers to these questions, although not directly relevant here, might help to unravel the puzzle of why linguistic knowledge rather than language use is still being stressed in the Senior III English course.

The other subgoal of the course—to help students develop NMET skills—can also be divided into lower level conceptual units in relation to the different sections of the NMET. According to the teachers and inspectors interviewed, each section, including cloze, has been treated as a skill and drilled excessively. This is done not only in class but also, and more frequently, outside class. Listening, reading, and writing assignments take a large portion of students' off-class time and vacations. Students are made to practice the NMET listening task before class early in the morning and during the self-study hours in the evening. One inspector (IB) interviewed said:

> Altogether they [Senior III students from a certain school] completed 60 sets of listening items in that year.[6] The trouble is there aren't enough practice materials for the NMET listening on sale in bookstores. Otherwise they could have done more. (IB)

Unlike listening, reading is mainly practiced on an individual rather than a group basis. The teachers gave students reading assignments to do after class and during holidays. One teacher said they once invited an experienced English inspector from Beijing to give a talk on how to prepare for the NMET and, "According to him [the inspector from Beijing], Senior III students should read at least 600 short passages[7] in the year. . . . Our students have read about 300 since the beginning of the term" (TE, L.633).

Writing is also a common target for skill training in the course. Five teachers mentioned that their students wrote at least one passage as homework each week in addition to performing the writing tasks in mock tests (TD, L.13; TE, L.22; TF, L.84; TH, L.11; TA, L.18). As class time is limited, teachers make students practice these skills after class.

Practice of listening, reading, and writing is what the test constructors intended. This provides added evidence for the belief, based on the results of a survey conducted by the NMET constructors (as cited in Li, 1990, p. 400), that the most telling changes following the introduction of the NMET occurred outside class. Nevertheless, the skills are practiced in ways that may well not have been anticipated by the test constructors. For instance, multiple-choice items have found their way into most reading activities. In fact, all the comprehension questions in the reading materials I saw during my visit to the eight schools were, without exception, in the multiple-choice format. The test constructors have explicitly expressed their objection to using multiple-choice items in teaching despite the fact that they have to use it in the test for the sake of reliability (see the section on the test constructors' general intentions).

The way listening is drilled merits mention as well. When asked what she thought of the new listening section in the NMET, one teacher said, "In the past, we gave our students short stories to listen to. Now, we make them do a lot of items exactly like the ones in the NMET. It's good to add a listening section" (TA, L.122).

It is disturbing to note that there used to be some more life-like listening activities in that teacher's school, but changes have been made to imitate the format of the NMET listening since it was introduced. Clearly, English

---

[6]A set of listening items, following the format of the NMET, includes several dialogues and monologues and 20 multiple-choice comprehension questions.

[7]A short passage is usually between 200 and 300 words. That is the average length of the NMET reading passages. From my observation, most of the reading passages used in Senior III are of that length.

Chronological structure / Conceptual structure	P1 Aug.-- Jan. Revision	P2 Feb.-- May Individual section training	P3 June -- July Comprehensive training
Overall goal: Raising NMET scores	****	****	****
Sub-goal 1: Reinforcing linguistic knowledge	****	----	----
Sub-goal 2: Developing NMET skills	----	****	****

FIG. 10.5. The foci of the Senior III English course.

practice at school is not only affected by the content of the NMET but also its format. It does seem likely that some teachers may tend to model learning activities on the test format.

But why does the format of the test have such a powerful impact? One explanation given by our teacher informants is that students and their parents will complain if the exercises at school do not look like the NMET. As far as the Senior III English course is concerned, developing NMET skills seems to be the only logical practice, in the eyes of at least some parents and students. Therefore, the second subgoal of the course is justified.

Putting the chronological and the conceptual structures together, the Senior III English course can be shown in Fig. 10.5.

The stars in Fig. 10.5 are used to denote the association of a goal or subgoal with the focus of a particular phase, while broken lines indicate that, although the relevant subgoal does not receive first priority in a phase, it is still one of its objectives. It is clear that the two main foci of the Senior III English course are the linguistic knowledge and the NMET skills.

Comparison of Intentions and Practices

As was previously stated, a comparison of the test constructors' intentions with the ELT practice in Senior III is necessary in order to find out whether the intended washback has occurred (see Fig. 10.6).

Intended by test constructors

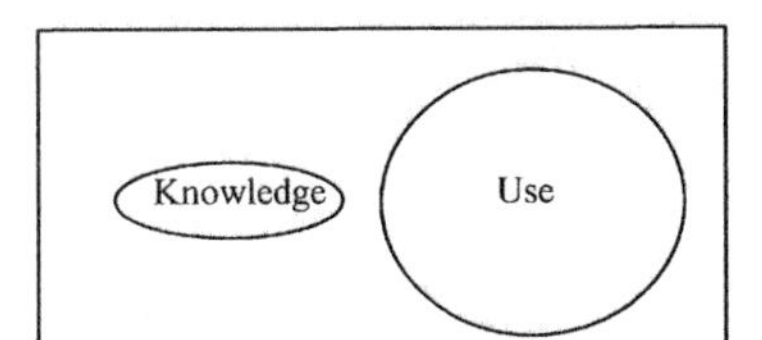

Reported by teachers and inspectors

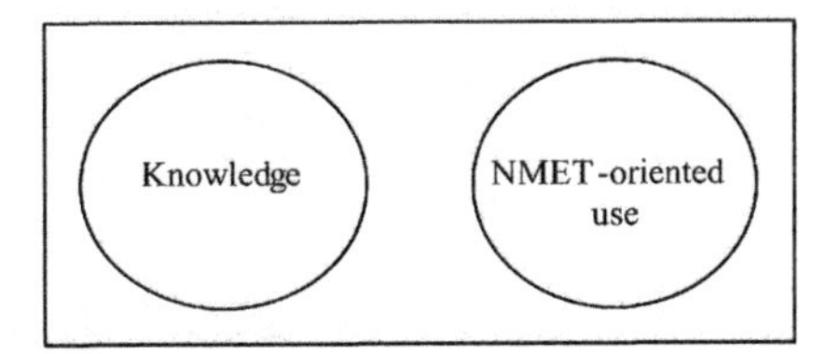

FIG. 10.6. Comparison of the intended ELT practice with the reported ELT practice.

From Fig. 10.6, it can be seen there is a mismatch and a partial match between what is intended and what is reported to be the practice. The mismatch concerns the teaching of linguistic knowledge, which shows that the test constructors' intention to de-emphasize formal linguistic knowledge has not materialized.

The partial match is between the test constructor's intention to encourage teaching of listening, reading, and writing as language use and how these skills are drilled in the Senior III English course. This intention to bring about skills teaching can be said to have achieved some results, especially in terms of the amount of time devoted to reading, listening, and writing, considering that these skills were hardly practiced before and in the early days of the NMET (Gui et al., 1988; Hu, 1990; Li, 1990). It can be regarded as a welcome move toward what is now widely regarded as more effective learning and teaching, as one test constructor put it, "From the point of view of input, it [practice of reading with multiple-choice questions] is OK. The students can read a lot and do some mc questions. This will enrich their knowledge and expose them more to the language" (CF, L.120). I tend to agree with this test constructor in that drilling in listening, reading, and writing can be beneficial to learning to some extent, as comprehensible input has a role to play in L2 acquisition (Krashen, 1998; VanPatten & Sanz, 1995) and the role of comprehensible output is also recognized by other researchers (Swain, 1995; Swain & Lapkin, 1995).

Nonetheless, the type of activities involved, particularly excessive use of multiple-choice items, are motivated by gaining higher test scores rather than the need to use language in real communication, as intended by the test constructors (Li, 1988). Thus, there seems to be only a partial match between the test constructors' intention to promote language use through practice of skills, and the actual practice reported in the course. The skills have been included in the content of teaching, but the teaching methodology is not what the test constructors have intended. The main reason for this seems to be that, with most of its items in the multiple-choice format, the NMET fails to realize the teaching methodology considered by the test constructors to be conducive to the effective development of language abilities.

CONCLUSIONS

Based on the findings of the study, the present author concludes that, after 15 years' use, the NMNET has produced only limited intended washback effects, as teaching of linguistic knowledge is still emphasized and the kind of language taught is restricted to the skills tested in the NMET. This conclusion is consistent with the findings from other washback studies in different contexts (Andrews, 1995; Cheng, 1997; Wall & Alderson, 1993). For example, Cheng's observation that "The changes tend to happen at the obvious and format level" (p. 52) has found support in the present study with respect to the reading and listening exercises in the Senior III English course. The present study also supports the claim that washback is neither simple nor direct, but circuitous and complicated (Wall & Alderson, 1993). This suggests that tests might not be a good lever for change, if this lever is used to set the educational machinery in motion. The machinery, in the sense of the educational systems or school practices, will not easily lend itself to the control of test constructors.

The conceptualization presented thus far has implications for the NMET constructors and policymakers in China. Because the NMET appears not to be an efficient tool to induce pedagogical changes, efforts should be made to investigate other factors in the educational system, so as to seek better means to promote the intended communicative approach to ELT in China's schools. Factors that are thought to hinder operation of intended washback include: teachers' beliefs about language teaching and test preparation; teachers' educational background; teaching style; teaching experience; and inadequate communication between test makers and test users (Alderson & Hamp-Lyons, 1996; Cheng, 1998a; Wall & Alderson, 1993; Watanabe, 1996b). Investigations into these factors and their interactions might deepen our understanding of the function of washback and suggest ways of improving this "lever" for positive, lasting, and widespread change.

APPENDIX[8]

The NMET Washback Project

Test constructor interview

Name of participant ________
Date of interview ________ Place of interview ________
Time started ___________ Time ended ______________

Two NMET past papers, one in the national version and one in the Guangdong version, are at hand for reference.

[8]The interviews were conducted in Chinese. The English version of the interview guide is provided for English-speaking readers.

Introductory statement: Thank you for agreeing to talk with me. The purpose of my research is to investigate the influence of the NMET on middle school teaching and learning. I'd like to have your views on this. The content of our talk will be confidential and used only for this research project.

Questions:

1. I heard that two ways concerning the writing task in the NMET are used by English teachers to prepare their students for the test. The first is to give up the writing task so as to concentrate on the mc questions. The second is to train students to decide on the important points in the input quickly and use simple sentences to express these points. Students are told not to use complex sentences to play safe. What do you think of these strategies?
2. What do you think of the proofreading item? Is it necessary to have it since there is already a writing task?
3. Besides the writing and the proofreading, all the other items are of the mc format, what do you think of this test format?
4. What do you think of the five items on pronunciation?
5. What do you think of the spelling items? Which are better, the present one or the one used before 1996?
6. In Guangdong a new version of the test is used. There have been many unexpected problems for the administration of the listening section. Do you think the listening section should be added? Why? (Why not?)
7. Would you like to add anything else concerning the influence of the NMET?

Teacher interview

Name of participant ________ Age ________ Gender ________
Degree held ______________ Training received __________
No. of years in ESL teaching ________
Date of interview ________ Place of interview ________
Time started ____________ Time ended ____________
Two past papers of the NMET, one in the national version and one in the Guangdong version, are at hand for reference.

Introductory statement: Thank you for agreeing to talk to me. This project I'm working on is called "English in Senior III". I am told that in this course you prepare your students for the NMET. Could you tell me how you do it by answering my questions? What you tell me will be used for this research project only. I won't let other people listen to the recording or see the transcripts. Before I ask questions can you tell me briefly your teaching plan for the course?

Questions:

1. How do you train your students for the writing task?
2. How do you train your students for the proofreading task?
3. What do you think of the mc question format?
4. What do you think of the first five items on the test?
5. What do you think of the spelling test? Which do you think is better? The present one or the one used before 1996?
6. Do you think it's necessary to have the listening section in the test? Why? (Why not?)
7. Would you like to add anything concerning the influence of the NMET?

Closing remarks: Thank you very much for sharing your views with me. We can talk again if you have something to add or clarify. I might have one or more questions to ask you, too. We'll see if we need to have another talk and when. Thank you very much indeed.

CHAPTER

11

The Washback of an EFL National Oral Matriculation Test to Teaching and Learning

Irit Ferman
Tel Aviv University

Although the connection between testing and the teaching–learning process is commonly made, it is not entirely clear whether this connection actually exists and, if it does, what the nature of its effect is. Washback definitions (see chap. 1, this volume) indicate that tests are held to have an influence on teaching, on learning, and on those involved. The introduction of national tests seems to trigger factors that affect the educational process (Shohamy, Donitsa-Schmidt, & Ferman, 1996, p. 298).

The present study examined the washback effects of a national EFL oral matriculation test, introduced by the Ministry of Education into the Israeli educational system, with the officially expressed intent to utilize it as a means of curriculum innovation and upgrading of language skills. The study attempted to find whether this high-stakes test affected the educational processes, the participants, and the products of teaching and learning, and if so, how; it attempted to find whether the washback of the examination innovation corresponded very closely to the effect intended by the policymakers.

CONTEXT OF THE STUDY

English is a first foreign language in Israel and one which constitutes the most honored linguistic resource besides Hebrew. It is perceived by the overall population as a status symbol and as a means of upward socioeconomic mobility (Ben-Rafael, 1994; Shohamy & Donitsa-Schmidt, 1995). The Israeli context is thus a reflection of the spread of English as a language of wider communication, its position in the global linguistic market, and its international status as a Lingua Franca (Phillipson, 1992; Quirk, 1995).

English is taught in Israeli schools from Grade 4 to Grade 12. The grades obtained by the students in English affect graduation from high school as well as entrance and acceptance to tertiary institutions. The English teaching policy here is based on an instrumental approach. English is perceived as a practical skill subject, with the aim of imparting as high a level of language proficiency as possible. The current approach to teaching English in Israeli schools with a focus on communicative competence was officially announced in the 1988 Ministry of Education syllabus.

THE TARGET TEST

The English Foreign Language (EFL) Oral Matriculation Test for Grade 12 was introduced nationally into the Israeli education system in 1986. Since its initial administration, the EFL Oral Test has become routine practice in the Israeli educational system. It constitutes an integral part of the national matriculation examination and makes up 20% of the final grade for the English subject in the matriculation examination. It is an achievement and proficiency test, administered in the twelfth grade to all students who take the written matriculation examination in the English subject at the end of the same school year. This high-stakes test decides success or failure in the matriculation exams and entrance to tertiary learning institutions.

The EFL oral matriculation test, introduced in 1986, consisted of a number of tasks representing several speech interactions (Camron, 1985). This oral test battery was first administered to individual students in 1986. The EFL oral matriculation test battery remained an integral part of the teaching of English, but over the years it underwent a number of changes. The new version of the test—announced and specified in a Director General Bulletin of the Ministry of Education (1998)—consisted of four parts:

1. An extended interview: Students were asked a series of warm-up questions which led to an extended monologue on any topic stemming directly or indirectly from the first stage of the interview.
2. A "modified" role-play: Students asked the tester a series of questions based on cue cards they had not seen before.
3. An extensive reading part: Students reported orally on two books (out of the six) they were required to have read by the time of the test. A reading file, which contained tasks on the six books the students had read over 2 years of studies preceding the test, was handed in to the teacher

one month prior to the oral test. The reading file was then returned to the student who presented it to the examiner at the time of the test.

4. A literature component: Students were tested on pieces of literature studied during the 2 school years preceding the test.

The rationale for introducing the new oral matriculation test battery as stated by the Chief Inspector for English, J. Steiner, was to increase the emphasis on teaching oral language, "... to provide an opportunity for authentic speech and communication and to gauge the pupil's overall level of oral proficiency" (Steiner, 1995a, p. 2). The purpose of the changes was to expand and emphasize the oral skills and to establish a variety of communicative ways of using English. The English Inspectorate's[1] aim was also to encourage pupils to read: "It is important to see the 'Reading for Pleasure' program as a process, and not as an end-product on the day of the oral matriculation exam. It is a process that should start in elementary school and continue up through all grade levels" (Steiner, 1995b, p. 2). Thus the oral test was used as a means to encourage students to read. The Chief Inspector for English, J. Steiner, quoted Krashen (1993) to support the rationale: "When children read for pleasure, ... they acquire, ... nearly all of the ... 'language skills' " (p. 84).

THE STUDY

The purpose of this study was to examine the washback of a new national EFL oral matriculation test battery–introduced into the education system by the Ministry of Education–immediately following its administration. The study examined educational domains, which are most likely to be affected by the introduction of a test. It attempted to find whether washback effects occurred, to see how and why they occurred, and if they did, what the nature of these effects was. The research question at its most general level was: Does the EFL oral matriculation test have washback on the educational processes, the participants, and the products of teaching and learning, in Israeli high schools?

METHOD

Sample

The sample of the study included teachers, students, and EFL inspectors.

---

[1]The English Inspectorate is a body comprised of the Chief Inspector for English and a staff of regional inspectors. Each of the regional inspectors is in charge of a region, which usually includes several towns or settlements.

- 18 teachers of EFL, in Grades 11 to 12, from three different types of high school.
- 120 EFL 12th grade, 3-, 4-, and 5-point students (to be explained below), from three different types of high school and from six different classes, according to ability levels.
- 4 EFL inspectors: (a) the Chief Inspector for English (b) three regional inspectors responsible for the English curriculum implementation in their respective regions.

The three schools where the 18 teachers and 120 students in this study were situated were an academic high school, a comprehensive high school, and a vocational high school. The three different ability levels within the student population were: *lowest ability level* (3-point students); *average ability level* (4-point students); and *highest ability level* (5-point students). The variety of schools and ability levels are of considerable importance, because tests might have different amounts and types of washback on some teachers and learners compared with other teachers and learners.

Instruments

Four types of instruments were used: structured questionnaires, structured interviews, open interviews, and document analyses. (a) Structured Questionnaires comprised of items based on the relevant literature and examined by a team of experts from the Tel-Aviv University School of Education. The questionnaire was then piloted (30 questionnaires were completed by students representing three ability levels, from the three types of schools described earlier) in order to obtain information regarding the relevance and clarity of the questions, the format, and the amount of time required to answer the questions. The questionnaire was then revised accordingly: Several questions were formulated more clearly and two questions were found to be irrelevant and were deleted. Furthermore, all the questions, except five, were changed from open to closed, as the students either ignored the open-ended questions or answered them in an incomplete fashion. The questionnaires were administered to the students in Hebrew to prevent any bias that might occur due to differential command of English among the students. The questionnaires included questions regarding three main variables: teaching, learning, and those involved (see Appendix). (b) Structured Interviews were held with teachers. The interview items were examined by a team of experts from the Tel-Aviv University School of Education, then piloted (3 interviews were held with teachers) to obtain information regarding, as before, the relevance and clarity of the questions, the format, and the amount of time required to answer the questions. The interview was revised accordingly: Several questions were formulated more clearly and three questions were withdrawn because of their repetitive nature. The interview consisted of questions defined from the start and presented to the interviewees. Teachers were encouraged to elaborate on their answers, as the aim was to generate in-depth information. The interview questions comprised of items examining the washback of the test with regard to the same variables: teaching, learning, and those involved. (c) Nonstructured interviews were held with the three regional inspectors, the overall topic of the interview being the EFL oral test and its potential impact on teaching and learning. The expectation was that by allowing the interviewees maximum freedom, ample and perhaps unexpected information would emerge. The interview, nevertheless, was accompanied by a preplanned agenda referring to test washback on teaching and learning. (d) Document Analyses of the Director General Bulletins and instructions issued by the Chief Inspector for English were performed to investigate the intentions of the test designers.

Data Collection Procedure

The data for the EFL test was collected immediately following the administration of the test. The questionnaires were completed by EFL students during class time, which took 25 to 30 minutes, and was preceded by a brief introduction, assuring students of confidentiality. The guided interviews with the teachers and the inspectors were held on a one-to-one basis. Each interview lasted for about 1 hour and was audiorecorded and then transcribed.

Data Analysis

The qualitative analysis was based on a system of categories (i.e., the variables established in the students' and teachers' questionnaires). The ordering system of categories was derived from the research questions that this study posed, and then investigated with the aid of descriptive statistics, such as frequencies, central tendencies, variabilities, and correlations. The descriptive statistics analysis was used to describe different aspects of the data and obtain insights into the data, which were subsequently used for quantitative and qualitative analysis.

RESULTS

In terms of test washback and for the sake of research validity, the results are discussed with reference to more than one dimension. With regard to the population, reference is made to (a) the student population as a whole, and (b) three different ability levels within the student population. Furthermore, there is reference both to the global effects of the test as a whole and to the profile of effects across the four different parts of the test: extended interview, modified role-play, extensive reading, and literature component. The results concerning test washback to teaching, learning, and those involved are examined with regard to the following areas: (a) teaching–learning focus, (b) time allotment, (c) employment of teaching strategies, (d) employment of learning strategies, (e) promotion of learning, (f) parental involvement, (g) anxiety level.

(a) Teaching–Learning Focus

Teaching–learning focus refers to the change resulting in concentrating on the oral skills as a result of the new EFL oral test. Teachers, students, and the inspectorate, stated that the introduction of the oral test had affected the teaching–learning activities in class by focusing teachers' and students' attention and efforts on the oral skills.

Furthermore, all the teachers reported that they would stop teaching oral proficiency immediately following the oral test and would engage in preparing for the written test only. Teachers' remarks include: Teacher I: "I will not go on with oral activities once the oral exam is over," Teacher II: "I certainly won't spend more time on oral tasks after the test!" and Teacher III: "There is no time for any oral activities lessons after the test. I have to prepare my students for the written test. If I had the time I would continue discussions."

Most of the students (66%, $n = 79$) reported that there had been an increased focus on learning the oral skills in class in preparation for the test. However, students' reports showed that this learning focus decreased as level of ability increased. Specifically, 3-point students had had statistically more significant intensive preparation for the test than other students.

The English Inspectors stated in interviews that the oral test had had a tremendous effect on the teaching–learning activities of all those involved. They firmly believed that what teachers taught and students learned, and how they did it, was largely dictated by official exam requirements. They maintained that were the oral test to be canceled, teachers would cease teaching oral skills, and students would stop developing oral proficiency. One of the regional inspectors stated: "There is a change concerning the teaching of English in the respect that you cannot learn a language without the communicative aspect—that is the real revolution!" Another regional inspector added: "The change in teaching has been tremendous! A teacher cannot teach his class anymore without incorporating some kind of communicative activity. The way of teaching has changed too: Techniques such as pair-work, group-work, etc., are employed. The fact is teachers no longer teach from the front of the classroom like they used to."

(b) Time Allotment

Time allotment refers to the amount of EFL classroom time spent on preparation for the test. This is reflected in the time spent weekly on learning for the oral test, as well as extra time and an accelerated pace of learning during the period of time immediately preceding the test.

Most of the teachers (83%, $n = 15$) reported spending 2 hours per week (i.e., 40% of the 5 weekly hours allotted to teaching English) with the 5- and 4-point students learning for the test. The teachers spent 1.5 hours (i.e., 50% of the 3 weekly hours) with the 3-point students, learning for the test. In both cases the time spent on preparation for the test was much larger than the weight assigned to the oral test (i.e., 20% of the total English matriculation test score). Moreover, teachers reported devoting even longer periods of time, including vacation time, on preparation for the test as the date of its administration approached. Teachers' responses include: Teacher I: "A lot of time and effort is devoted to teaching the oral skills . . . in fact, much more time than they deserve if you think of the value of the oral test in the final score!" and Teacher II: "We invest a lot of time and effort in preparation for the oral test. . . . Obviously, if there were no test, we wouldn't."

Most of the students' responses to questions regarding time allotted to learning for the test in class confirmed the teachers' responses. Eighty-six percent of the 5-point students and all of the 4-point students reported between 1 and 3 weekly hours of the 5 weekly hours allotted to learning English for the test, whereas 93.8% of the 3-point students reported having between 1 and 2 weekly hours out of the 3 weekly hours allotted to learning English for the test.

(c) Employment of Teaching Strategies

Teaching strategies refer to the specific techniques that teachers reported using in preparation for the test: student coaching; narrowing of scope and content; intensive drilling with weaker students; individual coaching; and employing integrative teaching techniques.

Student Coaching. Most of the teachers reported using the strategy of student coaching by employing simulations of the test form and content. Most of the twelfth-grade teachers (94%, $n = 17$) reported that their teaching focused on the specific oral tasks that were included in the test, explaining that they believed this was crucial to their students' success on the test.

The extent to which cue cards were practiced provided further indication of the test washback. Although the English Inspectorate recommended doing 10 forms and cue-cards tasks as adequate preparation for the test, most of the teachers (83%, n = 15) reported doing more than 10 tasks, assuming that the more they coached their students, the better they would do on the test. Teachers' remarks regarding this strategy include Teacher I: "I try to simulate the tasks of the new oral exam as best I can when I teach my students. I believe this is the best way to prepare them for what they will be tested on." Also Teacher II: "My aim is to help my students do well in the exam, so of course I teach the items that will be tested in the exam." and Teacher III: "I would certainly not have bothered with cue-cards without the test." Additional comments include Teacher IV: "I would not teach the way I had to because of the exam, but rather speak with my pupils about significant things" and Teacher V: "Let's be honest. What we do during the last TWO years of high school is teach our students how to succeed on their matriculation exams. NOT learn English! The kids know it, too!"

Students' responses to the questionnaires confirmed these findings, as most students (80.2%, n = 96) reported learning 10 to 15 cue cards, with the remainder reporting even more cards. It is worth noting that the 3-point students (the lowest ability level) learned a statistically significant number of cue cards more than the other students.

Narrowing of Scope and Content. The pattern of narrowing the scope and content of teaching to only what was to be tested was consistently repeated through all ability levels (3 = *low*; 4 = *average*; 5 = *high*). Moreover, given some latitude by the English Inspectorate in the choice of literary texts which students had to learn and then be tested on, most of the teachers (89%, n = 16) reported that they taught students shorter and easier texts whenever possible—in this case, stories rather than plays and essays—as one of the ways to help their students succeed on the test. Teachers' remarks include: Teacher I: "I want my pupils to be ready for the test. Why should I try to achieve the impossible by teaching them texts that are either too long or too difficult for them?" and Teacher II: "I usually choose to teach texts that are easier for the students to cope with. . . . This seems to me the best way to help the students prepare for the test."

Intensive Drilling With Weaker Students. Most of the teachers (83%, n = 15) reported drilling the material in an intensive manner and spending extra time with the weaker students. Teachers reported that the 3-point students were taught the highest number of cue cards and allotted more teaching time, compared with 4- and 5-point students. They explained that weaker students needed more drilling to ensure their success on the test, as their command of the target language was lower. One of the teachers stated: "The more you drill these questions with the students, the better their chances of doing well in the test!"

Individual Coaching. Teachers reported that some students were tutored individually and gradually encouraged to participate in class. Most of the teachers (77%, n = 14) stated that about 10% of the students in their classes found it too traumatic an experience to perform orally, simulating test-like tasks, in front of their peers. These students were coached individually, usually during the breaks, until at some stage of the learning process they were able to perform without too much anxiety in front of their peers.

Integrative Teaching Techniques. Most of the teachers (61%, n = 11) claimed that they taught oral skills employing an integrative approach, combining oral skills with other language skills. This enabled them to make more efficient use of the time at their disposal, and consequently to teach the oral skills more frequently. One teacher stated: "The oral test has even affected the way I teach composition. In my classes students don't just write compositions or prepare book tasks—they also have to be able to give an oral presentation of what they have written. I believe that by combining these two skills, I make more efficient use of the time. . . . Well, I have to prepare them for the exam as best I can."

(d) Employment of Learning Strategies

Learning strategies refer to the specific techniques that students reported using in preparation for the test. Specifically: intensive learning for the test; memorization; self-learning; and tutor-employment. It must be noted, however, that there is a differential impact, reflected in a difference in the extent and type of learning for the test, both with regard to the different ability levels of the students and the different parts of the oral test.

Intensive Learning to the Test. Students' reports with regard to learning to the oral test showed that most of the students (85.2%, n = 102) learned quite intensively for the test. It must be stressed that the lower the students' ability level, the higher the intensity of learning. Furthermore, most of the students (78%, n = 94) believed that they could attain a better score in the test by cramming for it, with 4-point students statistically significantly more convinced of this.

Memorization. Most of the students (77.5%, n = 93) claimed to have memorized large parts of test-related tasks in preparation for the test. A significant statistical difference ($p < .001$) was found between the various levels of students; the higher the students' ability level, the better informed they were with regard to which parts of the test they were to be examined on. Data show that 68.7% of the 3-point students and 72.4% of the 4-point students, compared with 81.4% of the 5-point students, knew in advance which and how many cue cards they would be tested on, and memorized them accordingly.

Self-Learning as a Compensation Strategy. Students reported that they often learned the material for the test on their own. On the whole, it seems that self-learning increased as learning in class decreased. The diversity in the extent of self-learning relates to the different parts of the oral test. It is worth noting that whenever students did not learn for some parts of the test in class, they generally compensated for it by self-learning (i.e., learning on their own).

Tutor Employment. Some students reported that tutors were employed to help them prepare for the test. According to students' reports, 51.7% (n = 62) of the students were tutored for the oral test either by private teachers or by higher ability fellow students. There was a statistically significant difference between 3-, 4-, and 5-point students in this respect: 3- and 4-point students were tutored for the test significantly more than 5-point students (i.e., the weaker the students, the more were they tutored for the test).

(e) Promotion of Language Skills

Promotion of language skills refers to the upgrading of students' oral skills and the promotion of their reading skills. Although the English Inspectorate and most of the students believed that the test had resulted in the upgrading of the oral skills and in the promotion of reading, most of the teachers claimed that not all the parts of the test had had the desired impact on upgrading the oral skills and they were doubtful about the promotion of reading. Moreover, findings showed that much less reading had been done by students than was presumed by the English Inspectorate and professed by students.

Upgrading Students' Oral Skills. Teachers stated that the oral test as such had had a considerable impact on upgrading the students' overall command of English or on the upgrading of the oral skills. Most of the teachers (89%, n = 16) stressed, however, that not all parts of the oral test had had the desired impact on upgrading students' oral language skills. Although they believed the extended interview and the literature parts had had an effect on the promotion of oral skills, they criticized the cue cards, claiming that this part had had a very minor effect on upgrading the students' overall command of English or on the improvement of oral language skills. The cue cards were intended by the inspectorate as a proficiency test (i.e., the students were to be tested on cue cards they had not seen before). However, in reality, the examiners tested them on the cue cards their classroom teachers had used in preparation for the test. Most of the teachers (94%, $n = 17$) admitted they coached their students for this part of the test, the end product being memorization of a certain number of cue cards, rather than learning to form and use questions in authentic, communicative contexts. They added that, as far as preparation for the test was concerned, this might be an adequate approach, but it did not do much toward promoting the oral skills.

Most of the students (80%, $n = 96$) believed that following the oral test there was an upgrading in their overall command of English. However, there is a statistically significant difference between the 3-, 4-, and 5-point students here, as 100% of the 4-point students were of this opinion.

The English Inspectorate claimed that the introduction of the oral test had had a very positive educational impact, with the optimal result of upgrading students' command of English, and the oral skills in particular. They were convinced that from an educational point of view, the oral test had been a great success in that although only the higher grades were tested, a focus on learning the oral skills had been achieved not only in the higher grades but in the lower ones as well. One of the regional inspectors stated: "In fact, the washback effect goes down all the way to the elementary school. The moment they added an oral component to the matriculation exam, they added oral component tests to the elementary school as well."

Promotion of Reading. Although teachers recognized the importance of reading in the process of second language acquisition, most of them (94%, $n = 17$) rejected this part of the test as an inadequate and inefficient means of promoting reading. They added that in this part of the oral test, there seemed to be a gap between teaching and testing. Consequently, the test was not an integral part of the teaching process and teachers doubted if in its current form this part of the test could really promote reading. Although the English Inspectorate was confident that students were reading and were in control of things, most of the teachers (94%, $n = 17$) stated that they were skeptical about any reading reported by students.

The teachers complained that they had very little control of what their students had read (because students could choose any reading text they liked, the only approval criterion employed by teacher being suitable language level) or whether they read at all. A minority of the teachers (11%, $n = 2$) believed that all their students had read the two extensive reading books required for the exam, as all of them had handed in their reading files as required. Some of the teachers (27%, $n = 5$) believed that many of their students had read the books, although they could not say how many. They added that all their students handed in reading files containing the assigned tasks. However, most of the teachers (62%, $n = 11$) stated they did not know whether their students had actually read the books, even though they had handed in the required reading files. Teachers' remarks include Teacher I: "How can I tell for sure if they have read the books?! It's impossible to check if they wrote the assignments by themselves or just copied from others!" and Teacher II: "One of my students has handed in the two assignments, but he really outdid himself. Each of them was in a different handwriting!!!" Also Teacher III: "It is really a process of recycling material, and mind you, it will be even worse next year! There will be huge numbers of summaries and students will just have to swap between them ..." and Teacher IV: "Is there any way to check that they have read it? I feel some kind of regression ... I feel 90% are not reading—They are copying!"

Most of the students (80%, $n = 96$) reported having read the required two books for the extensive reading part of the test. There is, however, a statistically significant difference between the students. Only 37% of the 3-point students compared with 79.3% of the 4-point and 89.3% of the 5-point students reported having read the required two books. These results point to a decrease in performance potentially parallel to a decrease in ability level.

However, when asked about their fellow students, only 60.8% ($n = 73$) of the students (compared to the 80%, $n = 96$, above) believed that the two required books had actually been read by their fellow students. Here again, there is a statistically significant difference between the students, as more of the 5-point students believed that the two books required for the test had actually been read by their fellow students. The obvious gap between the declared behavior of self as against the observed behavior of others is well worth noting here, and is extremely large in the case of the 4-point students. Moreover, 65% ($n = 78$) of the students agreed with the their teachers that handing in the reading files on two books, as required by the English Inspectorate, did not necessarily mean that the students had read the books. Here again, there is a statistically significant difference between the students: 3- and 4-point students believed significantly less in the correlation between handing in the reading files and having actually read the books than did the 5-point students.

When asked to explain the foregoing differences of opinion, students offered explanations such as: "I could easily copy the assignment from another student," "I could read the beginning and the ending of the book only and still do one of the optional reading tasks," and "It's obvious that you don't really have to read the book in order to do the written assignment and pass the test. The general nature of the questions makes them easy to answer even without having read the books." Also "Nobody in his right mind reads the whole book!" "I downloaded the summaries of the books from the Internet," "My private teacher helped me write the assignment. She actually summarized the books for me," "I didn't read the books. I got video-cassettes of the movies instead" and "Everybody knows one can pass the test without having read the books and no one will be the wiser."

In apparent contrast to the findings, 95.8% (n = 115) of the students reported having handed in completed reading files, containing the required two book assignments. There is a statistically significant difference, though, between the 3-point students, 81% of whom had handed in a complete reading file, the 4-point students, 100% of whom had handed in a complete reading file, and the 5-point students, 97.3% of whom had handed in a complete reading file. The minority of students (4.2%, n = 5) who had not handed in a reading file, in response to an open-ended question, made statements such as: "I could have easily copied the assignment from other students but I am morally opposed to cheating!" "I haven't handed in a file as a matter of principle! I won't cheat like some of the others!" and "To tell the truth . . . it's not worth the effort. I don't mind getting a slightly lower score because of that . . ."

The English Inspectorate declared that one of the new EFL oral test aims was to encourage pupils to read: "It is a process that should start in elementary school and continue up through all grade levels." The inspectors explained in the interviews that the extensive reading part of the test had been added with the specific intent of creating a washback effect, which they believed could already be witnessed in schools. They believed, for example, that the reading files the students had to prepare for the oral test had led students to read English not only in the upper level grades but also in the lower level ones. One of the regional inspectors stated: "It has led a lot to extensive reading. Extensive reading is the 'in' thing now and teachers are doing it much more extensively than they did in the past. This is mainly due to the fact that students are taking a matriculation exam in extensive reading. Even though in the exam it is only 5%, it has much wider applications!"

(f) Parental Involvement

According to 59.2% (n = 71) of the students, there was parental involvement in the test, expressed in parents urging the students to learn for the test. Parents of 4-point students showed statistically more significant involvement with the test than the other parents. Furthermore, 51.7% (n = 62) parents employed tutors to help students prepare for the test. There was a statistically significant difference between 3-, 4-, and 5-point students; the weaker the students, the more their parents employed tutors to help them prepare for the test.

(g) Anxiety Level

This aspect refers to test washback on teachers' and students' level of anxiety. Most of the teachers (83%, $n = 15$) admitted that the test aroused feelings of high anxiety and fear of test results, both in them and in their students. Teachers explained that because the oral test results were made public knowledge immediately following the test, and because students and teachers tended to compare results with other classes, they were quite anxious for their students to do well in the oral test. Teachers felt that the test results reflected on their competence as teachers. They admitted feeling pressure to cover the material for the test, and they stated that they were ready to invest extra time and effort to ensure better results. Teachers' remarks include Teacher I: "I'm never a hundred percent sure about my students' success in the test. It's a stressful situation" and Teacher II: "The oral test has an effect on all those involved. Teachers spend time teaching to and students spend time learning for the test. Schools and parents are involved too."

Most students' (77.5%, $n = 93$) reports showed that the test aroused in them feelings of anxiety to quite a high extent. There was also a statistically significant difference between 3-, 4-, and 5-point students here: 4-point students were the most anxious ones. Moreover, 78.3% ($n = 94$) of the students reported being adversely affected by potential failure in the test. On the whole, 3- and 4-point students were significantly more adversely affected than the 5-point students were by potential failure in the test.

CONCLUSION AND IMPLICATIONS

The Nature of the Washback Effect

The EFL oral matriculation test resulted in strong washback on the educational processes, the participants and the products of teaching and learning in Israeli high schools. There was an increased focus of teachers, students, and parents on the oral language skills. This resulted in an increase in time allotment for the development of these skills, and an accelerated pace of learning as well as an employment of teaching and learning strategies geared towards test success. There was an intense focus on content and a narrowing of scope, reflecting the test requirements. There was also an increase in parental involvement and in anxiety levels among teachers and students. This seems to confirm that what is tested is indeed taught and learned (Spolsky, 1995a).

The EFL oral matriculation test resulted in both positive and negative washback on the processes, the products, and those involved. The positive washback was: Focusing the attention of teachers, learners, and parents on the tested skills; the promotion of learning the oral skills; and the upgrading of the oral skills. Moreover, focus on test format while teaching to the test might be perceived as being aimed at positive washback, as the promotion of learning and test familiarization might possibly have the effect of alleviating test anxiety (Messick, 1996). The negative washback was: a narrowing of the scope and content of teaching and learning; increased pressure to cover the material; a high level of anxiety; and fear of test results among teachers and students. This negative washback has been referred to in the language testing literature as narrowing of the curriculum (Madaus, 1988) and the educational process (Spolsky, 1995a) and increasing anxiety (Shohamy, 1993b; Shohamy et al., 1996). Negative washback was also reflected in students' memorization of material, rather than acquisition and development of oral skills, referred to in literature as test score pollution, or increases in test scores without a parallel rise in ability in the construct tested (Haladyna, Nolan, & Haas, 1991). Additional evidence of negative washback was the preference for easier teaching tasks, which has been referred to in the measurement literature as reduced emphasis on skills that require complex thinking (Darling-Hammond & Wise, 1985; Fredericksen, 1984). Apparently, both positive and negative washback tend to be associated with high-stakes testing (Por & Ki, 1995). Messick (1996) perceived positive or negative washback as "good or bad practice that is evidently linked to the introduction and use of a test" (p. 254).

The EFL oral matriculation test resulted in differential washback. This was reflected in the extent and type of teaching and learning for the test, both with regard to the different parts of the oral test and the different ability levels of the students. Specifically: (a) Students compensated for not having learned for certain parts of the test in class by learning on their own. (b) The lower the students' ability level, the higher the extent of teaching and learning towards the test. One of the most obvious features of student–teacher culture is that teachers teach and students learn for success (Spolsky, 1995a). In the case of weaker students, obviously, more work needs to be invested both by teachers and by students in order to ensure success. (c) 4-point students (i.e., the average ability level), were significantly different from other students in that all of them handed in the reading files. Their anxiety level was the highest and they were most adversely affected by potential failure in the test. Furthermore, their parents showed significantly more involvement with the test, expressed in their urging their children to learn for the test. All the 4-point students believed that following the oral test there was an upgrading in their overall command of English. The 4-point students and their parents seem to be ambitious, to aspire to the highest achievement possible and willing to invest extra resources to do so. It might point to the upward mobility phenomenon of the average level aspiring to join the highest level and believing they can achieve it.

There were diverse perceptions with regard to the upgrading of the oral skills and the promotion of the reading skills. Specifically, although the English Inspectorate presumed this to be the case, and the students professed that the test had had a considerable effect on the upgrading of the oral skills and on the promotion of reading, teachers claimed that while some parts of the test had had considerable impact on the upgrading of the oral skills, it had had little impact on the promotion of reading. Moreover, findings supported the teachers' perceptions, showing that students had apparently done much less reading than presumed by the English Inspectorate. The reason for the different perceptions might be an intentional disregard of reality on the part of the Inspectorate and declarative level opinions on the part of the students, compared with teachers' unwillingness to support the Inspectorate's feeling of satisfaction regarding test effects.

Washback and Validity

This study found evidence of *validity*, as well as sources of bias and unfairness, resulting in *lack of validity*, while examining the consequences of the EFL national oral test battery in Israel. Positive washback or any positive consequences following the introduction of the test are perceived as related to *consequential validity*; negative washback or negative consequences are perceived as *lack of validity*.

Consequential validity was evidentially linked to the introduction of the test in that it had a positive washback effect, as specified before. However, there is evidence that this washback was incomplete: Test washback only partially fulfilled the goals of the test designers. Furthermore, it was a differential washback, in that the test had a more pronounced effect on some stakeholders than on others, i.e., on different ability levels among students and their respective teachers and parents.

Further evidence points to additional major sources of bias and unfairness: the uses the English Inspectorate made of the test. The test, which was intended as a test of oral skills, was used as a means to promote reading skills, which was done by the inclusion of a reading component in the oral test. The lack of fit between test content and teaching content reflects the Inspectorate's approach of taking advantage of the testing situation and manipulating the educational system.

In summary, the positive consequences point to the consequential validity of the test, and indicate that assessment can promote learning and washback can be beneficial for the educational system. However, the negative consequences point to a lack of validity, resulting in unfairness and bias, which eventually hinder learning.

Some Unresolved Ethical Issues: Recommendations

This study highlights the power and control the Inspectorate, that is, the test designers, attribute to the test. The test is viewed as the primary curriculum, as a means to impose new textbooks and new teaching methods (Shohamy, 1993a), and to dictate priorities within the system (Shohamy, 1997).

It has been shown that test washback does not always correspond to the effects intended by the Inspectorate. As a means for curriculum innovation and implementation, washback may have some predictable effects. However, it may also have much less predictable ones. Thus, to ensure the desired effect, the English Inspectorate needs to consider a variety of factors that may have a washback effect on the performance of the stakeholders. A detailed examination of the educational context is necessary, so test washback can be thoroughly understood and employed for beneficial effects in education. Pragmatically, it would then seem safe to assume that test impact may facilitate the promotion of curriculum innovation and implementation in an educational context where all those involved collaborate to promote learning.

APPENDIX

Students' Questionnaire

Dear Student,

We are conducting a research with regard to the new EFL oral matriculation test. The questionnaire is confidential and will be used for research purposes only.

Thank you for your cooperation
The research team

Sex: boy/girl Grade:__________ Level of English studies: 3/4/5/ points

School:___________________________________

The EFL oral matriculation test includes four parts as follows:

(a) Interview (b) Cue-cards (c) Extensive reading (d) Literature

Please circle your answer to the following questions or answer with a phrase/sentence wherever necessary:

1. Have you studied for the following parts of the test in class and/or by self-learning?

If so, where?

(a) Interview - yes/no (i) in class (ii) self-learning (iii) both
(b) Cue-cards - yes/no (i) in class (ii) self-learning (iii) both
(c) Extensive reading - yes/no (i) in class (ii) self-learning (iii) both
(d) Literature - yes/no (i) in class (ii) self-learning (iii) both

2. Answer with regard to the number of items studied for each part of the test:

cue-cards: ___ play:_____ stories:______ essays:______ poems:______
extensive-reading books: __________________

3. Does handing in a reading file mean that a student has read the required books?

(i) yes (ii) not necessarily

Could you explain?

____

____

4. In your opinion, how many books have most of the other students read for the test?

1 2 0 other ____

5. The reading file of most of the students reported on their having read the following number of books: 1 2 0

6. How many weekly hours were dedicated in class to studying for the EFL oral test?

0 15 minutes 30 minutes 1 hour 1.5 hours 2 hours 2.5 hours 3 hours
other __________

Please read the following questions and circle for each one the answer which seems most appropriate to you: 1 = not at all; 2 = to a slight extent; 3 = to some extent; 4 = to a large extent; 5 = definitely yes.

7. When you studied for the **interview** part of the test, you have improved your language skills as follows:

reading **1 2 3 4 5**
writing **1 2 3 4 5**
speaking **1 2 3 4 5**

8. When you studied for the **cue-cards** part of the test, you have improved your language skills as follows:

reading **1 2 3 4 5**
writing **1 2 3 4 5**
speaking **1 2 3 4 5**

9. When you studied for the **literature** part of the test, you have improved your language skills as follows:

reading **1 2 3 4 5**
writing **1 2 3 4 5**
speaking **1 2 3 4 5**

10. When you studied for the **extensive-reading** part of the test, you have improved your language skills as follows:

reading **1 2 3 4 5**
writing **1 2 3 4 5**
speaking **1 2 3 4 5**

11. Did you have private tutors or were tutored by your friends while studying for the test? **1 2 3 4 5**

12. Has studying for the test improved your English? **1 2 3 4 5**

13. My parents have been aware of the test. **1 2 3 4 5**

14. My parents urged me to study intensively for the test. **1 2 3 4 5**

15. Has your English teacher dedicated extra time to studying for the test (during breaks, on account of other lessons, during the Passover holiday, etc.)? **1 2 3 4 5**

16. The students were very anxious about the results of the test. **1 2 3 4 5**

17. The students were very anxious while being tested. **1 2 3 4 5**

18. One can do well in this test without studying too much for it. 1 2 3 4 5

19. It is very important for the students to get a good grade in the test. 1 2 3 4 5

20. One can do well in the test by cramming to it. 1 2 3 4 5

21. I approve of the four parts of this test. 1 2 3 4 5

22. It is a test of high importance. 1 2 3 4 5

References

Adams, R. S., & Chen, D. (1981). *The process of educational innovation: An international perspective*. London: Kogan Page.

AEL. (2000). Notes from the field: KERA in the classroom. *Notes from the field: Education reform in rural Kentucky, 7*(1), 1–18.

Alderson, J. C. (1986). Innovations in language testing. In M. Portal (Ed.), *Innovations in language testing: Proceedings of the IUS/NFER conference* (pp. 93–105). Windsor: NFER-Nelson.

Alderson, J. C. (1990). The relationship between grammar and reading in an English for academic purposes test battery. In D. Douglas & C. Chappelle (Eds.), *A new decade of language testing research: Selected papers from the Annual Language Testing Research Colloquium* (pp. 203–219). Alexandria, VA: Teachers of English to Speakers of Other Languages.

Alderson, J. C. (1992). Guidelines for the evaluation of language education. In J. C. Alderson & A. Beretta (Eds.), *Evaluating second language education* (pp. 274–304). Cambridge, England: Cambridge University Press.

Alderson, J. C., & Banerjee, J. (1996). *How might impact study instruments be validated?* Cambridge, England: University of Cambridge Local Examinations Syndicate.

Alderson, J. C., & Banerjee, J. (2001). Impact and washback research in language testing. In C. Elder, A. Brown, E. Grove, K. Hill, N. Iwashita, T. Lumley, K. McLoughlin, & T. McNamara (Eds.), *Experimenting with uncertainty: Essays in honor of Alan Davies* (pp. 150–161). Cambridge, England: Cambridge University Press.

Alderson, J. C., & Hamp-Lyons, L. (1996). TOEFL preparation courses: A study of washback. *Language Testing, 13*, 280–297.

Alderson, J. C., & Scott, M. (1992). Insiders and outsiders and participatory evaluation. In J. C. Alderson & A. Beretta (Eds.), *Evaluating second language curriculum* (pp. 25–60). Cambridge, England: Cambridge University Press.

Alderson, J. C., & Wall, D. (1993). Does washback exist? *Applied Linguistics, 14*, 115–129.

Alderson, J. C., & Wall, D. (Eds.). (1996). [Special issue]. *Language Testing, 13*(3).

Allwright, D., & Bailey, K. M. (1991). *Focus on the language classroom: An introduction to classroom research for language teachers*. Cambridge, England: Cambridge University Press.

Amano, I. (1990). *Education and examination in modern Japan* (W. K. Cummings & F. Cummings, Trans.). Tokyo: University of Tokyo Press. (Original work published 1983)

Anderson, J. O., Muir, W., Bateson, D. J., Blackmore, D., & Rogers, W. T. (1990). *The impact of provincial examinations on education in British Columbia: General report.* Victoria: British Columbia Ministry of Education.

Andrews, S. (1994). The washback effect of examinations: Its impact upon curriculum innovation in English language teaching. *Curriculum Forum, 4*(1), 44–58.

Andrews, S. (1995). Washback or washout? The relationship between examination reform and curriculum innovation. In D. Nunan, V. Berry, & R. Berry (Eds.), *Bringing about change in language education* (pp. 67–81). Hong Kong: University of Hong Kong.

Andrews, S., & Fullilove, J. (1993). Backwash and the use of English oral: Speculations on the impact of a new examination upon sixth form English language testing in Hong Kong. *New Horizons, 34,* 46–52.

Andrews, S., & Fullilove, J. (1994). Assessing spoken English in public examinations—Why and how? In J. Boyle & P. Falvey (Eds.), *English language testing in Hong Kong* (pp. 57–85). Hong Kong: Chinese University Press.

Andrews, S., & Fullilove, J. (1997, December). *The elusiveness of washback: Investigating the impact of a new oral exam on students' spoken language performance.* Paper presented at the International Language in Education Conference, University of Hong Kong, Hong Kong.

Andrews, S., Fullilove, J., & Wong, Y. (2002). Targeting washback: A case-study. *System, 30,* 207–223.

Ariyoshi, H., & Senba, K. (1983). Daigaku nyushi junbi kyoiku ni kansuru kenkyu [A study on preparatory teaching for entrance examination]. *Fukuoka Kyoiku Daigaku Kiyo, 33,* 1–21.

Arnove, R. F., Altback, P. G., & Kelly, G. P. (Eds.). (1992). *Emergent issues in education: Comparative perspectives.* Albany, NY: State University of New York Press.

Aschbacher, P. R., Baker, E. L., & Herman, J. L. (Eds.). (1988). *Improving large-scale assessment* (Resource Paper No. 9). Los Angeles: University of California, National Center for Research on Evaluation, Standards, and Student Testing.

Aschbacher, P. R. (1990). *Monitoring the impact of testing and evaluation innovations projects: State activities and interest concerning performance-based assessment.* Los Angeles: University of California, National Center for Research on Evaluation, Standards, and Student Testing.

Association of Language Testers in Europe. (1995). *Development and descriptive checklists for tasks and examinations.* Cambridge, England: Author.

Association of Language Testers in Europe. (1998). *ALTE handbook of language examinations and examination systems.* Cambridge, England: University of Cambridge Local Examinations Syndicate.

Bachman, L., Davidson, F., Ryan, K., & Choi, I. C. (Eds.). (1993). *An investigation into the comparability of two tests of English as a foreign language.* Cambridge, England: Cambridge University Press.

Bachman, L. F., & Palmer, A. S. (1996). *Language testing in practice.* Oxford, England: Oxford University Press.

Bachman, L. F., Purpura, J. E., & Cushing, S. T. (1993). *Development of a questionnaire item bank to explore test-taker characteristics.* Cambridge, England: University of Cambridge Local Examinations Syndicate.

Bailey, K. M. (1996). Working for washback: A review of the washback concept in language testing. *Language Testing, 13,* 257–279.

Bailey, K. M. (1999). *Washback in language testing.* Princeton, NJ: Educational Testing Service.

Baker, E. L. (1989). *Can we fairly measure the quality of education?* (Tech. Rep. No. 290). Los Angeles: University of California, Center for the Study of Evaluation.

Baker, E. L. (1991, September). *Issues in policy, assessment, and equity.* Paper presented at the national research symposium on limited English proficient students' issues: Focus on evaluation and measurement, Washington, DC.

Baker, E., Aschbacher, P., Niemi, D., & Sato, E. (1992). *Performance assessment models: Assessing content area explanations*. Los Angeles: University of California, National Center for Research on Evaluation, Standards, and Student Testing.

Banerjee, J. V. (1996). *The design of the classroom observation instruments*. Cambridge, England: University of Cambridge Local Examinations Syndicate.

Ben-Rafael, E. (1994). *Language, identity, and social division: The case of Israel*. Oxford, England: Clarendon Press.

Bergeson, T., Wise, B. J., Fitton, R., Gill, D. H., & Arnold, N. (2000). *Guidelines for participation and testing accommodations for special populations on the Washington assessment of student learning (WASL)*. Olympia, WA: Office of Superintendent of Public Instruction.

Berry, V., Falvey, P., Nunan, D., Burnett, M., & Hunt, J. (1995). Assessment and change in the classroom. In D. Nunan, R. Berry & V. Berry (Eds.), *Bringing about change in language education* (pp. 31–54). Hong Kong: University of Hong Kong, Department of Curriculum Studies.

Berwick, R., & Ross, S. (1989). Motivation after matriculation: Are Japanese learners of English still alive after exam hell? *Japan Association for Language Teaching Journal, 11*, 193–210.

Biggs, J. B. (1992). The psychology of assessment and the Hong Kong scene. *Bulletin of the Hong Kong Psychological Society, 29*, 1–21.

Biggs, J. B. (1995). Assumptions underlying new approaches to educational assessment. *Curriculum Forum, 4*(2), 1–22.

Biggs, J. B. (Ed.). (1996). *Testing: To educate or to select? Education in Hong Kong at the cross-roads*. Hong Kong: Hong Kong Educational Publishing.

Biggs, J. B. (1998). Assumptions underlying new approaches to assessment. In P. G. Stimpson & P. Morris (Eds.), *Curriculum and assessment for Hong Kong* (pp. 351–384). Hong Kong: Open University of Hong Kong Press.

Biggs, J. B. (1999). *Teaching for quality learning at university*. Buckingham, England: Open University Press.

Black, P., & Wiliam, D. (1998). Assessment and classroom learning. *Assessment in education: Principles, policy and practice 5*(1), 7–75.

Blenkin, G. M., Edwards, G., & Kelly, A. V. (1992). *Change and the curriculum*. London: P. Chapman.

Blewchamp, P. (1994). *Washback in TOEFL classrooms: An exploratory investigation into the influence of the TOEFL test on teaching content and methodology*. Unpublished master's thesis, Lancaster University, England.

Bonkowski, F. (1996). *Instrument for the assessment of teaching materials*. Unpublished manuscript, Lancaster University, England.

Borko, H., & Elliott, R. (1999). "Hands-on" pedagogy vs. "hands-off" accountability: Tensions between competing commitments for exemplary teachers of mathematics in Kentucky. *Phi Delta Kappa, 80*, 394–400.

Bracey, G. W. (1987). Measurement-driven instruction: Catchy phrase, dangerous practice. *Phi Delta Kappa, 68*, 683–686.

Bracey, G. W. (1989). The $150 million redundancy. *Phi Delta Kappa, 70*, 698–702.

Bray, M., & Steward, L. (Eds.). (1998). *Examination systems in small states: Comparative perspectives on policies, models and operations*. London: Commonwealth Secretariat.

Briggs, C. L. (1986). *Learning how to ask: A sociolinguistic appraisal of the role of the interview in social science research*. Cambridge, England: Cambridge University Press.

Brindley, G. (1989). *Assessing achievement in the learner-centered curriculum*. Sydney, Australia: National Center for English Language Teaching and Research.

Brindley, G. (1994). Competency-based assessment in second language programs: Some issues and questions. *Prospect, 9*(2), 41–55.

Broadfoot, P. (1998, April). *Categories, standards and instrumentalism: Theorizing the changing discourse of assessment policy in English primary education*. Paper presented at the annual conference of the American Educational Research Association, San Diego, CA.

Broadfoot, P. (1999, September). *Empowerment or performativity? English assessment policy in the late twentieth century.* Paper presented at the British Educational Research Association Annual Conference, Sussex, England.

Brooke, N., & Oxenham, J. (1984). The influence of certification and selection on teaching and learning. In J. Oxenham (Ed.), *Education versus qualifications?* (pp. 147–175). London: Allen and Unwin.

Brown, J. D. (1997). Do tests washback on the language classroom? *The TESOLANZ Journal, 5*(5), 63–80.

Brown, J. D. (2001). *Using surveys in language programs.* Cambridge, England: Cambridge University Press.

Bude, U. (1989). *The challenge of quality in primary education in Africa.* Bonn, Germany: German Foundation for International Development, Education, Science and Documentation Center.

Burrows, C. (1993). *Assessment guidelines for the certificate in spoken and written English: Educational Draft* (Vols. 1–5). Sydney, Australia: New South Wales Adult Migrant English Service.

Burrows, C. (1998). *Searching for washback: An investigation into the impact on teachers of the implementation into the adult migrant English program of the certificate in spoken and written English.* Unpublished doctoral dissertation, Macquarie University, Sydney, Australia.

Burrows, C. (1999, July). *Adopters, adapters, and resisters: Did the assessment of the certificates in spoken and written English change teaching in AMEP.* Paper presented at the Language Testing Research Colloquium, Tsukuba, Japan.

Burrows, C. (2001). Searching for washback: The impact of assessment in the Certificate in Spoken and Written English. In G. Brindley & C. Burrows (Eds.), *Studies in immigrant English language assessment: Vol. 2.* Sydney, Australia: National Center for English Language Teaching and Research.

Bush, M. (1998). *A sociocultural view of washback in Japanese university entrance exams.* Unpublished manuscript, Ontario Institute for Studies in Education, Toronto, Ontario, Canada.

Calder, P. (1990). *Impact of diploma examinations on the teaching-learning process.* Admonition, Alberta, Canada: Alberta Teacher Association.

Calder, P. (1997). *Impact of Alberta achievement tests on the teaching-learning process.* Admonition, Alberta, Canada: Alberta Teacher Association.

Camron, H. (1985). *Guide to the oral Bagrut examination.* Jerusalem: Ministry of Education and Culture, English Inspectorate.

Cannell, J. J. (1987). Nationally-normed elementary achievement testing in America's public schools: How all 50 states are above the national average. *Educational Measurement: Issues and Practice, 7*(4), 12–15.

Chapman, D. W., & Snyder, C. W. (2000). Can high-stakes national testing improve instruction: Reexamining conventional wisdom. *International Journal of Educational Development, 20,* 457–474.

Chaudron, C. (1986). The interaction of quantitative and qualitative approaches to research: A view of the second language classroom. *TESOL Quarterly, 20,* 709–717.

Chaudron, C. (1988). *Second language classrooms: Research on teaching and learning.* Cambridge, England: Cambridge University Press.

Cheng, L. (1997). How does washback influence teaching? Implications for Hong Kong. *Language and Education, 11,* 38–54.

Cheng, L. (1998a). *The washback effect of public examination change on classroom teaching: An impact study of the 1996 Hong Kong certificate of education in English on the classroom teaching of English in Hong Kong secondary schools.* Unpublished doctoral dissertation, University of Hong Kong, Hong Kong.

Cheng, L. (1998b). Impact of a public English examination change on students' perceptions and attitudes toward their English learning. *Studies in Educational Evaluation, 24,* 279–301.

Cheng, L. (1999). Changing assessment: Washback on teacher perspectives and actions. *Teaching and Teacher Education, 15,* 253–271.

Cheng, L. (2001). Washback studies: Methodological considerations. *Curriculum Forum, 10*(2), 17–32.

Cheng, L., & Couture, J. C. (2000). Teachers' work in the global culture of performance. *Alberta Journal of Educational Research, 46*(1), 65–74.

Chin, R., & Benne, K. D. (1976). General strategies for effecting changes in human systems. In W. G. Bennis, K. D. Benne, R. Chin, & K. E. Corey (Eds.), *The planning of change* (3rd ed., pp. 22–45). New York: Holt, Rinehart and Winston.

Clark, J. L. (1987). *Curriculum renewal in school foreign language learning*. Oxford, England: Oxford University Press.

Cohen, L. (1976). *Educational research in classrooms and schools: A manual of materials and methods*. London: Harper & Row.

Cohen, L., & Manion, L. (1989). *Research methods in education* (3rd ed.). London: Routledge.

Cohen, L., Manion, L., & Morrison, K. (2000). *Research methods in education* (5th ed.). London: Routledge Falmer.

Cooley, W. W. (1991). State-wide student assessment. *Educational Measurement: Issues and Practice, 10*, 3–6.

Cooper, R. (1989). *Language planning and social change*. Cambridge, England: Cambridge University Press.

Corbett, H. D., & Wilson, B. L. (1988). Raising the stakes in statewide mandatory minimum competency testing. In W. L. Boyd & C. T. Kerchner (Eds.), *The politics of excellence and choice in education: The 1987 politics of education association yearbook* (pp. 27–39). New York: Falmer Press.

Corbett, H. D., & Wilson, B. L. (1991). *Testing, reform and rebellion*. Norwood, NJ: Ablex.

Council of Chief State School Officers. (1998). *Annual Survey of State Student Assessment Programs, Summary Report*. Washington, DC: Author.

Council of Ministers of Education, Canada. (1994). *School achievement indicators program*. Toronto, Ontario, Canada: Author.

Cronbach, L. J. (1982). Prudent aspirations for social inquiry. In W. H. Kruskal (Ed.), *The social sciences: Their nature and uses* (pp. 61–81). Chicago: University of Chicago Press.

Cronbach, L. J. (1988). Five perspectives on the validity argument. In H. Wainer & H. I. Braun (Eds.), *Test validity* (pp. 3–17). Hillsdale, NJ: Lawrence Erlbaum Associates.

Crooks, T. J. (1988). The impact of classroom evaluation practices on students. *Review of Educational Research, 58*, 438–481.

Csikszentmihalyi, M. (1992). *Flow: The psychology of happiness*. London: Rider.

Curriculum Development Council. (1982). *The syllabus for English (Forms I–V)*. Hong Kong: Hong Kong Government Printer.

Curtis, A. (2000). A problem-solving approach to the management of change in language education. *Korea TESOL Journal, 3*(1), 1–12.

Darling-Hammond, L., & Wise, A. E. (1985). Beyond standardization: State standards and school improvement. *The Elementary School Journal, 85*, 315–336.

Davies, A. (Ed.). (1968). *Language testing symposium: A psycholinguistic approach*. Oxford: Oxford University Press.

Davies, A. (1985). Follow my leader: Is that what language tests do? In Y. P. Lee, C. Y. Y. Fok, R. Lord, & G. Low (Eds.), *New directions in language testing* (pp. 1–12). Oxford: Pergamon Press.

Davies, A. (1997). Demands of being professional in language testing. *Language Testing, 14*, 328–339.

Davis, K. A. (1992). Validity and reliability in qualitative research on second language acquisition and teaching: Another researcher comments. *TESOL Quarterly, 26*, 605–608.

Davis, K. A. (1995). Qualitative theory and methods in applied linguistics research. *TESOL Quarterly, 29*, 427–453.

Docking, R. (1993, May). *Competency-based approaches to education and training: Progress and promise.* Paper presented at the annual meeting of the National Centre for English Language Teaching and Research, Sydney, Australia.

Dore, R. P. (1976). *The diploma disease.* London: Allen and Unwin.

Dore, R. P. (1997). Reflections on the diploma disease twenty years later. *Assessment in Education, 4*, 189–206.

Ebel, R. L. (1966). The social consequences of educational testing. In A. Anastasi (Ed.), *Testing problems in perspective* (pp. 18–29). Washington, DC: American Council on Education.

Eckstein, M. A., & Noah, H. J. (Eds.). (1992). *Examinations: Comparative and international studies.* Oxford: Pergamon Press.

Education Week. (1997, January). *Quality counts '97: A report card on the conditions of education in 50 states.* Bethesda, MD: Editorial Projects in Education. Retrieved April 3, 2000, from http://www.edweek.org/sreports/qc97/

Education Week. (1999, January 11). *Quality counts '99: Rewarding results, punishing failure.* Bethesda, MD: Editorial Projects in Education.

Education Week. (2000, January 13). *Quality counts 2000: Who should teach?* Bethesda, MD: Editorial Project in Education.

Eisenhart, M. A., & Howe, K. R. (1992). Validity in educational research. In M. D. Lecompte, W. L. Millroy, & J. Preissle (Eds.), *Handbook of qualitative research in education* (pp. 643–680). San Diego, CA: Academic Press.

Elliott, N., & Ensign, G. (1999). *The Washington assessment of student learning: An update on writing.* Olympia, WA: Office of the Superintendent of Public Instruction. Retrieved January 2, 2001, from: http://www.k12.wa.us/assessment/assessproginfo/subdocuments/writupdate.asp

Elton, L., & Laurillard, D. (1979). Trends in student learning. *Studies in Higher Education, 4*, 87–102.

English, F. W. (1992). *Deciding what to teach and test: Developing, aligning, and auditing the curriculum.* Newbury Park, CA: Corwin Press.

Erickson, F. (1986). Qualitative methods in research on teaching. In M. Wittrock (Ed.), *Handbook of research on teaching* (3rd ed., pp. 119–161). New York: Macmillan.

Falvey, P. (1995). The education of teachers of English in Hong Kong: A case for special treatment. In F. Lopez-Real (Ed.), *Proceedings of ITEC '95* (pp. 107–113). Hong Kong: University of Hong Kong, Department of Curriculum Studies.

Fish, J. (1988). *Responses to mandated standardized testing.* Unpublished doctoral dissertation, University of California, Los Angeles.

Frederiksen, J. R., & Collins, A. (1989). A system approach to educational testing. *Educational Researcher, 18*(9), 27–32.

Frederiksen, N. (1984). The real test bias: Influences of testing on teaching and learning. *American Psychology, 39*, 193–202.

Fullan, M. G. (1993). *Change forces: Probing the depth of educational reform.* London: Falmer Press.

Fullan, M. G. (1998). Linking change and assessment. In P. Rea-Dickins & K. P. Germaine (Eds.), *Managing evaluation and innovation in language teaching: Building bridges* (pp. 253–262). London: Longman.

Fullan, M., & Park, P. (1981). *Curriculum implementation: A resource booklet.* Toronto, Ontario, Canada: Ontario Ministry of Education.

Fullan, M. G., with Stiegelbauer, S. (1991). *The new meaning of educational change* (2nd ed.). London: Cassell.

Gardner, H. (1992). Assessment in context: The alternative to standardized testing. In B. R. Gifford & M. C. O'Connor (Eds.), *Changing assessments: Alternative views of aptitude, achievement and instruction* (pp. 77–119). London: Kluwer Academic.

Geertz, C. (1973). *The interpretation of culture.* New York: Basic Books.

Genesee, F. (1994). Assessment alternatives. *TESOL Matters, 4*(5), 2.

Gifford, B. R., & O'Connor, M. C. (Eds.). (1992). *Changing assessments: Alternative views of aptitude, achievement and instruction.* London: Kluwer Academic.

Gipps, C. V. (1994). *Beyond testing: Toward a theory of educational assessment.* London: Falmer Press.

Glaser, R. (1981). The future of testing: A research agenda for cognitive psychology and psychometrics. *American Psychologist, 36*, 923–936.

Glaser, R. (1990). Towards new models of assessment. *International Journal for Educational Research, 14*, 475–483.

Glaser, R., & Bassok, M. (1989). Learning theory and the study of instruction. *Annual Review of Psychology, 40*, 631–666.

Glaser, R., & Silver, E. (1994). *Assessment, testing, and instruction: Retrospect and prospect* (Tech. Rep. 379). Pittsburgh, PA: University of Pittsburgh, Learning Research and Development Center.

Goetz, J. P., & LeCompte, M. D. (1984). *Ethnography and qualitative design in educational research.* Orlando, FL: Academic Press.

Goldstein, H. (1989). Psychometric test theory and educational assessment. In H. Simons & J. Elliot (Eds.), *Rethinking appraisal and assessment* (pp. 140–148). Milton Keynes, England: Open University Press.

Grove, E. (1997, October). *Accountability in competency-based language programs: Issues of curriculum and assessment.* Paper presented at the meeting of the Applied Linguistics Association of Australia, Toowoomba, Australia.

Gui, S., Li, X., & Li, W. (1988). A reflection on experimenting with the National Matriculation English Test. In National Education Examination Authorities (Ed.), *Theory and practice of standardized test* (pp. 70–85). Guangzhou, China: Guangdong Higher Education Press.

Hagan, P. (1994). Competency-based curriculum: The NSW AMES experience. *Prospect, 9*(2), 30–40.

Hagan, P., Hood, S., Jackson, E., Jones, M., Joyce, H., & Manidis, M. (1993). *Certificate in spoken and written English* (2nd ed.). Sydney, Australia: New South Wales Adult Migrant English Service.

Haladyna, T. M., Nolen, S. B., & Haas, N. S. (1991). Raising standardized achievement test scores and the origins of test score pollution. *Educational Research, 20*(5), 2–7.

Hamp-Lyons, L. (1997). Washback, impact and validity: Ethical concerns. *Language Testing, 14*, 295–303.

Han, J. (1997). *The educational statistics yearbook of China*. Beijing, China: People's Education Press.

Hargreaves, A. (1994). *Changing teachers, changing times: Teachers' work and culture in the postmodern age*. London: Cassell.

Hayek, F. A. (1952). *The counter-revolution of science: Studies on the abuse of reason.* Indianapolis, IN: Liberty Press.

Henrichsen, L. E. (1989). *Diffusion of innovations in English language teaching: The ELEC effort in Japan, 1956–1968.* New York: Greenwood Press.

Herman, J. L. (1989). *Priorities of educational testing and evaluation: The testimony of the CRESST National Faculty* (Tech. Rep. 304). Los Angeles: University of California, Center for the Study of Evaluation.

Herman, J. L. (1992). *Accountability and alternative assessment: Research and development issues* (Tech. Rep. 384). Los Angeles: University of California, Center for the Study of Evaluation.

Herman, J. L., & Golan, S. (1993). The effects of standardized testing on teaching and schools. *Educational Measurement: Issues and Practice, 12*(4), 20–25, 41–42.

Herman, J. L., & Golan, S. (n.d.). *Effects of standardized testing on teachers and learning. Another look* (CSE Tech. Rep. 334). Los Angeles: University of California National Center for Research on Evaluation, Standards, and Student Testing.

Herrington, R. (1996). *Test-taking strategies and second language proficiency: Is there a relationship?* Unpublished master's thesis, Lancaster University, England.

Heyneman, S. P. (1987). Use of examinations in developing countries: Selection, research, and education sector management. *International Journal of Education Development, 7*, 251–263.

Heyneman, S. P., & Ransom, A. W. (1990). Using examinations and testing to improve educational quality. *Educational Policy, 4*, 177–192.

Hivela, A., & Law, E. (1991). A survey of local English teachers' attitudes towards English and E. L. T. *Institute of Language in Education Journal, 8*, 25–28.

Hong Kong Examinations Authority. (1993). *Hong Kong certificate of education examination 1996—Proposed English language syllabus.* Hong Kong: Author.

Hong Kong Examinations Authority. (1994a). *Hong Kong certificate of education examination 1996—English language.* Hong Kong: Author.

Hong Kong Examinations Authority. (1994b). *The work of the Hong Kong examinations authority—1977–93.* Hong Kong: Author.

Hong Kong Government. (1993). *Enrolment survey 1993.* Hong Kong: Education Department.

Hood, S. (1995). From curriculum to courses: Why do teachers do what they do? In A. Burns & S. Hood (Eds.), *Teachers' voices: Exploring course design in a changing curriculum* (pp. 21–34). Sydney, NSW, Australia: National Center for English Language Teaching and Research.

Hopkins, D. (1985). *A teacher's guide to classroom research.* Milton Keynes, UK: Open University Press.

Horak, T. (1996). *IELTS impact study project.* Unpublished manuscript, Lancaster University, England.

Hu, C. T. (1984). The historical background: Examinations and controls in pre-modern China. *Comparative Education, 20*, 7–26.

Hu, Y. (1990). Teaching English in Chinese secondary schools. In Y. F. Dzau (Ed.), *English in China* (pp. 59–67). Hong Kong: API Press.

Huberman, A. M. (1973). *Understanding change in education: An introduction.* Paris: Organization for Economic Co-operation and Development.

Hughes, A. (1988). Introducing a needs-based test of English language proficiency into an English-medium university in Turkey. In A. Hughes (Ed.), *Testing English for university study* (pp. 134–153). London: Modern English Publications.

Hughes, A. (1989). *Testing for language teachers.* Cambridge, England: Cambridge University Press.

Hughes, A. (1993). *Backwash and TOEFL 2000.* Unpublished manuscript, University of Reading, England.

Ingram, D. E. (1984). *Australian second language proficiency ratings.* Canberra, Australia: Department of Immigration and Ethnic Affairs.

Jaeger, R. M. (1988). Survey research methods in education. In R. M. Jaeger (Ed.), *Complementary methods for research in education* (pp. 303–330). Washington, DC: American Educational Research Association.

James, M. (2000). Measured lives: The rise of assessment as the engine of change in English schools. *Curriculum Journal, 11*, 343–364.

James, M., & Gipps, C. (1998). Broadening the basis of assessment to prevent the narrowing of learning. *The Curriculum Journal, 9*, 285–297.

Japan Association of College English Teachers (JACET). (1993). *21 seki ni muketeno eigo kyoiku* [English education for 21 centuries]. Tokyo: Taishukan shoten.

Johnson, R. K. (Ed.). (1989). *The second language curriculum.* Cambridge, England: Cambridge University Press.

Johnston, P. (1989). Constructive evaluation and the improvement of teaching and learning. *Teachers College Record, 90*, 509–528.

Kellaghan, T., & Greaney, V. (1992). *Using examinations to improve education: A study of fourteen African countries.* Washington, DC: World Bank.

Kellaghan, T., Madaus, G. F., & Airasian, P. (1982). *The effects of standardized testing.* Boston, MA: Kluwer-Nijhoff.

Kemmis, S., & McTaggart, R. (1988). *The action research planner* (3rd ed.). Melbourne, Victoria, Australia: Deakin University Press.

Kennedy, C. (1988). Evaluation of the management of change in ELT projects. *Applied Linguistics, 9*, 329–342.

Khaniyah, T. R. (1990). *Examinations as instruments for educational change: Investigating the washback effect of the Nepalese English exams*. Unpublished doctoral dissertation, University of Edinburgh, Scotland.

King, R. (1997). Can public examinations have a positive washback effect on classroom teaching? In P. Grundy (Ed.), *IATEFL 31th International Annual Conference Brighton, April 1997* (pp. 33–38). London: International Association of Teachers of English as a Foreign Language.

Koretz, D., Barron, S., Mitchell, K., & Stecher, B. (1996). *The perceived effects of the Kentucky instructional results information system (KIRIS)* (Document No. MR-792-PCT/FF). Santa Monica, CA: RAND.

Koretz, D., Stecher, B., Klein, S., & McCaffrey, D. (1994). The Vermont portfolio assessment program: Findings and implications. *Educational Measurement: Issues and Practice, 13*(3), 5–16.

Krashen, S. D. (1993). *The power of reading*. Englewood, CO: Libraries Unlimited, Inc.

Krashen, S. D. (1998). Comprehensible output? *System, 26*, 175–182.

Kuckartz, U. (1998). *WinMax. Scientific text analysis for the social sciences: User's guide*. Thousand Oaks, CA: Sage.

Kunnan, A. (2000). *IELTS impact study project*. Cambridge, England: University of Cambridge Local Examinations Syndicate.

Lai, C. T. (1970). *A scholar in imperial China*. Hong Kong: Kelly & Walsh.

Lam, H. P. (1993). *Washback—Can it be quantified? A study on the impact of English Examinations in Hong Kong*. Unpublished master's thesis, University of Leeds, Leeds, England.

Latham, H. (1877). *On the action of examinations considered as a means of selection*. Cambridge, England: Deighton, Bell and Company.

Lazaraton, A. (1995). Qualitative research in applied linguistics: A progress report. *TESOL Quarterly, 29*, 455–472.

LeCompte, M. D., & Preissle, J. (1993). *Ethnography and qualitative design in educational research* (2nd ed.). New York: Academic Press.

LeCompte, M. D., Millroy, W. L, & Preissle, J. (1992). *The handbook of qualitative research in education*. San Diego, CA: Academic Press.

Lewkowicz, J. A. (2000). Authenticity in language testing: Some outstanding questions. *Language Testing, 17*, 43–64.

Li, X. (1984). In defense of the communicative approach. *ELT Journal, 38*(1), 2–13.

Li, X. (1988). Teaching for use, learning by use and testing through use. In H. Xiao (Ed.), *Standardized English test and ELT in the middle schools* (pp. 80–90). Guangzhou: Guangdong Education Press.

Li, X. (1990). How powerful can a language test be? The MET in China. *Journal of Multilingual and Multicultural Development, 11*, 393–404.

Li, X., Gui, S., & Li, W. (1990). The design of the NMET and ELT in middle schools. *English Language Teaching and Research in Primary Schools and Middle Schools, 1*, 1–27.

Lincoln, Y. S., & Guba, E. G. (1985). *Naturalistic inquiry*. Beverly Hills, CA: Sage.

Linn, R. L. (1983). Testing and instruction: Links and distinctions. *Journal of Educational Measurement, 20*, 179–189.

Linn, R. L. (1992). *Educational assessment: Expanded expectations and challenges* (Tech. Rep. 351). Boulder: University of Colorado at Boulder, Center for the Study of Evaluation.

Linn, R. L. (2000). Assessments and accountability. *Educational Researcher, 29*(2), 4–16.

Linn, R. L., & Herman, J. L. (1997, February). *Standards-led assessment: Technical and policy issues in measuring school and student progress (CSE technical report 426)*. Los Angeles: University of California National Center for Research on Evaluation, Standards, and Student Testing.

Linn, R. L., Baker, E. L., & Dunbar, S. B. (1991). Complex, performance-based assessment: Expectations and validation criteria. *Educational Researcher, 20*(8), 15–21.

Liu, Y. (Ed.). (1992). *Book of major educational events in China*. Hangzhou, China: Zhejiang Education Press.

Lock, C. L. (2001). *The influence of a large-scale assessment program on classroom practices*. Unpublished doctoral dissertation, Queen's University, Kingston, Ontario, Canada.

London, N. (1997). A national strategy for system-wide curriculum improvement in Trinidad and Tobago. In D. W. Chapman, L. O. Mahlck, & A. Smulders (Eds.), *From planning to action: Government initiatives for improving school level practice* (pp. 133–146). Paris: International Institute for Educational Planning.

Low, G. D. (1988). The semantics of questionnaire rating scales. *Evaluation and Research in Education, 22*, 69–79.

Macintosh, H. G. (1986). The prospects for public examinations in England and Wales. In D. L. Nuttall (Ed.), *Assessing educational achievement* (pp. 19–34). London: Falmer Press.

Madaus, G. F. (1985a). Public policy and the testing profession: You've never had it so good? *Educational Measurement: Issues and Practice, 4*(4), 5–11.

Madaus, G. F. (1985b). Test scores as administrative mechanisms in educational policy. *Phi Delta Kappa, 66*, 611–17.

Madaus, G. F. (1988). The influence of testing on the curriculum. In L. N. Tanner (Ed.), *Critical issues in curriculum: Eighty-seventh yearbook of the National Society for the Study of Education* (pp. 83–121). Chicago: University of Chicago Press.

Madaus, G. F., & Kellaghan, T. (1992). Curriculum evaluation and assessment. In P. W. Jackson (Ed.), *Handbook of research on curriculum* (pp. 119–154). New York: Macmillan.

Maeher, M. L., & Fyans, L. J., Jr. (1989). School culture, motivation, and achievement. In M. L. Maehr & C. Ames (Eds.), *Advances in motivation and achievement: Vol. 6. Motivation enhancing environments* (pp. 215–247). Greenwich, CT: JAI Press.

Markee, N. (1993). The diffusion of innovation in language teaching. *Annual Review of Applied Linguistics, 13*, 229–243.

Markee, N. (1997). *Managing curricular innovation*. Cambridge, England: Cambridge University Press.

Marton, F., Hounsell, D. J., & Entwistle, N. J. (Eds.). (1984). *The experience of learning*. Edinburgh, Scotland: Scottish Academic Press.

McCallum, B., Gipps, C., McAlister, S., & Brown, M. (1995). National curriculum assessment: Emerging models of teacher assessment in the classroom. In H. Torrance (Ed.), *Evaluating authentic assessment: Problems and possibilities in new approaches to assessment* (pp. 88–104). Buckingham, England: Open University Press.

McEwen, N. (1995a). Educational accountability in Alberta. *Canadian Journal of Education, 20*, 27–44.

McEwen, N. (1995b). Introducing accountability in education in Canada. *Canadian Journal of Education, 20*, 1–17.

McIver, M. C., & Wolf, S. A. (1999). The power of the conference is the power of suggestion. *Language Arts, 77*, 54–61.

McNamara, T. (1996). *Measuring second language performance*. London: Longman.

Merriam, S. B. (1988). *Case study research in education: A qualitative approach*. San Francisco: Jossey Bass.

Messick, S. (1975). The standard problem: Meaning and values in measurement and evaluation. *American Psychologist, 30*, 955–966.

Messick, S. (1989). Validity. In R. Linn (Ed.), *Educational measurement* (3rd ed., pp. 13–103). New York: Macmillan.

Messick, S. (1992, April). *The interplay between evidence and consequences in the validation of performance assessments*. Paper presented at the annual meeting of the National Council on Measurement in Education, San Francisco.

Messick, S. (1994). The interplay of evidence and consequences in the validation of performance assessments. *Educational Researcher, 23*(2), 13–23.

Messick, S. (1996). Validity and washback in language testing. *Language Testing, 13*, 241–256.

Milanovic, M., & Saville, N. (1996). *Considering the impact of Cambridge EFL examinations*. Cambridge, England: University of Cambridge Local Examinations Syndicate.

Miles, M. B., & Huberman, A. M. (1994). *Qualitative data analysis: An expanded sourcebook* (2nd ed.). Thousand Oaks, CA: Sage.

Ministry of Education, Science and Culture. (1992). *Atarashii jidai ni taio suru kyoiku no shosedo no kaikaku–dai 14 ki chuo kyoiku shingikai toshin* [Reforming educational systems for a new era–a report from 14th conference on education]. Tokyo: Author.

Ministry of Education. (1998). *Director General Bulletin*. Jerusalem: English Inspectorate.

Ministry of Education. (1999). *Internal document: No. 3*. Beijing, China: Author.

Morris, N. (1961). An historian's view of examinations. In S. Wiseman (Ed.), *Examinations and English education*. Manchester, England: Manchester University Press.

Morris, P. (1985). Teachers' perceptions of the barriers to the implementation of a pedagogic innovation: A South East Asian case study. *International Review of Education, 31*, 3–18.

Morris, P. (1990). Teachers' perceptions of the barriers to the implementation of a pedagogic innovation. In P. Morris (Ed.), *Curriculum development in Hong Kong* (pp. 45–60). Hong Kong: Hong Kong University Press.

Morris, P. (1995). *The Hong Kong school curriculum: Development, issues and policies*. Hong Kong: Hong Kong University Press.

Morris, P., Adamson, R., Au, M. L., Chan, K. K., Chan, W. Y., Yuk, K. P., et al. (1996). *Target oriented curriculum evaluation project: Interim report*. Hong Kong: University of Hong Kong, Faculty of Education.

Morrow, K. (1986). The evaluation of tests of communicative performance. In M. Portal (Ed.), *Innovations in language testing: Proceedings of the IUS/NFER conference* (pp. 1–13). London: NFER/Nelson.

Mosier, C. I. (1947). A critical examination of the concepts of face validity. *Educational and Psychological Measurement, 7*, 191–205.

Munby, J. (1978). *Communicative syllabus design*. Cambridge, England: Cambridge University Press.

Nagano, S. (1984). *Kyoiku hyoka ron* [Evaluation of education]. Tokyo: Daiichi hoki.

National Teaching Syllabus. (1990). China: Ministry of Education, PRC.

National Teaching Syllabus. (1996). China: Ministry of Education, PRC.

New South Wales Adult Migrant English Service. (1995). *Certificates I, II, III and IV in spoken and written English*. Sydney, Australia: Author.

New South Wales Adult Migrant English Service. (1997). *Certificates I, II, III and IV in spoken and written English*. Sydney, Australia: Author.

Noble, A. J., & Smith, M. L. (1994a). *Measurement-driven reform: Research on policy, practice, repercussion* (Tech. Rep. 381). Tempe, AZ: Arizona State University, Center for the Study of Evaluation.

Noble, A. J., & Smith, M. L. (1994b). *Old and new beliefs about measurement-driven reform: 'The more things change, the more they stay the same'* (Tech. Rep. 373). Tempe, AZ: Arizona State University, Center for the Study of Evaluation.

Nolen, S. B., Haladyna, T. M., & Haas, N. S. (1992). Uses and abuses of achievement test scores. *Educational Measurement: Issues and Practice, 11*(2), 9–15.

Nunan, D. (1989). *Understanding language classrooms: A guide for teacher-initiated action*. New York: Prentice-Hall.

Office of the Superintendent of Public Instruction. *The Washington assessment of student learning: An update on writing*. Retrieved February 15, 2000, from http://www.k12.wa.us/assessment/assessproginfo/subdocuments/writupdate.asp

Ogawa, Y. (1981). *Hanaseru dake ga eigo ja nai* [Beyond English conversation: Making school English work for you]. Tokyo: Simul Press.

Oppenheim, A. N. (1992). *Questionnaire design, interviewing and attitude measurement*. London: Pinter.

Oxenham, J. (Ed.). (1984). *Education versus qualifications?* London: Allen and Unwin.

Paris, S. G., Lawton, T. A., Turner, J. C., & Roth, J. L. (1991). A developmental perspective on standardized achievement testing. *Educational Researcher, 20*(5), 12–19.

Patton, M. Q. (1987). *How to use qualitative methods in evaluation*. London: Sage.

Pearson, I. (1988). Tests as levers for change. In D. Chamberlain & R. J. Baumgardner (Eds.), *ESP in the classroom: Practice and evaluation* (pp. 98–107). London: Modern English.

Petrie, H. G. (1987). Introduction to evaluation and testing. *Educational Policy, 1*, 175–180.

Phillipson, R. (1992). *Linguistic imperialism*. Oxford, England: Oxford University Press.

Popham, W. J. (1983). Measurement as an instructional catalyst. In R. B. Ekstrom (Ed.), *New directions for testing and measurement: Measurement, technology, and individuality in education* (pp. 19–30). San Francisco: Jossey-Bass.

Popham, W. J. (1987). The merits of measurement-driven instruction. *Phi Delta Kappa, 68*, 679–682.

Popham, W. J. (1993). Measurement-driven instruction as a 'quick-fix' reform strategy. *Measurement and Evaluation in Counseling and Development, 26*, 31–34.

Popham, W. J., Cruse, K. L., Rankin, S. C., Standifer, P. D., & Williams, P. L. (1985). Measurement-driven instruction: It is on the road. *Phi Delta Kappa, 66*, 628–634.

Por, L. H., & Ki, C. S. (1995). Methodology washback: An insider's view. In D. Nunan, R. Berry, & V. Berry (Eds.), *Bringing about change in language education* (pp. 217–235). Hong Kong: University of Hong-Kong, Department of Curriculum Studies.

Purpura, J. (1999). *Learner strategy use and performance on language tests*. Cambridge, England: Cambridge University Press.

Quinn, T. J. (1993). The competency movement, applied linguistics and language testing: Some reflections and suggestions for a possible research agenda. *Melbourne Papers in Language Testing, 2*(2), 55–87.

Quirk, R. (1995, December). *The threat and promise of English*. Paper presented at the Language Planning and Policy Conference, Ramat Gan, Israel.

Read, J. (1999, July). *The policy context of English testing for immigrants*. Paper presented at the Language Testing Research Colloquium, Tsukuba, Japan.

Reischauer, E. O., Kobayashi, H., & Naya, Y. (1989). *Nihon no kokusaika* [The internationalization of Japan]. Tokyo: Bunge Shunju Sha.

Resnick, L. B. (1989). Toward the thinking curriculum: An overview. In L. B. Resnick & L. E. Klopfer (Eds.), *Toward the thinking curriculum: Current cognitive research* (pp. 1–18). Reston, VA: Association for Supervision and Curriculum Development.

Resnick, L. B., & Resnick, D. P. (1992). Assessing the thinking curriculum: New tools for educational reform. In B. R. Gifford & M. C. O'Connor (Eds.), *Changing assessments: Alternative views of aptitude, achievement and instruction* (pp. 37–75). London: Kluwer Academic.

Robinson, P. (1993). *Teachers facing change*. Adelaide, Australia: National Center for Vocational Education Research.

Rogers, E. M. (1983). *The diffusion of innovations* (3rd ed.). New York: Macmillan.

Rohlen, T. P. (1983). *Japan's high schools*. Berkeley: University of California Press.

Rumsey, D. (1993, November). *A practical model for assessment of workplace competence within a competency-based system of training*. Paper presented at the Testing Times Conference, Sydney, NSW, Australia.

Runte, R. (1998). The impact of centralized examinations on teacher professionalism. *Canadian Journal of Education, 23*, 166–181.

Saito, T., Arita, S., & Nasu, I. (1984). *Tashi-sentaku tesuto ga igaku kyoiku ni oyobosu eikyo* [The influence of multiple-choice test on medical education] (*Nihon igaku kyoiku shinko zaidan kenkyu jose ni yoru kenkyu hokoku sho* [Technical report of the Japan Medical Education Research Fund]). Okayama: Kawasaki Medical School.

Sanders, W. L., & Horn, S. P. (1995). Educational assessment reassessed: The usefulness of standardized and alternative measures of student achievement as indicators for the assessment of educational outcomes. *Education Policy Analysis Archives, 3*(6), 1–15.

Saville, N. (1998). *Predicting impact on language learning and the classroom. UCLES internal report.* Cambridge, England: University of Cambridge Local Examinations Syndicate.

Saville, N. (2000). *Investigating the impact of international language examinations* (Research Notes No. 2). Available from University of Cambridge Local Examinations Syndicate Web site, http://www.cambridge-efl.org/rs_notes.

Scaramucci, M. (1999, July). *A study of washback in Brazil.* Paper presented at the Language Testing Research Colloquium, Tsukuba, Japan.

Schiefelbein, E. (1993). The use of national assessments to improve primary education in Chile. In D. W. Chapman & L. O. Mahlck (Eds.), *From data to action: Information systems in educational planning* (pp. 117–146). Paris, France: UNESCO.

Seliger, H. W., & Shohamy, E. G. (1989). *Second language research methods*. Oxford: Oxford University Press.

Shavelson, R. J., & Stern, P. (1981). Research on teachers' pedagogical thoughts, judgments, decisions, and behavior. *Review of Educational Research, 51*, 455–498.

Shepard, L. A. (1990). Inflated test score gains: Is the problem old norms or teaching the test? *Educational Measurement: Issues and Practice, 9*, 15–22.

Shepard, L. A. (1991a). Interview on assessment issues with Lorrie Shepard. *Educational Researcher, 20*(2), 21–27.

Shepard, L. A. (1991b). Psychometricians' beliefs about learning. *Educational Researcher, 20*(6), 2–16.

Shepard, L. A. (1992). What policy makers who mandate tests should know about the new psychology of intellectual ability and learning. In B. R. Gifford & M. C. O'Connor (Eds.), *Changing assessments: Alternative views of aptitude, achievement and instruction* (pp. 301–327). London: Kluwer Academic.

Shepard, L. A. (1993). The place of testing reform in educational reform: A reply to Cizek. *Educational Researcher, 22*(4), 10–14.

Shepard, L. A., & Dougherty, K. C. (1991, April). *Effects of high-stakes testing on instruction.* Paper presented at the annual meeting of the American Educational Research Association and the National Council on Measurement in Education, Chicago.

Shiozawa, T. (1983). *Daigaku nyushi—genjo to kadai* [University entrance examinations—the present situation and problems]. *Eigo Kyoiku Sokan 30-shunen Kinen Zokango [English Teacher's Magazine, 30th Anniversary Special Issue]*, 39–41.

Shohamy, E. (1992). Beyond proficiency testing: A diagnostic feedback testing model for assessing foreign language learning. *Modern Language Journal, 76*, 513–521.

Shohamy, E. (1993a). *The power of test: The impact of language testing on teaching and learning.* Washington, DC: National Foreign Language Center Occasional Papers. The National Foreign Language Center, Washington, DC.

Shohamy, E. (1993b). *The exercise of power and control in the rhetorics of testing.* Center for Applied Language Studies, Carleton University, Ottawa, Canada, 10:48–62.

Shohamy, E. (1997). Testing methods, testing consequences: Are they ethical? Are they fair? *Language Testing, 14*, 340–349.

Shohamy, E. (1999). Language testing: Impact. In B. Spolsky (Ed.), *Concise Encyclopedia of Educational Linguistics* (pp. 711–714). Oxford, England: Pergamon.

Shohamy, E. (2000). Using language tests for upgrading knowledge. *Hong Kong Journal of Applied Linguistics, 5*(1), 1–18.

Shohamy, E., & Donitsa-Schmidt, S. (1995, April). *The perceptions and stereotypes of Hebrew vs. English among three different ethnic groups in Israel.* Paper presented at the meeting of the American Association of Applied Linguistics, Long Beach, CA.

Shohamy, E., Donitsa-Schmidt, S., & Ferman, I. (1996). Test Impact revisited: Washback effect over time. *Language Testing, 13*, 298–317.

Silverman, D. (1993). *Interpreting qualitative data: Methods for analyzing talk, text and interaction*. London: Sage.

Simon, B. (1974). *The two nations and educational structure 1780–1870*. London: Lawrence & Wishart.

Smith, M. L. (1991a). Meanings of test preparation. *American Educational Research Journal, 28*, 521–542.

Smith, M. L. (1991b). Put to the test: The effects of external testing on teachers. *Educational Researcher, 20*(5), 8–11.

Snyder, C. W., Jr., Prince, B., Johanson, G., Odaet, C., Jaji, L., & Beatty, M. (1997). *Exam fervor and fever: Case studies of the influence of primary leaving examinations on Uganda classrooms, teachers, and pupils: Vol. 1*. Washington, DC: Academy for Educational Development, Advancing Basic Education and Literacy Project.

Somerset, A. (1983). *Examination reform: The Kenya experience*. Washington, DC: World Bank.

Spada, N., & Froehlich, M. (1995). *COLT: Communicative orientation of language teaching observation scheme, coding conventions and applications*. Sydney, NSW: Macquarie University, National Center for English Language Teaching and Research.

Spolsky, B. (1995a). The examination of classroom backwash cycle: Some historical cases. In D. Nunan, V. Berry, & R. Berry (Eds.), *Bringing about change in language education* (pp. 55–66). Hong Kong: University of Hong Kong, Department of Curriculum Studies.

Spolsky, B. (1995b). *Measured words*. Oxford: Oxford University Press.

Stecher, B., & Barron, S. (1999). *Quadrennial milepost accountability testing in Kentucky* (Tech. Rep. 505). Los Angeles: University of California, National Center for Research on Evaluation, Standards, and Student Testing.

Stecher, B., Barron, S., Chun, T., Krop, C., & Ross, K. (2000). *The effects of Washington education reform on schools and classrooms* (Tech. Rep. 525). Los Angeles: University of California, National Center for Research on Evaluation, Standards, and Student Testing.

Stecher, B., Barron, S., Kaganoff, T., & Goodwin, J. (1998). *The effects of standards-based assessment on classroom practices: Results of the 1996–97 RAND survey of Kentucky teachers of mathematics and writing* (Tech. Rep. 482). Los Angeles: University of California, National Center for Research on Evaluation, Standards, and Student Testing.

Stecher, B., & Chun, T. (2002). *School and classroom practices during two years of education reform in Washington state* (CSE Tech. Rep. No. 550). Los Angeles: University of California, National Center for Research on Evaluation, Standards, and Student Testing.

Steiner, J. (1995a). *Changes in the English Bagrut exam*. Jerusalem: Ministry of Education, English Inspectorate.

Steiner, J. (1995b). *Reading for pleasure*. Jerusalem: Ministry of Education, English Inspectorate.

Stevenson, D. K., & Riewe, U. (1981). Teachers' attitudes towards language tests and testing. In T. Culhane, C. Klein-Braley, & D. K. Stevenson (Eds.), *Practice and problems in language testing. Occasional Papers, 26* (pp. 146–155). Essex, UK: University of Essex.

Stiggins, R., & Faires-Conkin, N. (1992). *In teachers' hands*. Albany, NY: State University of New York Press.

Stoller, F. (1994). The diffusion of innovations in intensive ESL programs. *Applied Linguistics, 15*, 300–327.

Swain, M. (1984). Large-scale communicative language testing: A case study. In S. J. Savignon & M. Berns (Eds.), *Initiatives in communicative language teaching* (pp. 185–201). Reading, MA: Addison-Wesley.

Swain, M. (1985). Large-scale communicative language testing: A case study. In Y. P. Lee, A. C. Y. Y. Fok, R. Lord, & G. Low (Eds.), *New directions in language testing* (pp. 35–46). Oxford: Pergamon.

Swain, M. (1995). Three functions of output in second language learning. In G. Cook & B. Scidelhofer (Eds.), *Principle and practice in applied linguistics: Studies in honor of J. G. Woddowson* (pp. 125–144). Oxford, England: Oxford University Press.

Swain, M., & Lapkin, S. (1995). Problems in output and the cognitive processes they generate: A step towards second language learning. *Applied Linguistics, 16*, 371–391.

Takano, F. (1992). Daigaku nyushi no kaizen ni mukete [Towards a reform of university entrance examination]. *Shizen, 7*, 13–26.

Tang, C., & Biggs, J. B. (1996). How Hong Kong students cope with assessment. In D. A. Watkins & J. B. Biggs (Eds.), *The Chinese learner: Cultural, psychological and contextual influences* (pp. 159–182). Hong Kong: Center for Comparative Research in Education.

Troman, G. (1989). Testing tension: The politics of educational assessment. *British Educational Research Journal, 15*, 279–295.

University of Cambridge Local Examinations Syndicate (UCLES). (1999). *The IELTS handbook*. Cambridge, England: Authors.

University of Cambridge Local Examinations Syndicate (UCLES). (2000). *IELTS handbook*. Cambridge, England: Author.

Valette, R. M. (1967). *Modern language testing*. New York: Harcourt Brace.

van Lier, L. (1988). *The classroom and the language learner*. New York: Longman.

VanPatten, B., & Sanz, C. (1995). From input to output: Processing instruction and communicative task. In F. R. Eckman, D. Highland, P. W. Lee, J. Mileham, & R. R. Weber (Eds.), *Second language acquisition: Theory and pedagogy* (pp. 169–186). Mahwah, NJ: Lawrence Erlbaum Associates.

Vernon, P. E. (1956). *The measurement of abilities* (2nd ed.). London: University of London Press.

Vogel, E. F. (1979). *Japan as number one: Lessons for America*. Tokyo: Charles E. Tuttle.

Wall, D. (1996). Introducing new tests into traditional systems: Insights from general education and from innovation theory. *Language Testing, 13*, 334–354.

Wall, D. (1997). Impact and washback in language testing. In C. Clapham & D. Corson (Eds.), *Encyclopedia of language and education: Vol. 7. Language testing and assessment* (pp. 291–302). Dordrecht: Kluwer Academic.

Wall, D. (1999). *The impact of high-stakes examinations on classroom teaching: A case study using insights from testing and innovation theory*. Unpublished doctoral dissertation, Lancaster University, UK.

Wall, D. (2000). The impact of high-stakes testing on teaching and learning: Can this be predicted or controlled? *System, 28*, 499–509.

Wall, D., & Alderson, J. C. (1993). Examining washback: The Sri Lankan impact study. *Language Testing, 10*, 41–69.

Wall, D., & Alderson, J. C. (1996). Examining washback: The Sri Lanka impact study. In A. Cumming & R. Berwick (Eds.), *Validation in language testing* (pp. 194–221). Philadelphia: Multilingual Matters.

Wall, D., Kalnberzina, V., Mazuoliene, Z., & Truus, K. (1996). The Baltic States Year 12 examination project. *Language Testing Update, 19*, 15–27.

Washington State Commission on Student Learning. (1997). *Essential academic learning requirements: Technical manual*. Olympia, WA: Author.

Watanabe, Y. (1996a). Investigating washback in Japanese EFL classrooms: Problems of methodology. In G. Wigglesworth & C. Elder (Eds.), *The language testing circle: From inception to washback* (pp. 208–239). Melbourne, Victoria, Australia: Applied Linguistics Association of Australia.

Watanabe, Y. (1996b). Does grammar translation come from the entrance examination? Preliminary findings from classroom-based research. *Language Testing, 13*, 318–333.

Watanabe, Y. (1997a). Nyushi kara eigo o hazusu to jugyo wa kawaru ka [Will elimination of English from the entrance examination change classroom instruction?] *Eigo kyoiku [English teachers magazine], September, special issue*, 30–35. Tokyo: Taihukan shoten.

Watanabe, Y. (1997b). *Washback effects of the Japanese university entrance examination: Classroom-based research.* Unpublished doctoral dissertation, Lancaster University, UK.

Watanabe, Y. (2000). Washback effects of the English section of the Japanese university entrance examinations on instruction in pre-college level EFL. *Language Testing Update, 27,* 42–47.

Watanabe, Y. (2001). Does the university entrance examination motivate learners? A case study of learner interviews. In Akita Association of English Studies (Eds.), *Trans-equator exchanges: A collection of academic papers in honor of Professor David Ingram* (pp. 100–110). Akita, Japan: Author.

Watson-Gegeo, K. A. (1988). Ethnography in ESL: Defining the essentials. *TESOL Quarterly, 22,* 575–592.

Watson-Gegeo, K. A. (1997). Classroom ethnography. In N. H. Hornberger & D. Corson (Eds.), *Encyclopedia of language and education: Vol. 8. Research methods in language and education* (pp. 135–144). London: Kluwer Academic.

Weir, C. J. (2002). *Continuity and innovation: The revision of CPE 1913–2013.* Cambridge, England: Cambridge University Press/UCLES.

Whetton, C. (1999, May). *Attempting to find the true cost of assessment systems.* Paper presented at the annual meeting of the International Association for Educational Assessment, Bled, Slovenia.

White, R. V. (1988). *The ELT curriculum: Design, innovation and management.* Oxford: Blackwell.

White, R. V. (1991). Managing curriculum development and innovation. In R. V. White, M. Martin, M. Stimson, & R. Hodge (Eds.), *Management in English language teaching* (pp. 166–195). Cambridge, England: Cambridge University Press.

Widen, M. F., O'Shea, T., & Pye, I. (1997). High-stakes testing and the teaching of science. *Canadian Journal of Education, 22,* 428–444.

Wiggins, G. (1989a). A true test: Toward more authentic and equitable assessment. *Phi Delta Kappa, 70,* 703–713.

Wiggins, G. (1989b). Teaching to the (authentic) test. *Educational Leadership, 46*(7), 41–47.

Wiggins, G. (1993). Assessment: Authenticity, context, and validity. *Phi Delta Kappa, 75,* 200–214.

Wilkins, D. (1976). *Notional syllabuses.* Oxford, England: Oxford University Press.

Williams, M., & Burden, R. (1997). *Psychology for language teachers: A social constructivist approach.* Cambridge, England: Cambridge University Press.

Winetroube, S. (1997). *The design of the teachers' attitude questionnaires.* Cambridge, England: University of Cambridge Local Examinations Syndicate.

Wiseman, S. (Ed.). (1961). *Examinations and English education.* Manchester, England: Manchester University Press.

Wolf, S. A., Borko, H., Elliot, R., & McIver, M. (2000). "That dog won't hunt!": Exemplary school change efforts within the Kentucky reform. *American Educational Research Journal, 37,* 349–393.

Woods, A., Fletcher, P., & Hughes, A. (1986). *Statistics in language studies.* Cambridge, England: Cambridge University Press.

Woods, D. (1996). *Teacher cognition in language teaching: Beliefs, decision-making and classroom practice.* Cambridge, England: Cambridge University Press.

Yang, H. (1999, August 5). *The validation study of the National College English Test.* Paper presented at the annual meeting of Association Internationale de Linguistique Appliquée (AILA), Tokyo.

Yue, W. W. (1997). *An investigation of textbook materials designed to prepare students for the IELTS test: A study of washback.* Unpublished master's thesis, Lancaster University, England.

Author Index

I

J

K

L

M

T

U

Subject Index

J

L

M

N

O

P

Q

R

S